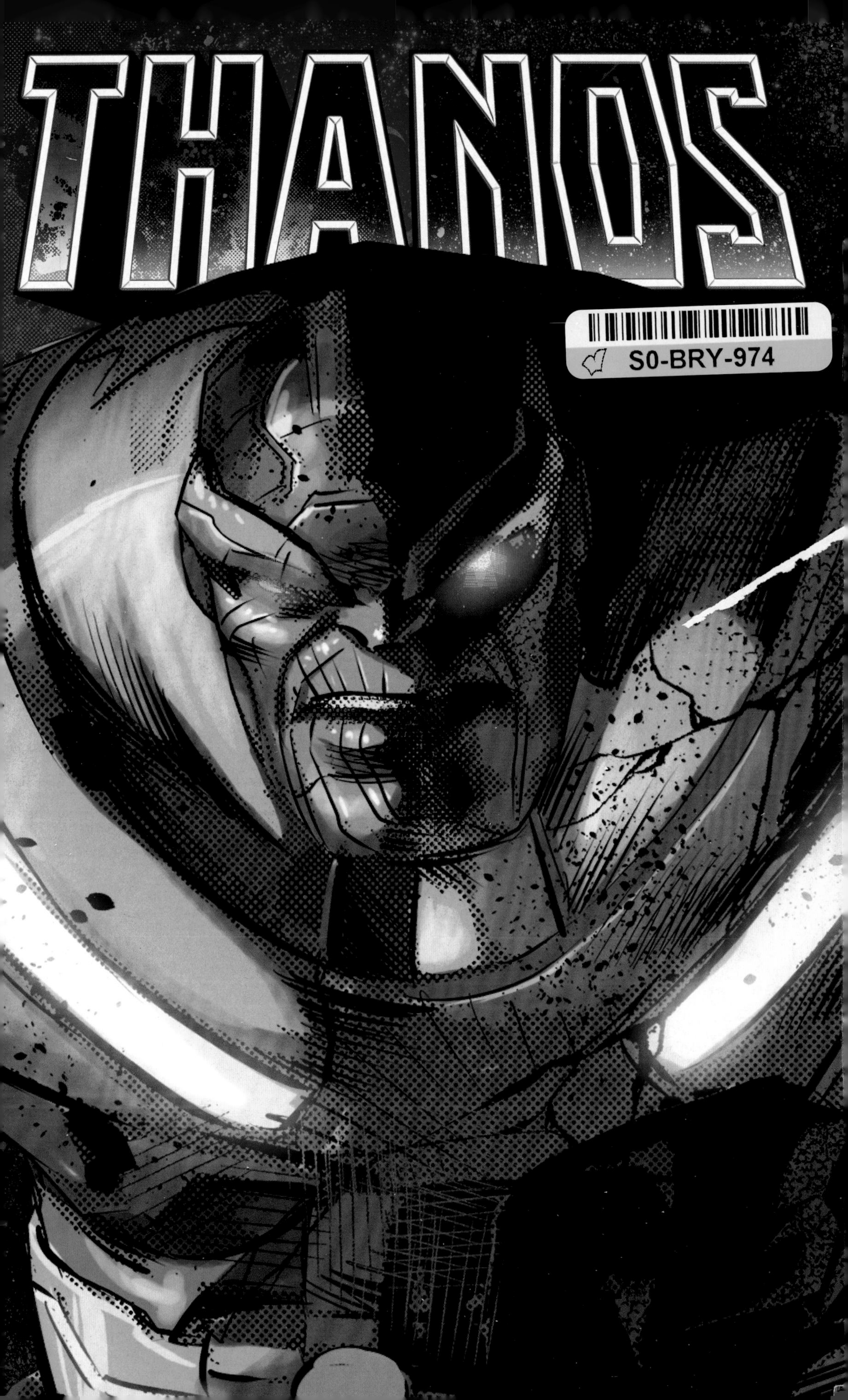
THANOS

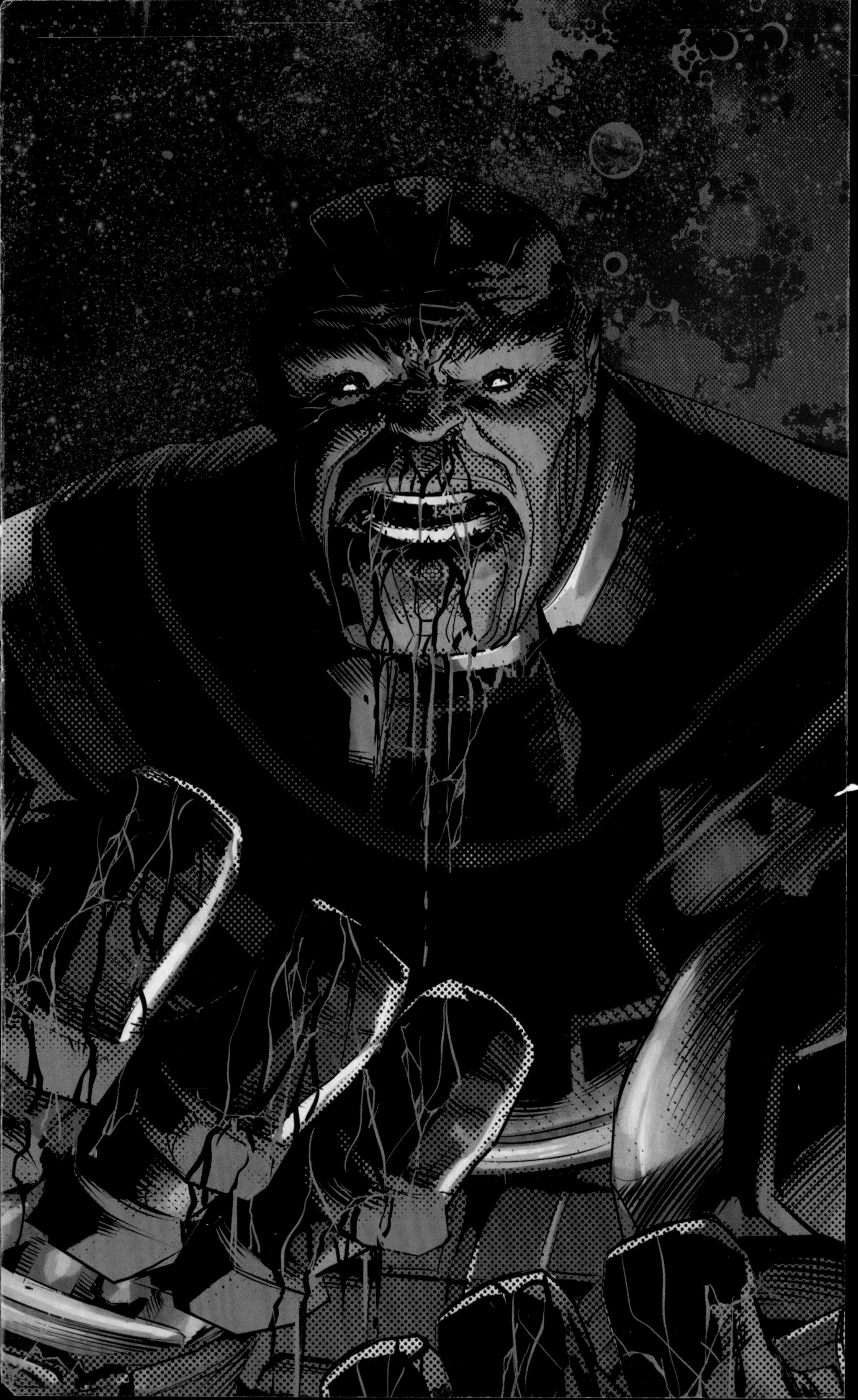

THANOS

THANOS RETURNS

JEFF LEMIRE
WRITER

MIKE DEODATO JR.
ARTIST

FRANK MARTIN
COLOR ARTIST

VC's CLAYTON COWLES
LETTERER

MIKE DEODATO JR. & FRANK MARTIN
COLOR ART

KATHLEEN WISNESKI
ASSISTANT EDITOR

DARREN SHAN
ASSOCIATE EDITOR

JORDAN D. WHITE
EDITOR

COLLECTION EDITOR **JENNIFER GRÜNWALD**
ASSOCIATE MANAGING EDITOR **KATERI WOODY**
ASSISTANT EDITOR **CAITLIN O'CONNELL**
EDITOR, SPECIAL PROJECTS **MARK D. BEAZLEY**

VP PRODUCTION & SPECIAL PROJECTS **JEFF YOUNGQUIST**
SVP PRINT, SALES & MARKETING **DAVID GABRIEL**
BOOK DESIGNER **ADAM DEL RE**

EDITOR IN CHIEF **AXEL ALONSO**
CHIEF CREATIVE OFFICER **JOE QUESADA**
PUBLISHER **DAN BUCKLEY**
EXECUTIVE PRODUCER **ALAN FINE**

THANOS VOL. 1: THANOS RETURNS. Contains material originally published in magazine form as THANOS #1-6. First printing 2017. ISBN# 978-1-302-90557-6. Published by MARVEL WORLDWIDE, INC., a subsidiary of MARVEL ENTERTAINMENT, LLC. OFFICE OF PUBLICATION: 135 West 50th Street, New York, NY 10020. Copyright © 2017 MARVEL. No similarity between any of the names, characters, persons, and/or institutions in this magazine with those of any living or dead person or institution is intended, and any such similarity which may exist is purely coincidental. **Printed in Canada.** DAN BUCKLEY, President, Marvel Entertainment; JOE QUESADA, Chief Creative Officer; TOM BREVOORT, SVP of Publishing; DAVID BOGART, SVP of Business Affairs & Operations, Publishing & Partnership; C.B. CEBULSKI, VP of Brand Management & Development, Asia; DAVID GABRIEL, SVP of Sales & Marketing, Publishing; JEFF YOUNGQUIST, VP of Production & Special Projects; DAN CARR, Executive Director of Publishing Technology; ALEX MORALES, Director of Publishing Operations; SUSAN CRESPI, Production Manager; STAN LEE, Chairman Emeritus. For information regarding advertising in Marvel Comics or on Marvel.com, please contact Vit DeBellis, Integrated Sales Manager, at vdebellis@marvel.com. For Marvel subscription inquiries, please call 888-511-5480. **Manufactured between 5/5/2017 and 6/6/2017 by SOLISCO PRINTERS, SCOTT, QC, CANADA.**

10 9 8 7 6 5 4 3 2 1

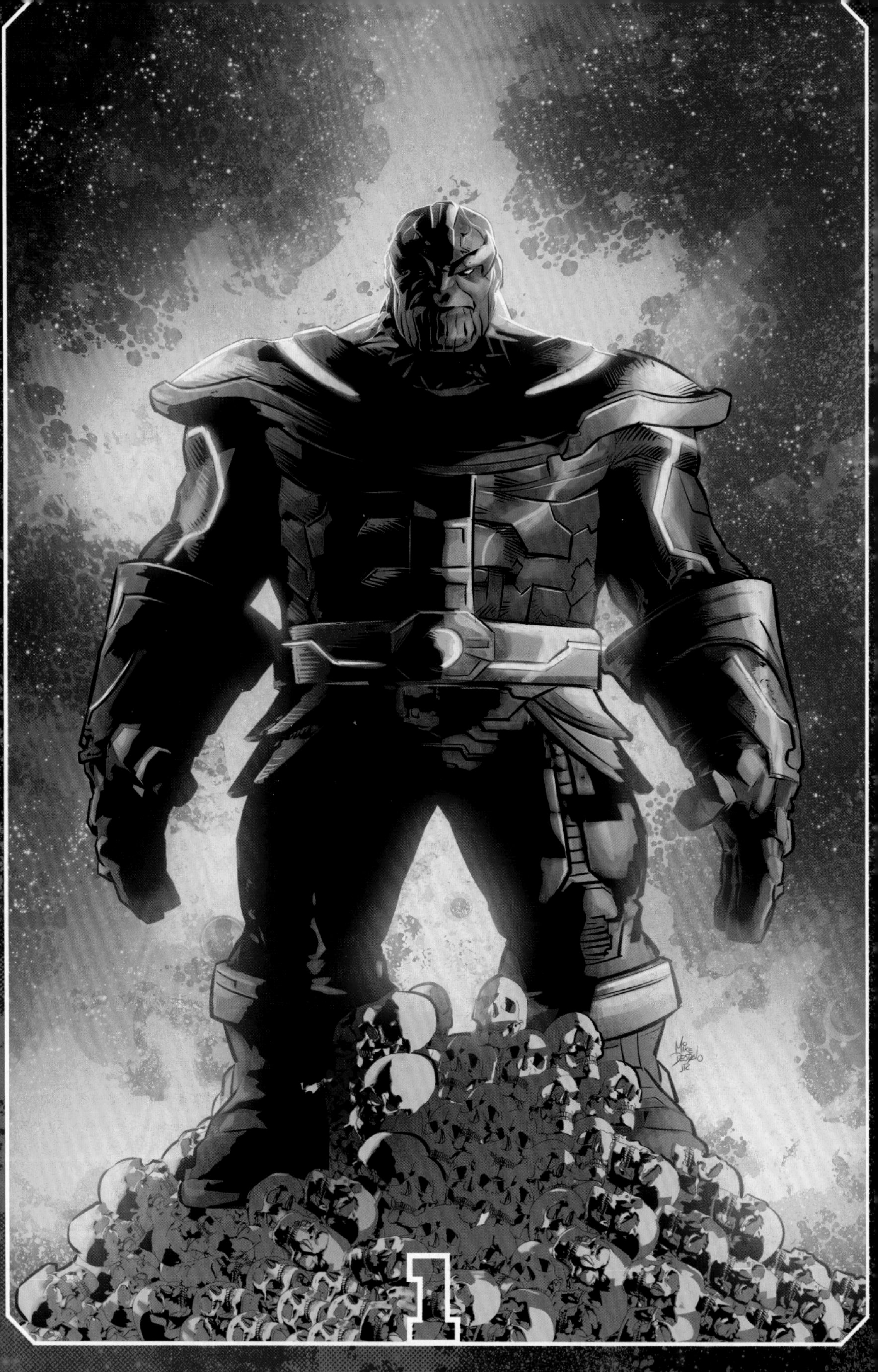
1

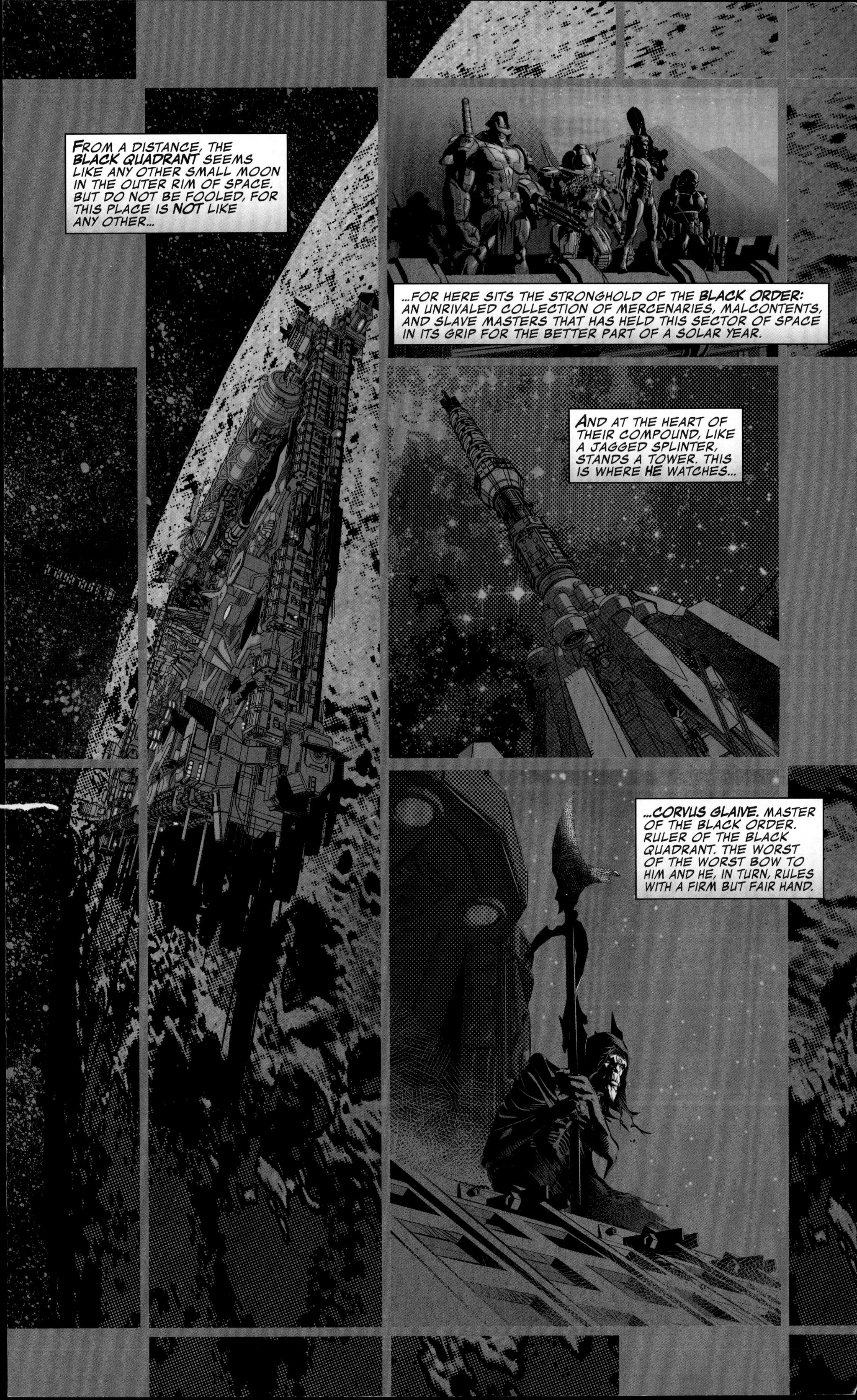
FROM A DISTANCE, THE BLACK QUADRANT SEEMS LIKE ANY OTHER SMALL MOON IN THE OUTER RIM OF SPACE. BUT DO NOT BE FOOLED, FOR THIS PLACE IS NOT LIKE ANY OTHER...
...FOR HERE SITS THE STRONGHOLD OF THE BLACK ORDER: AN UNRIVALED COLLECTION OF MERCENARIES, MALCONTENTS, AND SLAVE MASTERS THAT HAS HELD THIS SECTOR OF SPACE IN ITS GRIP FOR THE BETTER PART OF A SOLAR YEAR.
AND AT THE HEART OF THEIR COMPOUND, LIKE A JAGGED SPLINTER, STANDS A TOWER. THIS IS WHERE HE WATCHES...
...CORVUS GLAIVE. MASTER OF THE BLACK ORDER. RULER OF THE BLACK QUADRANT. THE WORST OF THE WORST BOW TO HIM AND HE, IN TURN, RULES WITH A FIRM BUT FAIR HAND.

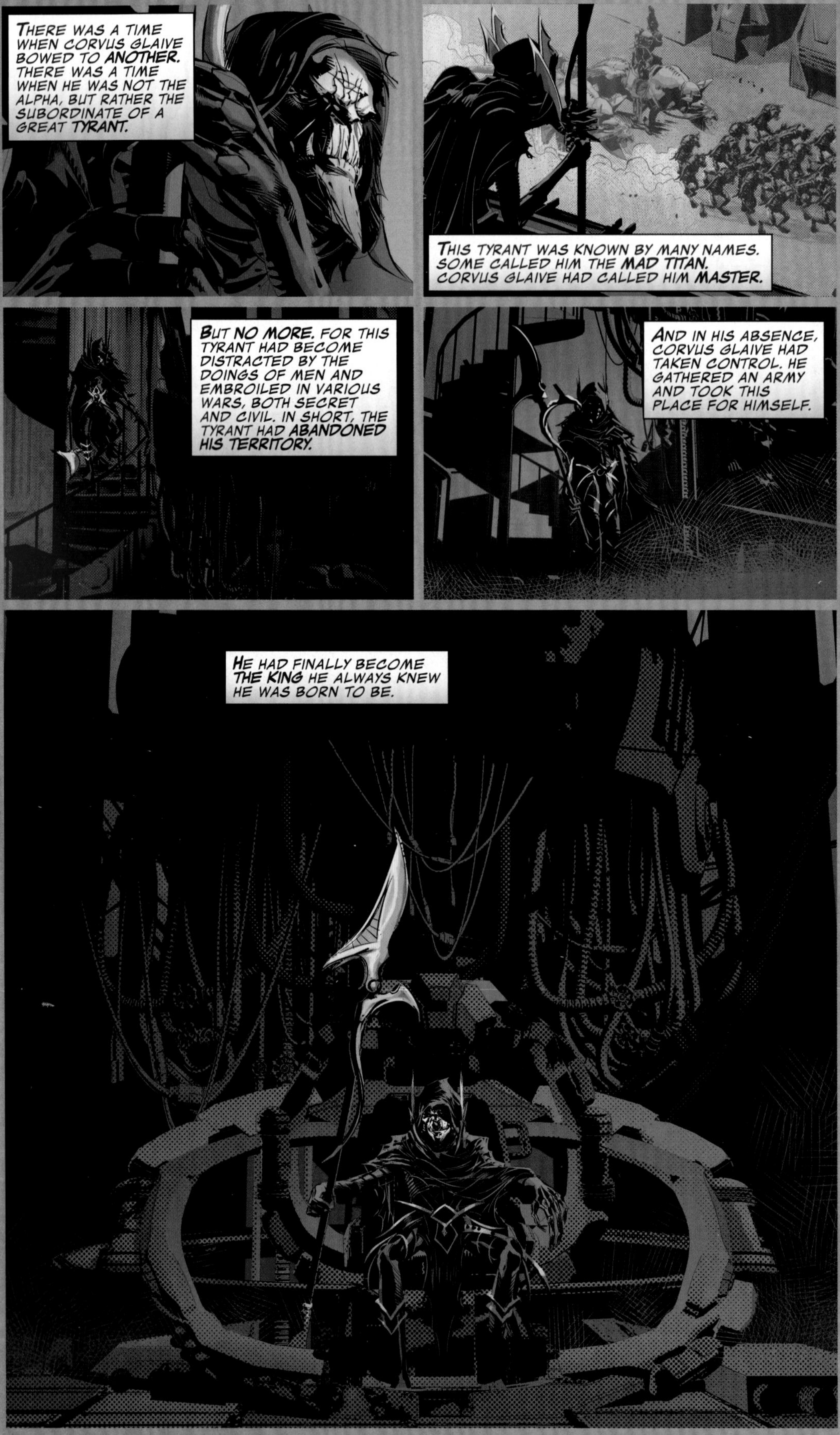
THERE WAS A TIME WHEN CORVUS GLAIVE BOWED TO ANOTHER. THERE WAS A TIME WHEN HE WAS NOT THE ALPHA, BUT RATHER THE SUBORDINATE OF A GREAT TYRANT.
THIS TYRANT WAS KNOWN BY MANY NAMES. SOME CALLED HIM THE MAD TITAN. CORVUS GLAIVE HAD CALLED HIM MASTER.
BUT NO MORE. FOR THIS TYRANT HAD BECOME DISTRACTED BY THE DOINGS OF MEN AND EMBROILED IN VARIOUS WARS, BOTH SECRET AND CIVIL. IN SHORT, THE TYRANT HAD ABANDONED HIS TERRITORY.
AND IN HIS ABSENCE, CORVUS GLAIVE HAD TAKEN CONTROL. HE GATHERED AN ARMY AND TOOK THIS PLACE FOR HIMSELF.
HE HAD FINALLY BECOME THE KING HE ALWAYS KNEW HE WAS BORN TO BE.

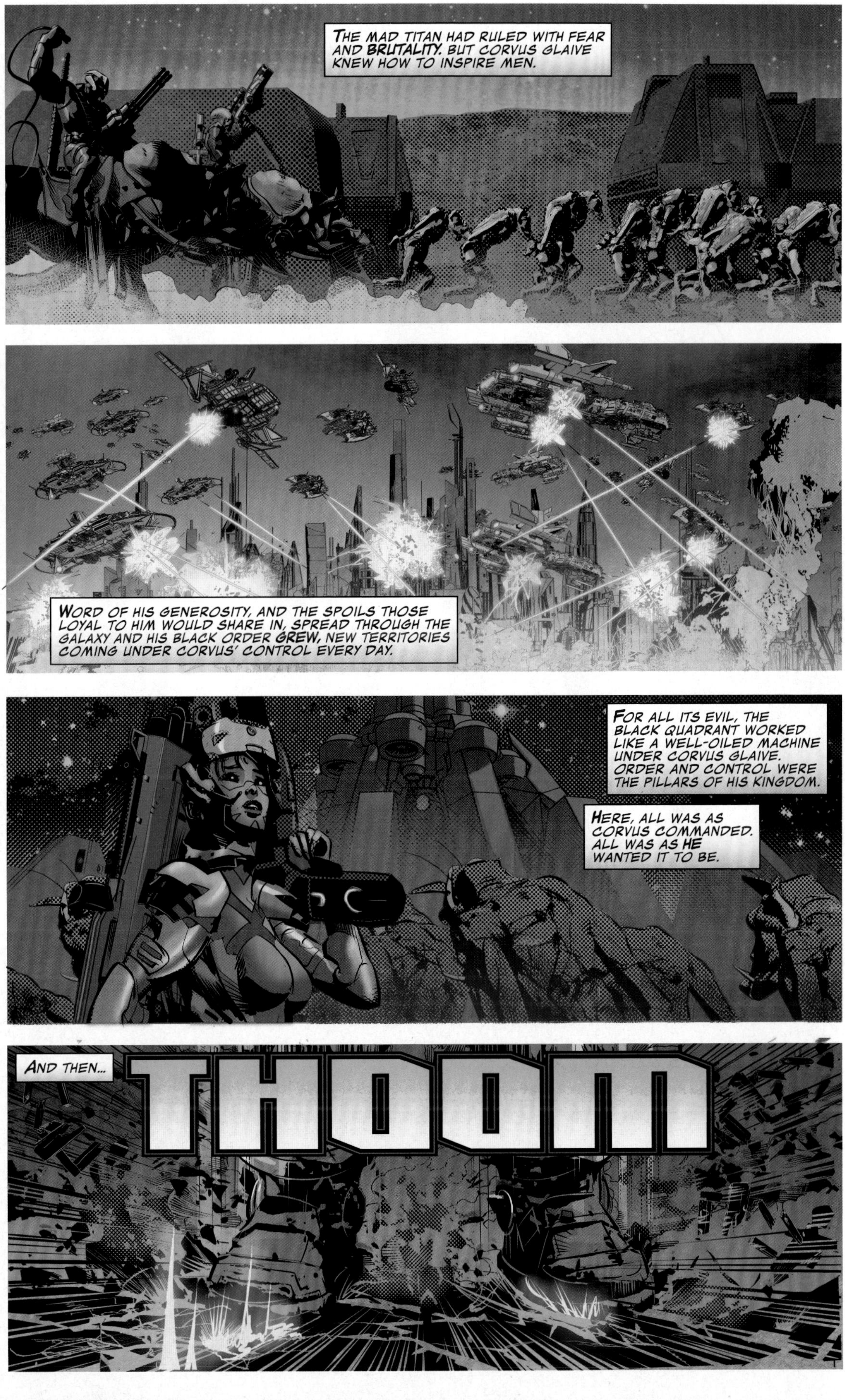
THE MAD TITAN HAD RULED WITH FEAR AND BRUTALITY. BUT CORVUS GLAIVE KNEW HOW TO INSPIRE MEN.
WORD OF HIS GENEROSITY, AND THE SPOILS THOSE LOYAL TO HIM WOULD SHARE IN, SPREAD THROUGH THE GALAXY AND HIS BLACK ORDER GREW, NEW TERRITORIES COMING UNDER CORVUS' CONTROL EVERY DAY.
FOR ALL ITS EVIL, THE BLACK QUADRANT WORKED LIKE A WELL-OILED MACHINE UNDER CORVUS GLAIVE. ORDER AND CONTROL WERE THE PILLARS OF HIS KINGDOM.
HERE, ALL WAS AS CORVUS COMMANDED. ALL WAS AS HE WANTED IT TO BE.
AND THEN...
THOOM

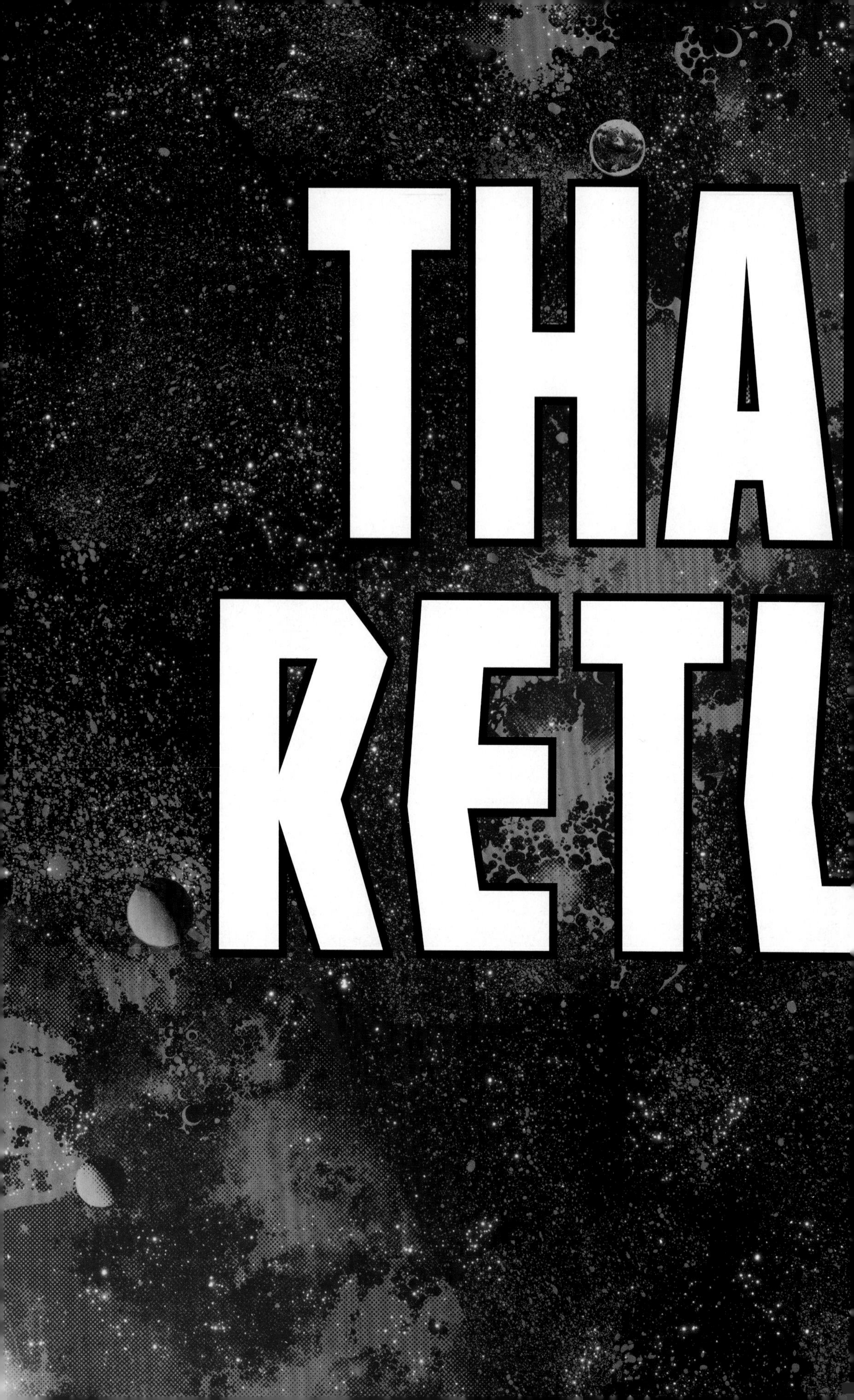
THA
RET

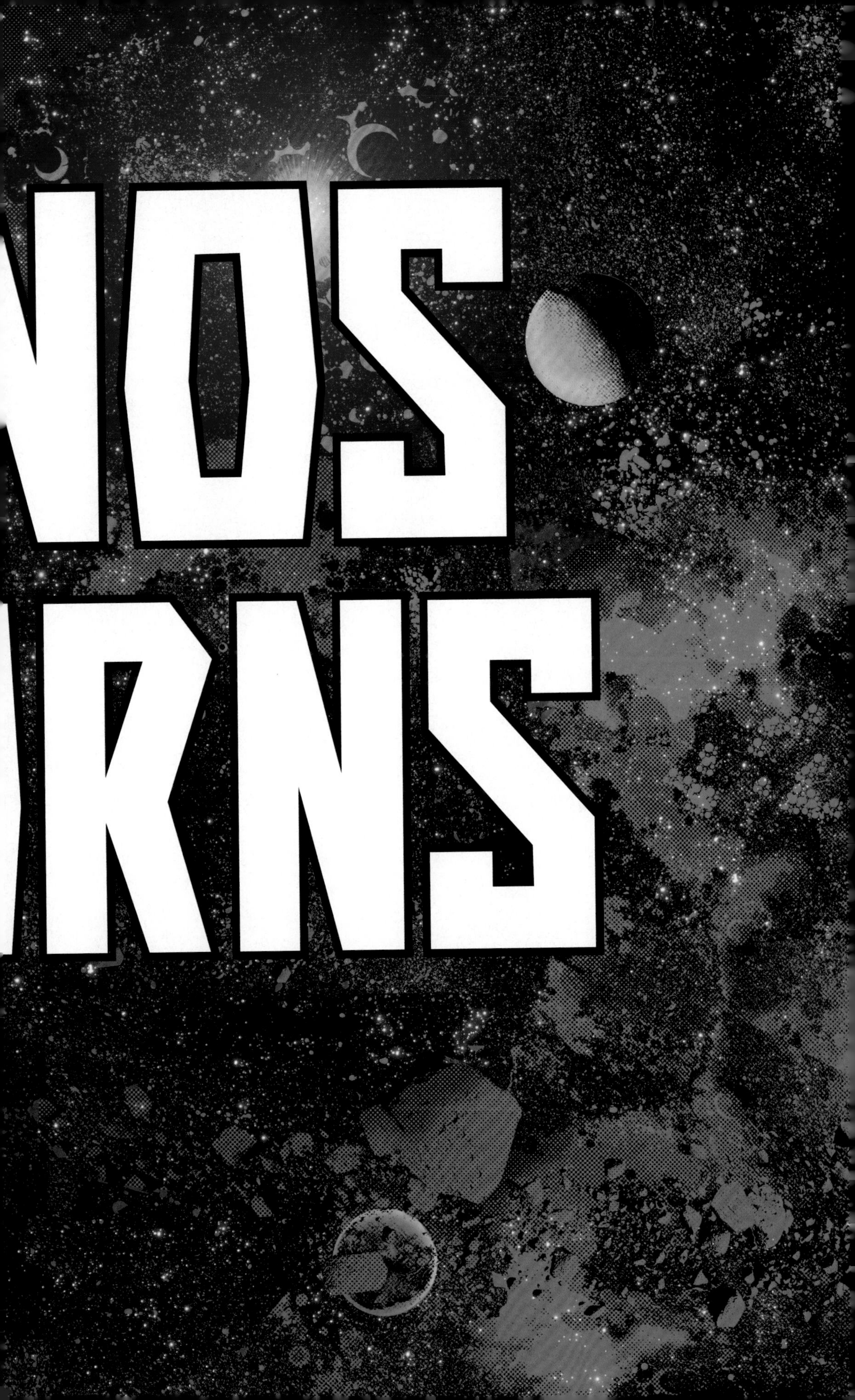
NOS
RNS

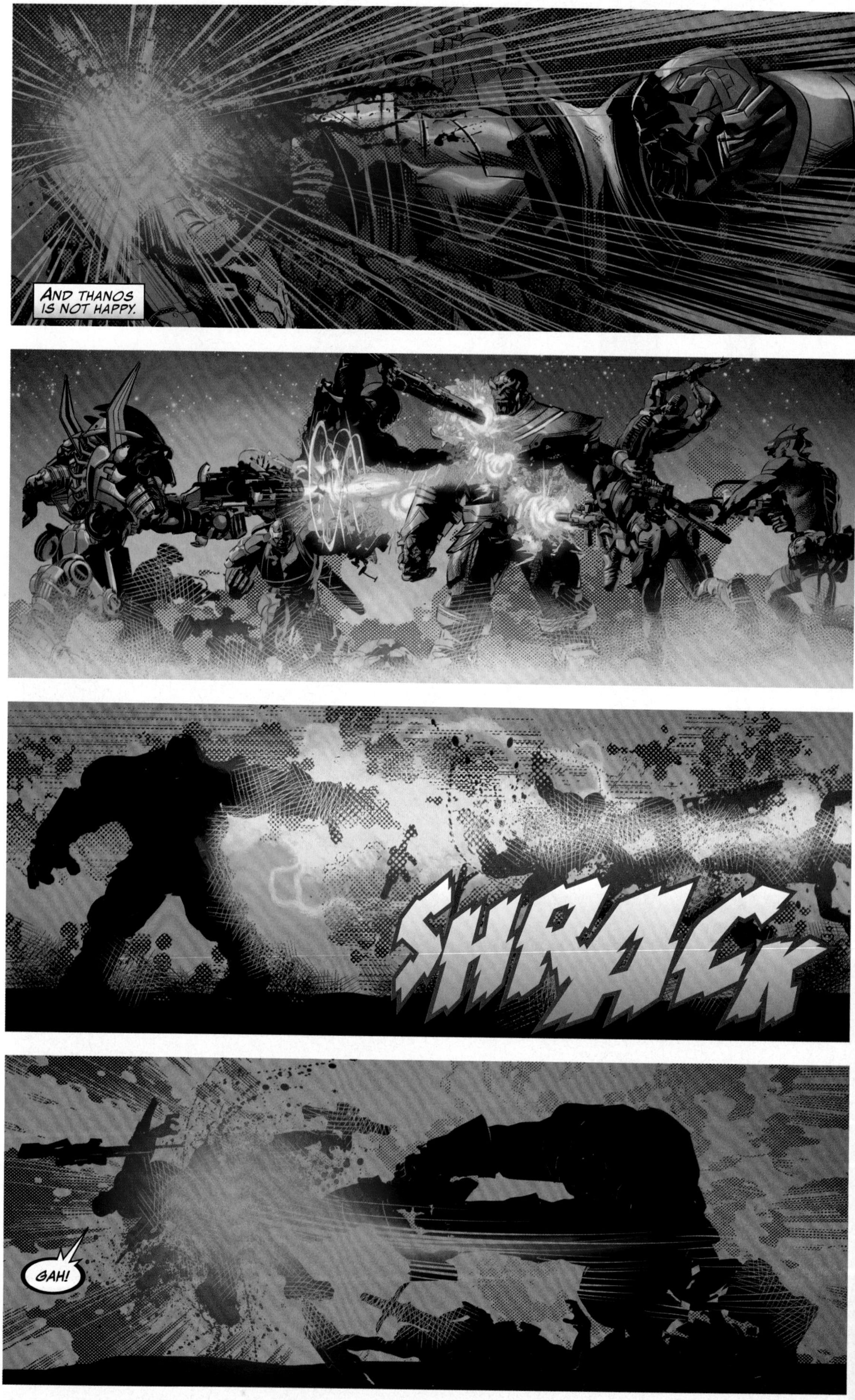
AND THANOS IS NOT HAPPY.
SHRACK
GAH!

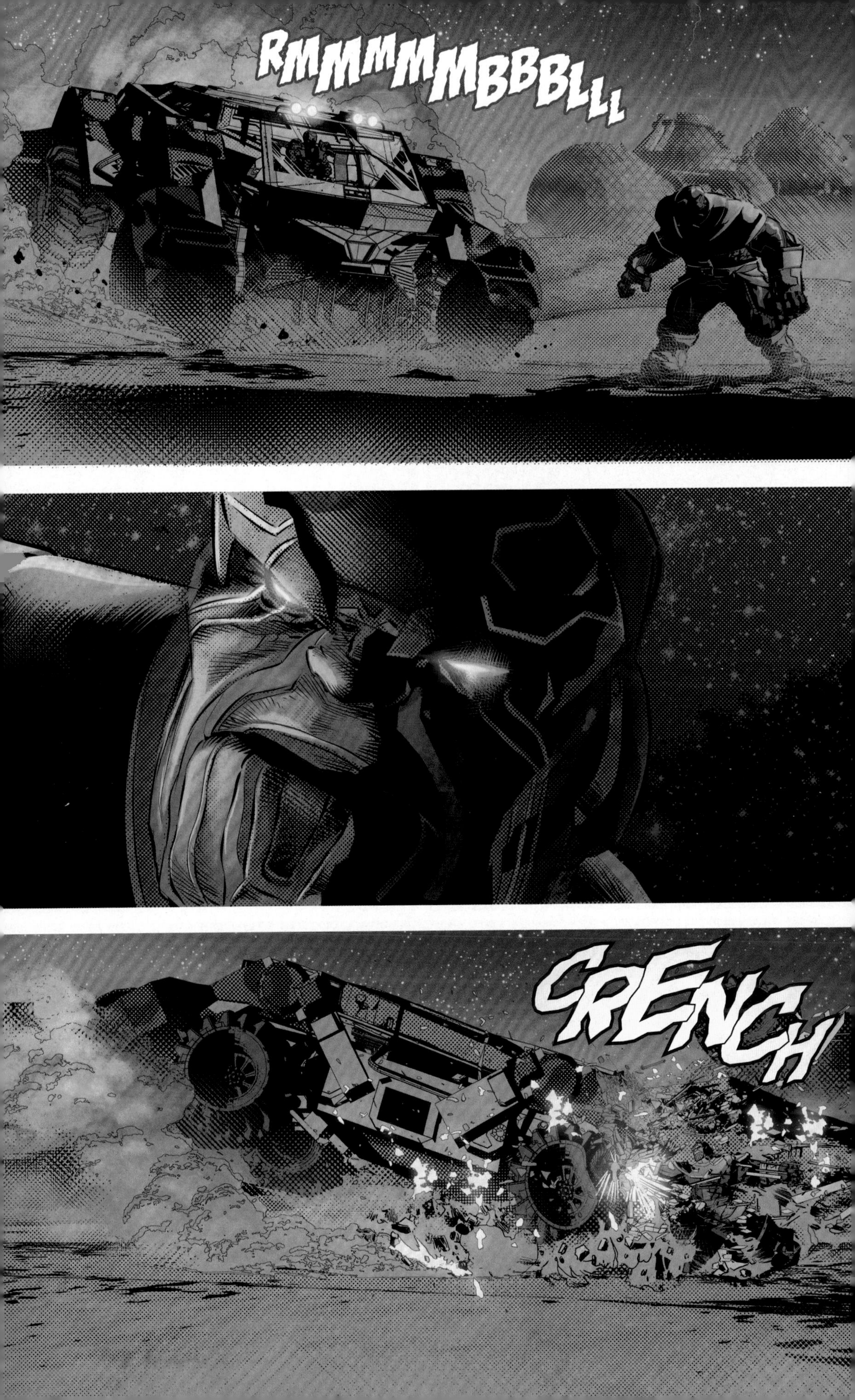
RMMMMMBBBLLL
CRENCH

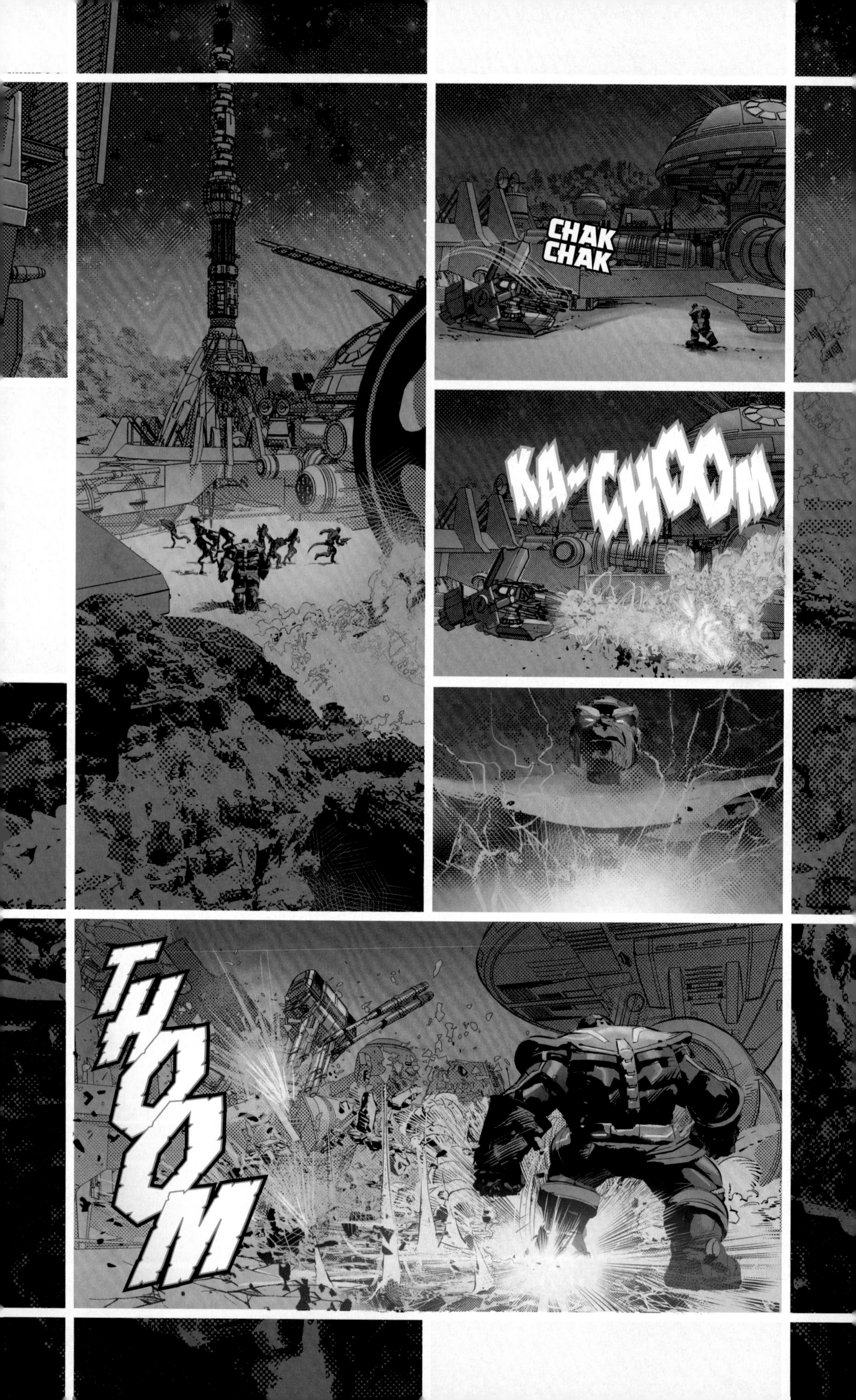
CHAK
CHAK
KA-CHOOM
THOOM

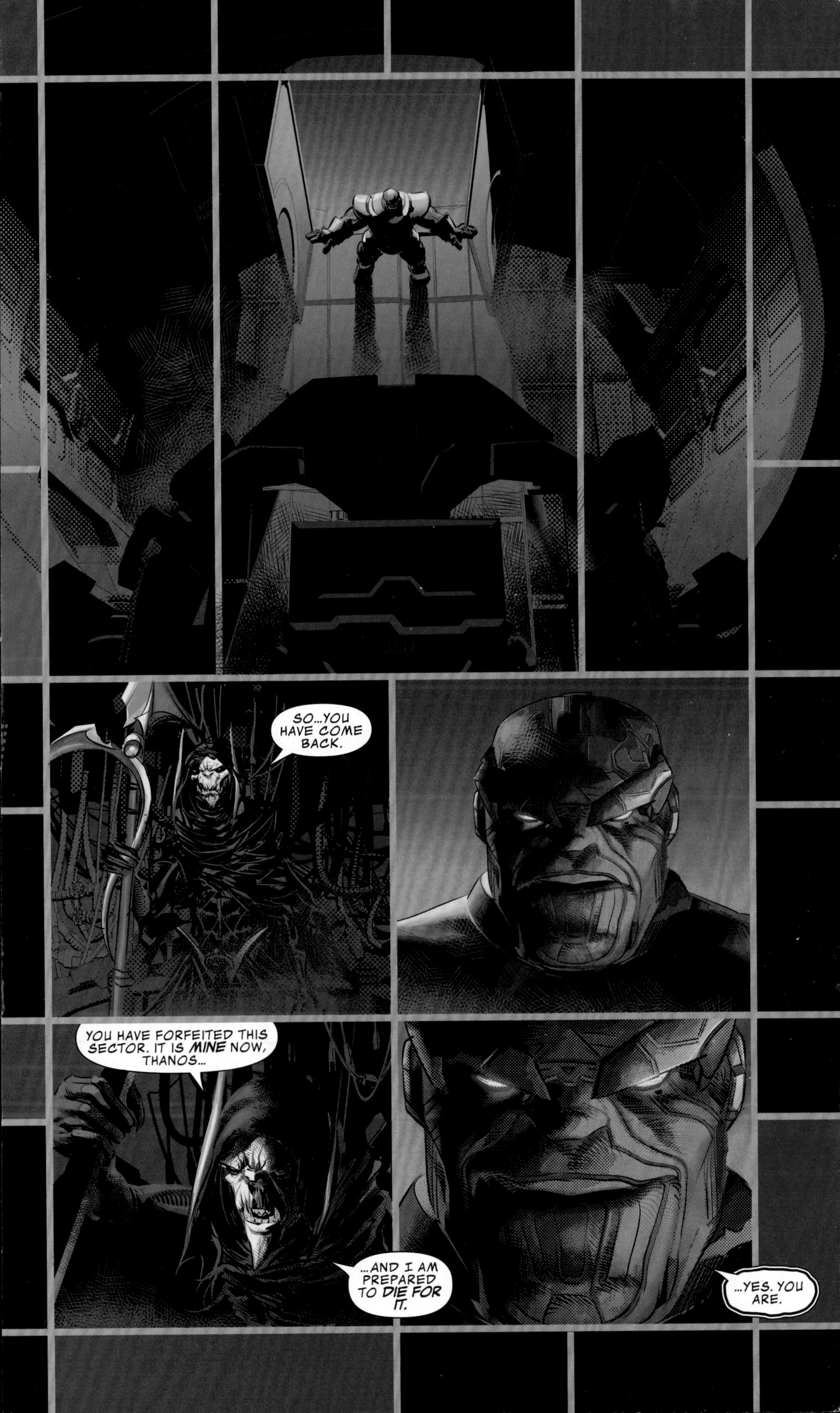
SO...YOU HAVE COME BACK.
YOU HAVE FORFEITED THIS SECTOR. IT IS MINE NOW, THANOS...
...AND I AM PREPARED TO DIE FOR IT.
...YES. YOU ARE.

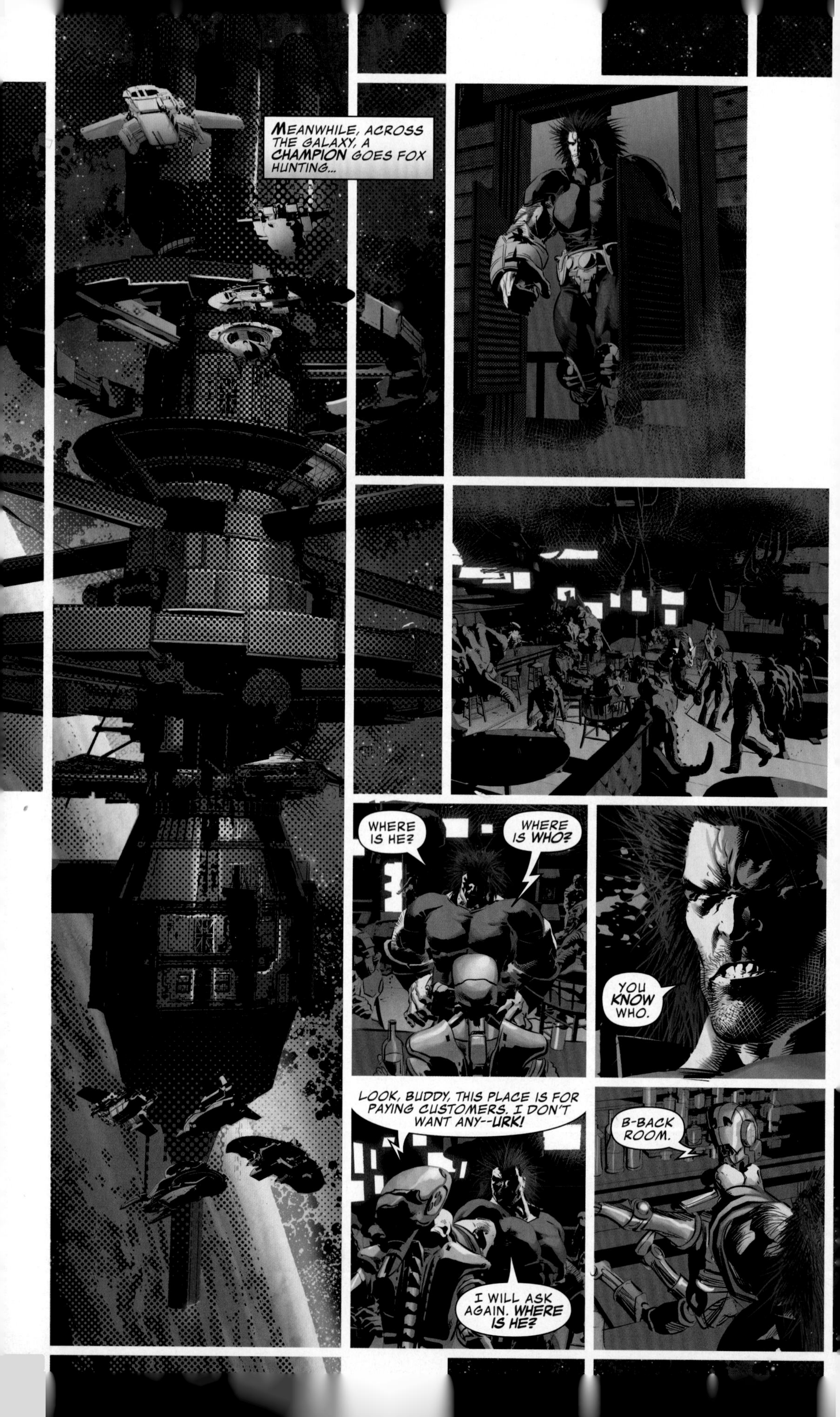
MEANWHILE, ACROSS THE GALAXY, A CHAMPION GOES FOX HUNTING...
WHERE IS HE?
WHERE IS WHO?
YOU KNOW WHO.
LOOK, BUDDY, THIS PLACE IS FOR PAYING CUSTOMERS. I DON'T WANT ANY--URK!
I WILL ASK AGAIN. WHERE IS HE?
B-BACK ROOM.

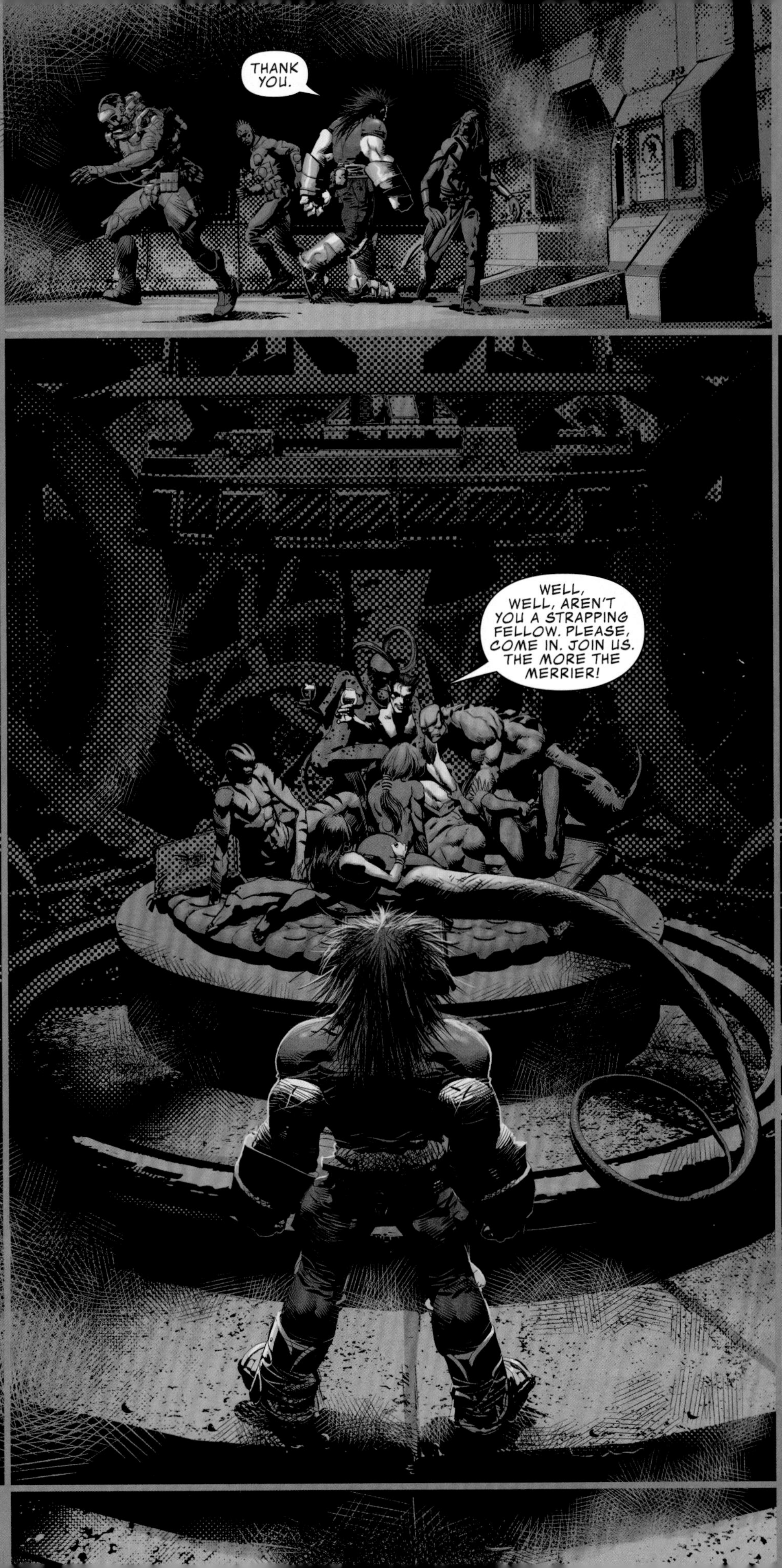
THANK YOU.
WELL, WELL, AREN'T YOU A STRAPPING FELLOW. PLEASE, COME IN. JOIN US. THE MORE THE MERRIER!

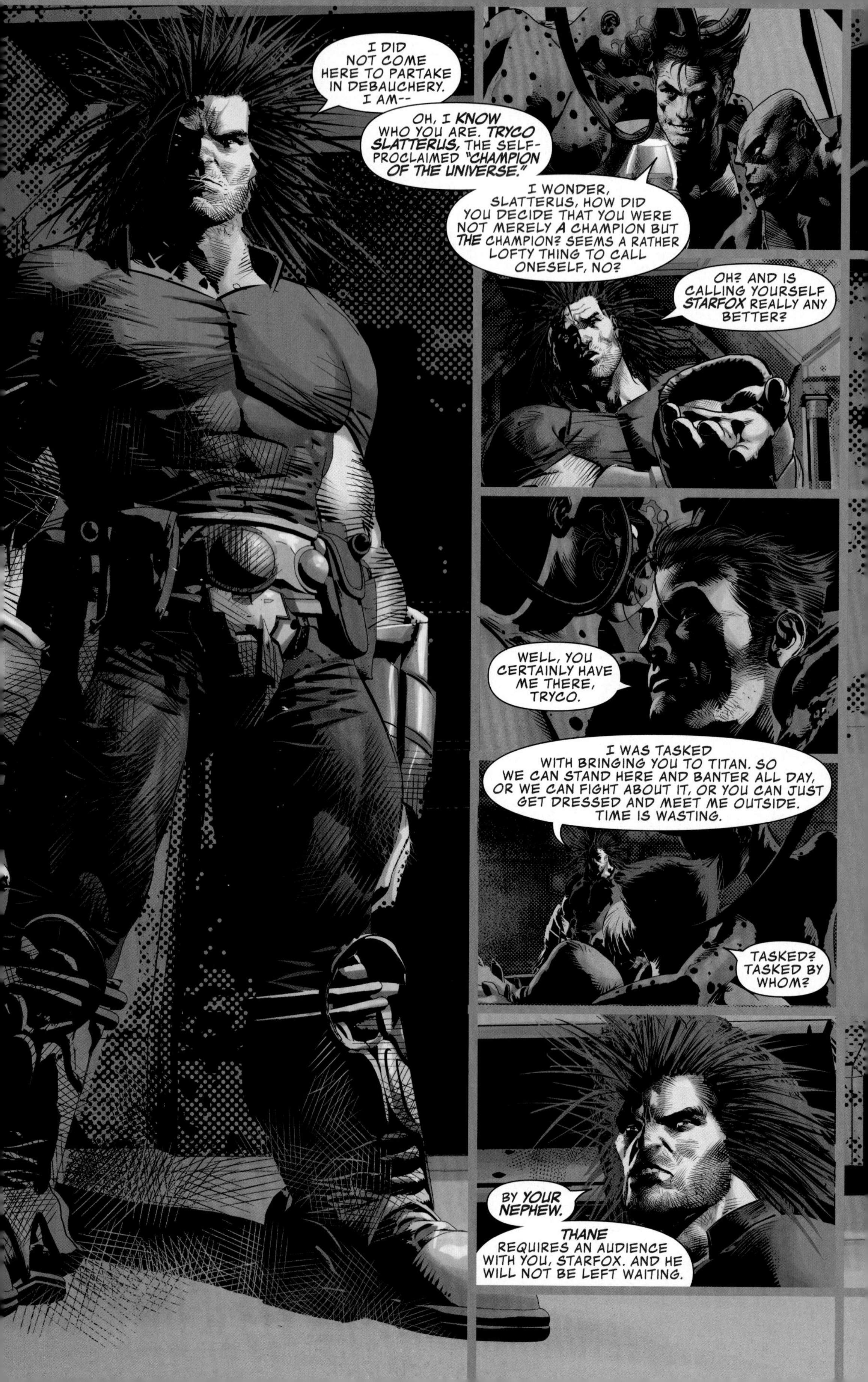

I DID NOT COME HERE TO PARTAKE IN DEBAUCHERY. I AM--
OH, I KNOW WHO YOU ARE. TRYCO SLATTERUS, THE SELF-PROCLAIMED "CHAMPION OF THE UNIVERSE."
I WONDER, SLATTERUS, HOW DID YOU DECIDE THAT YOU WERE NOT MERELY A CHAMPION BUT THE CHAMPION? SEEMS A RATHER LOFTY THING TO CALL ONESELF, NO?
OH? AND IS CALLING YOURSELF STARFOX REALLY ANY BETTER?
WELL, YOU CERTAINLY HAVE ME THERE, TRYCO.
I WAS TASKED WITH BRINGING YOU TO TITAN. SO WE CAN STAND HERE AND BANTER ALL DAY, OR WE CAN FIGHT ABOUT IT, OR YOU CAN JUST GET DRESSED AND MEET ME OUTSIDE. TIME IS WASTING.
TASKED? TASKED BY WHOM?
BY YOUR NEPHEW.
THANE REQUIRES AN AUDIENCE WITH YOU, STARFOX. AND HE WILL NOT BE LEFT WAITING.

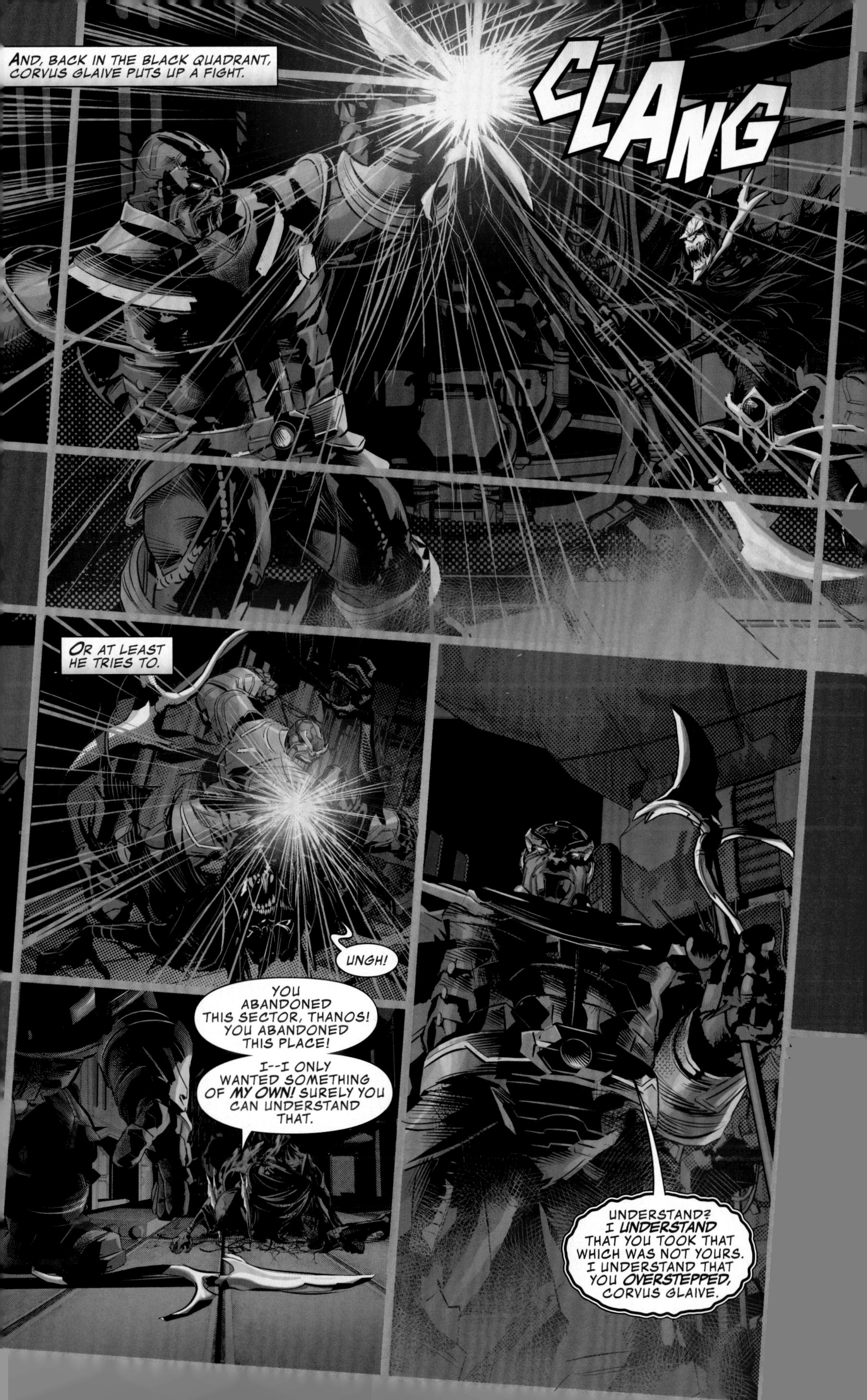
AND, BACK IN THE BLACK QUADRANT, CORVUS GLAIVE PUTS UP A FIGHT.
CLANG
OR AT LEAST HE TRIES TO.
UNGH!
YOU ABANDONED THIS SECTOR, THANOS! YOU ABANDONED THIS PLACE!
I--I ONLY WANTED SOMETHING OF MY OWN! SURELY YOU CAN UNDERSTAND THAT.
UNDERSTAND? I UNDERSTAND THAT YOU TOOK THAT WHICH WAS NOT YOURS. I UNDERSTAND THAT YOU OVERSTEPPED, CORVUS GLAIVE.

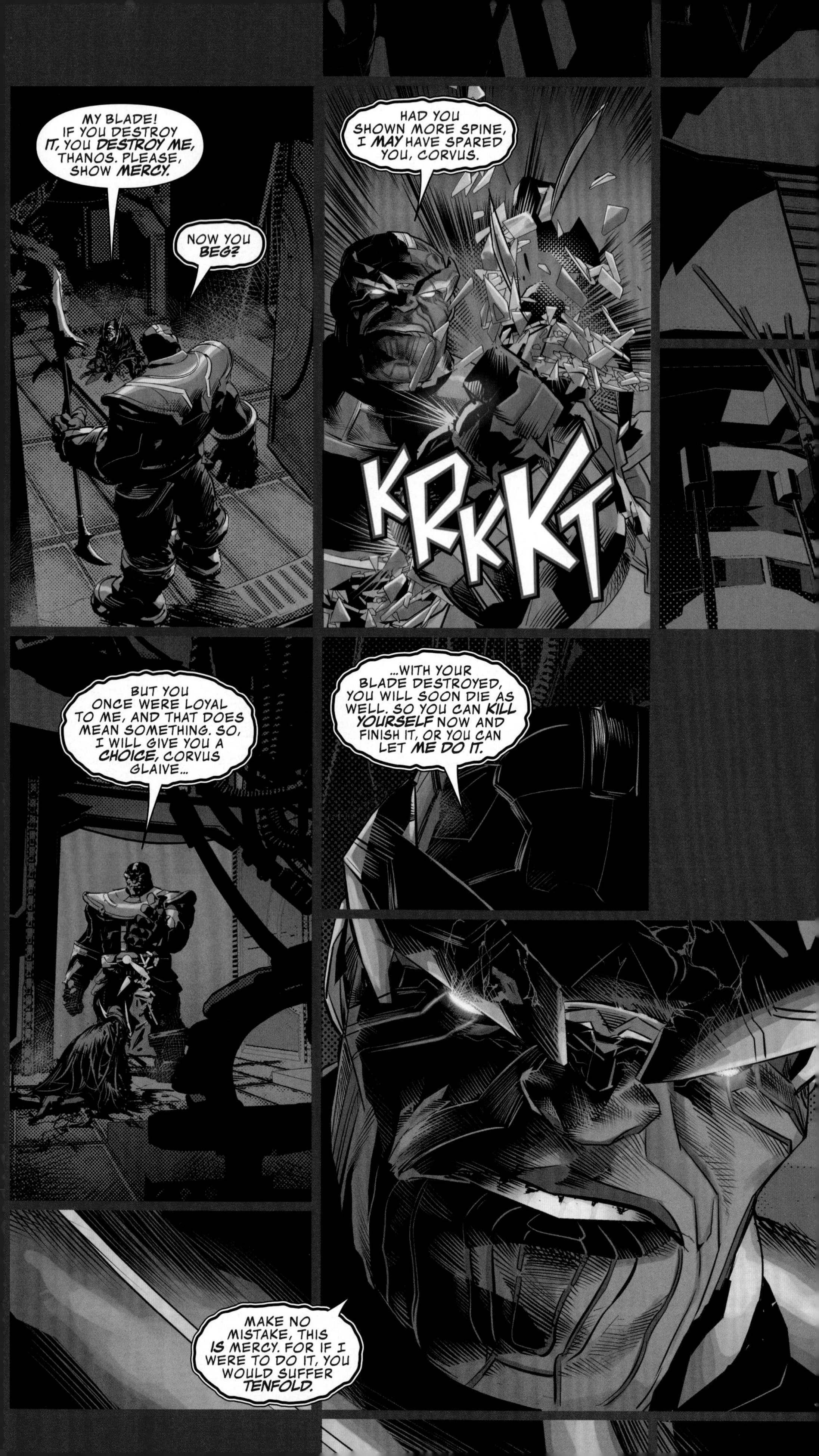
MY BLADE! IF YOU DESTROY IT, YOU DESTROY ME, THANOS. PLEASE, SHOW MERCY.
NOW YOU BEG?
HAD YOU SHOWN MORE SPINE, I MAY HAVE SPARED YOU, CORVUS.
KRKKT
BUT YOU ONCE WERE LOYAL TO ME, AND THAT DOES MEAN SOMETHING. SO, I WILL GIVE YOU A CHOICE, CORVUS GLAIVE...
...WITH YOUR BLADE DESTROYED, YOU WILL SOON DIE AS WELL. SO YOU CAN KILL YOURSELF NOW AND FINISH IT, OR YOU CAN LET ME DO IT.
MAKE NO MISTAKE, THIS IS MERCY. FOR IF I WERE TO DO IT, YOU WOULD SUFFER TENFOLD.

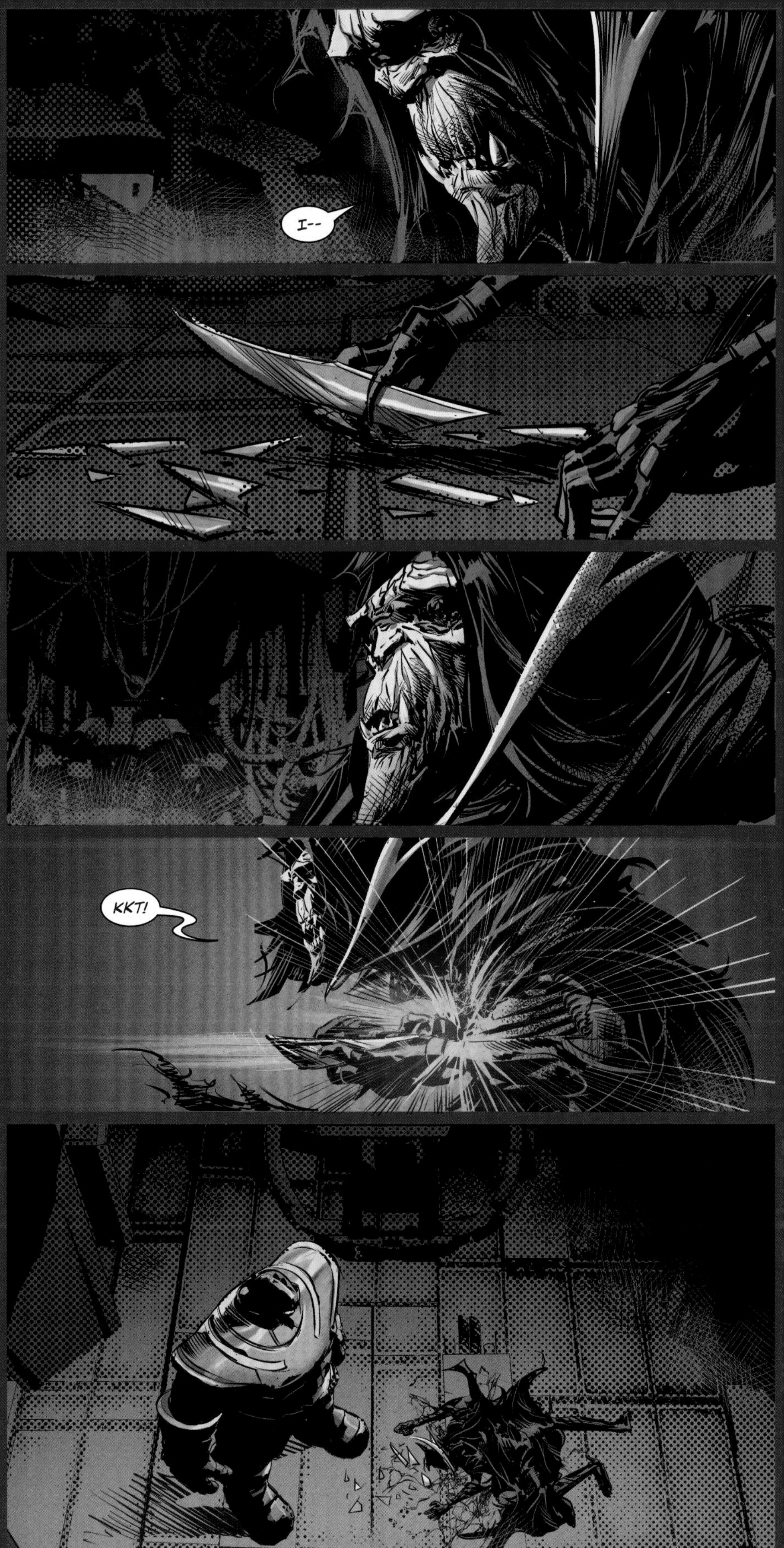
I--
KKT!

AND SO, THANOS TAKES HIS THRONE BACK.

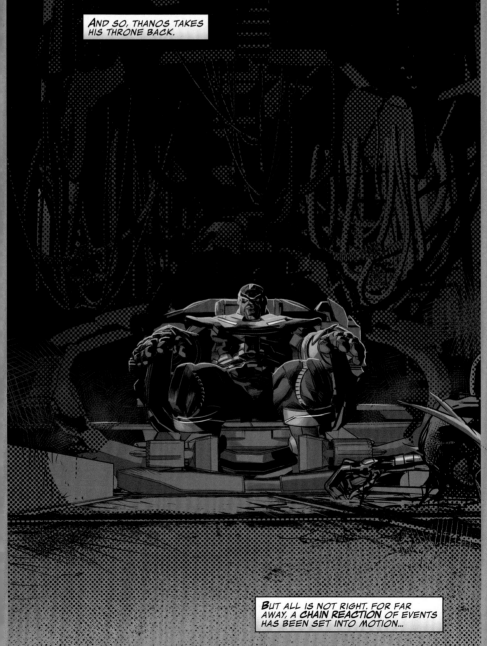

BUT ALL IS NOT RIGHT. FOR FAR AWAY, A *CHAIN REACTION* OF EVENTS HAS BEEN SET INTO MOTION...

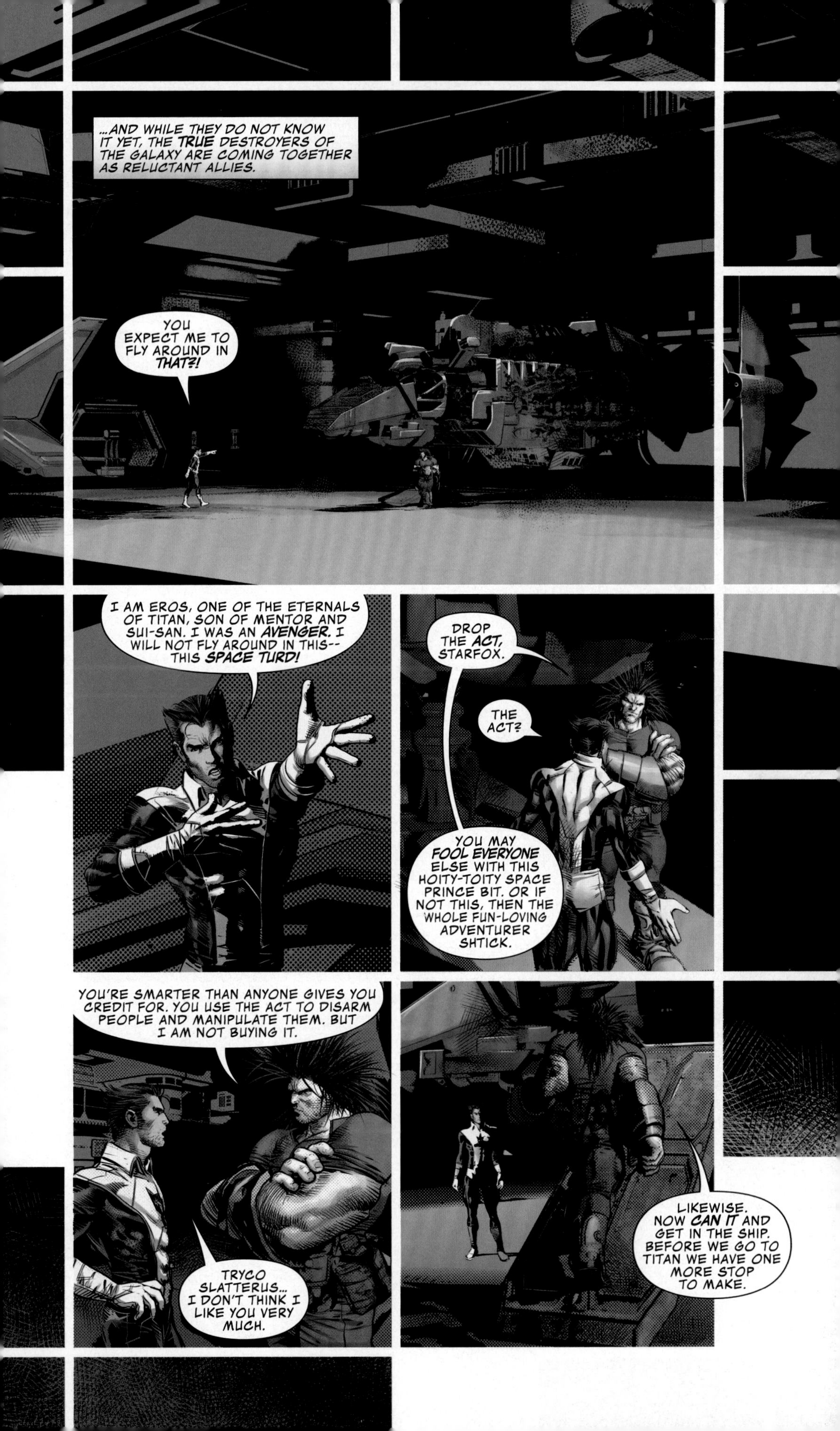
...AND WHILE THEY DO NOT KNOW IT YET, THE TRUE DESTROYERS OF THE GALAXY ARE COMING TOGETHER AS RELUCTANT ALLIES.
YOU EXPECT ME TO FLY AROUND IN THAT?!
I AM EROS, ONE OF THE ETERNALS OF TITAN, SON OF MENTOR AND SUI-SAN. I WAS AN AVENGER. I WILL NOT FLY AROUND IN THIS-- THIS SPACE TURD!
DROP THE ACT, STARFOX.
THE ACT?
YOU MAY FOOL EVERYONE ELSE WITH THIS HOITY-TOITY SPACE PRINCE BIT. OR IF NOT THIS, THEN THE WHOLE FUN-LOVING ADVENTURER SHTICK.
YOU'RE SMARTER THAN ANYONE GIVES YOU CREDIT FOR. YOU USE THE ACT TO DISARM PEOPLE AND MANIPULATE THEM. BUT I AM NOT BUYING IT.
TRYCO SLATTERUS... I DON'T THINK I LIKE YOU VERY MUCH.
LIKEWISE. NOW CAN IT AND GET IN THE SHIP. BEFORE WE GO TO TITAN WE HAVE ONE MORE STOP TO MAKE.

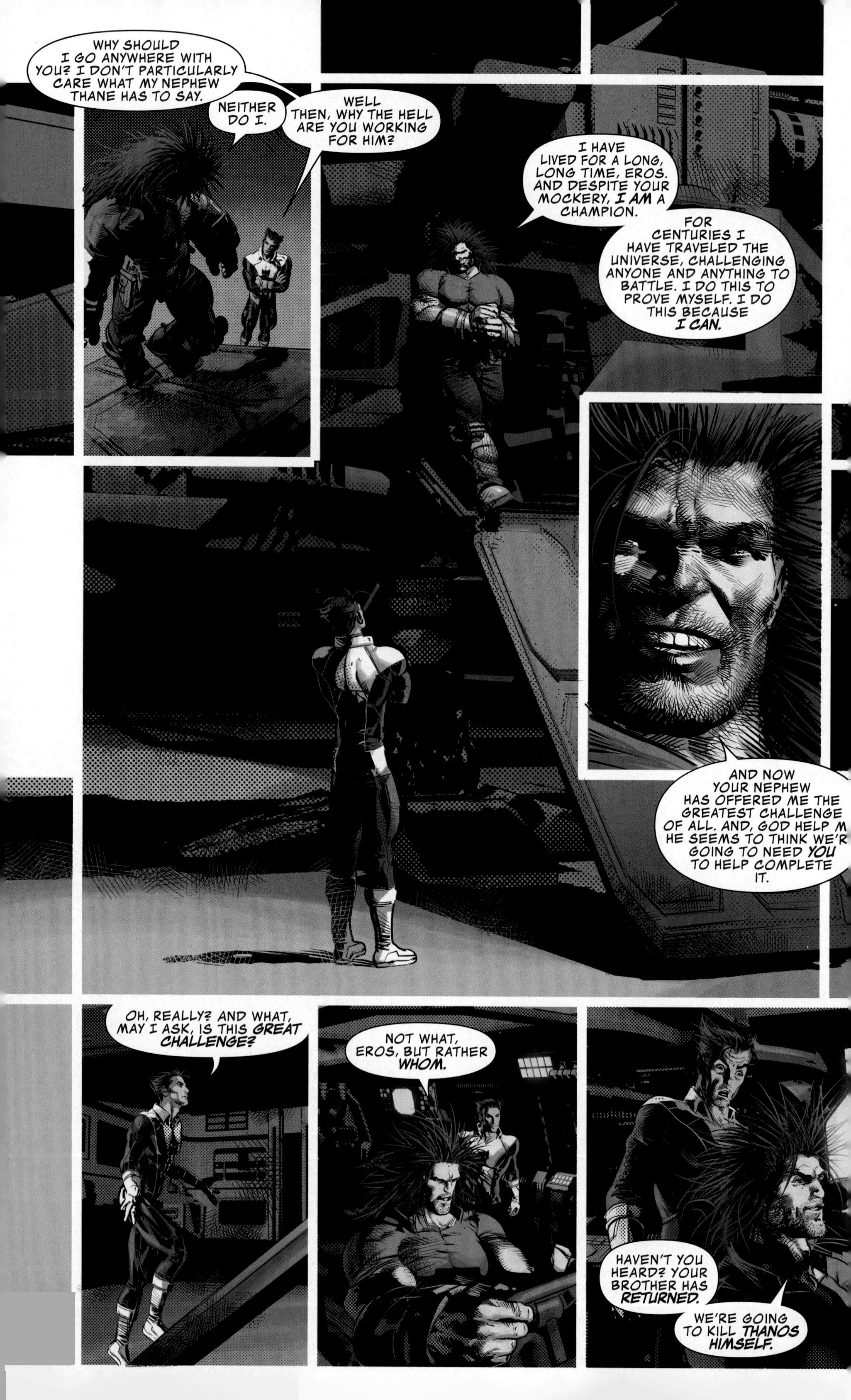
WHY SHOULD I GO ANYWHERE WITH YOU? I DON'T PARTICULARLY CARE WHAT MY NEPHEW THANE HAS TO SAY.
NEITHER DO I.
WELL THEN, WHY THE HELL ARE YOU WORKING FOR HIM?
I HAVE LIVED FOR A LONG, LONG TIME, EROS. AND DESPITE YOUR MOCKERY, I AM A CHAMPION.
FOR CENTURIES I HAVE TRAVELED THE UNIVERSE, CHALLENGING ANYONE AND ANYTHING TO BATTLE. I DO THIS TO PROVE MYSELF. I DO THIS BECAUSE I CAN.
AND NOW YOUR NEPHEW HAS OFFERED ME THE GREATEST CHALLENGE OF ALL. AND, GOD HELP M HE SEEMS TO THINK WE'R GOING TO NEED YOU TO HELP COMPLETE IT.
OH, REALLY? AND WHAT, MAY I ASK, IS THIS GREAT CHALLENGE?
NOT WHAT, EROS, BUT RATHER WHOM.
HAVEN'T YOU HEARD? YOUR BROTHER HAS RETURNED.
WE'RE GOING TO KILL THANOS HIMSELF.

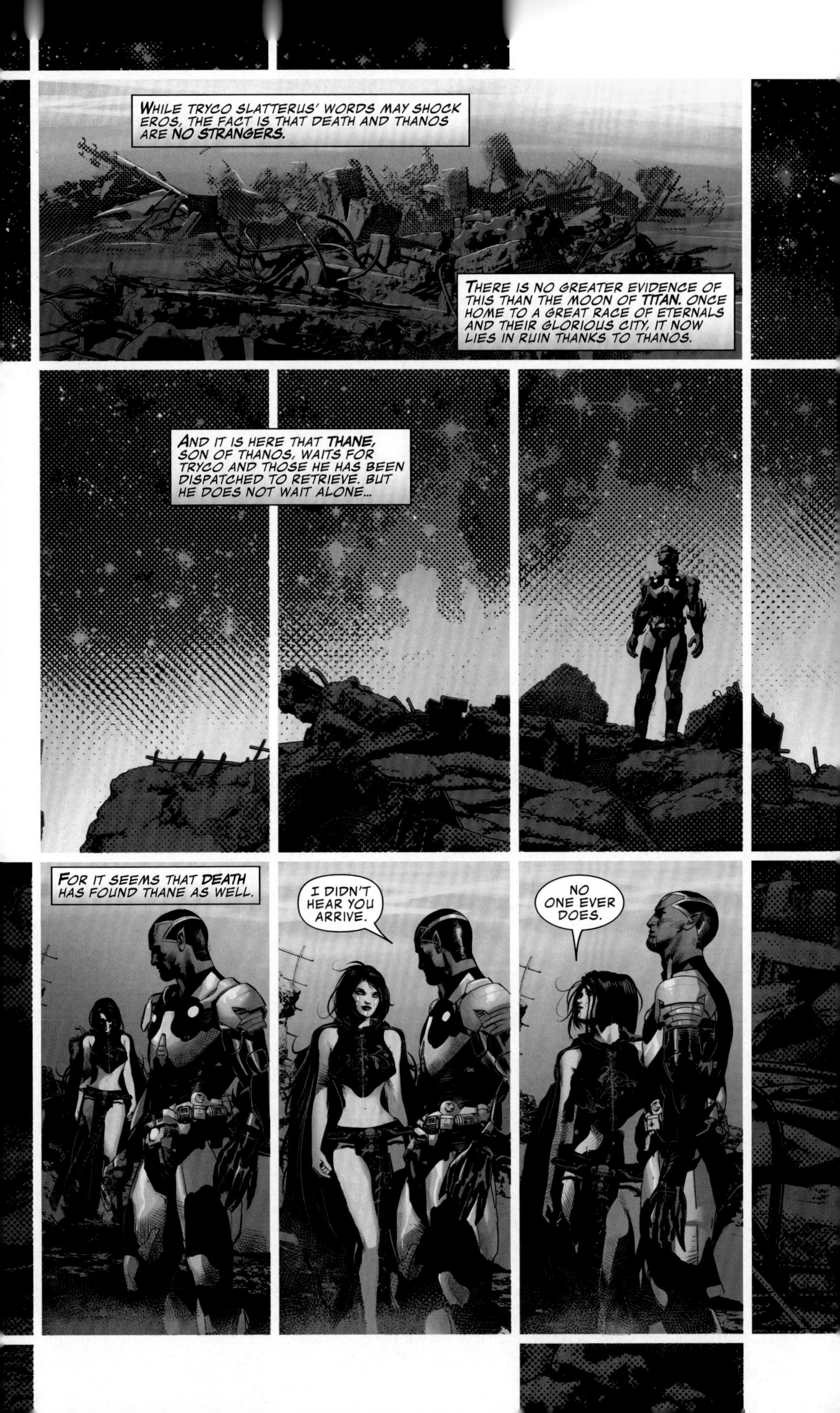
WHILE TRYCO SLATTERUS' WORDS MAY SHOCK EROS, THE FACT IS THAT DEATH AND THANOS ARE NO STRANGERS.
THERE IS NO GREATER EVIDENCE OF THIS THAN THE MOON OF TITAN. ONCE HOME TO A GREAT RACE OF ETERNALS AND THEIR GLORIOUS CITY, IT NOW LIES IN RUIN THANKS TO THANOS.
AND IT IS HERE THAT THANE, SON OF THANOS, WAITS FOR TRYCO AND THOSE HE HAS BEEN DISPATCHED TO RETRIEVE. BUT HE DOES NOT WAIT ALONE...
FOR IT SEEMS THAT DEATH HAS FOUND THANE AS WELL.
I DIDN'T HEAR YOU ARRIVE.
NO ONE EVER DOES.

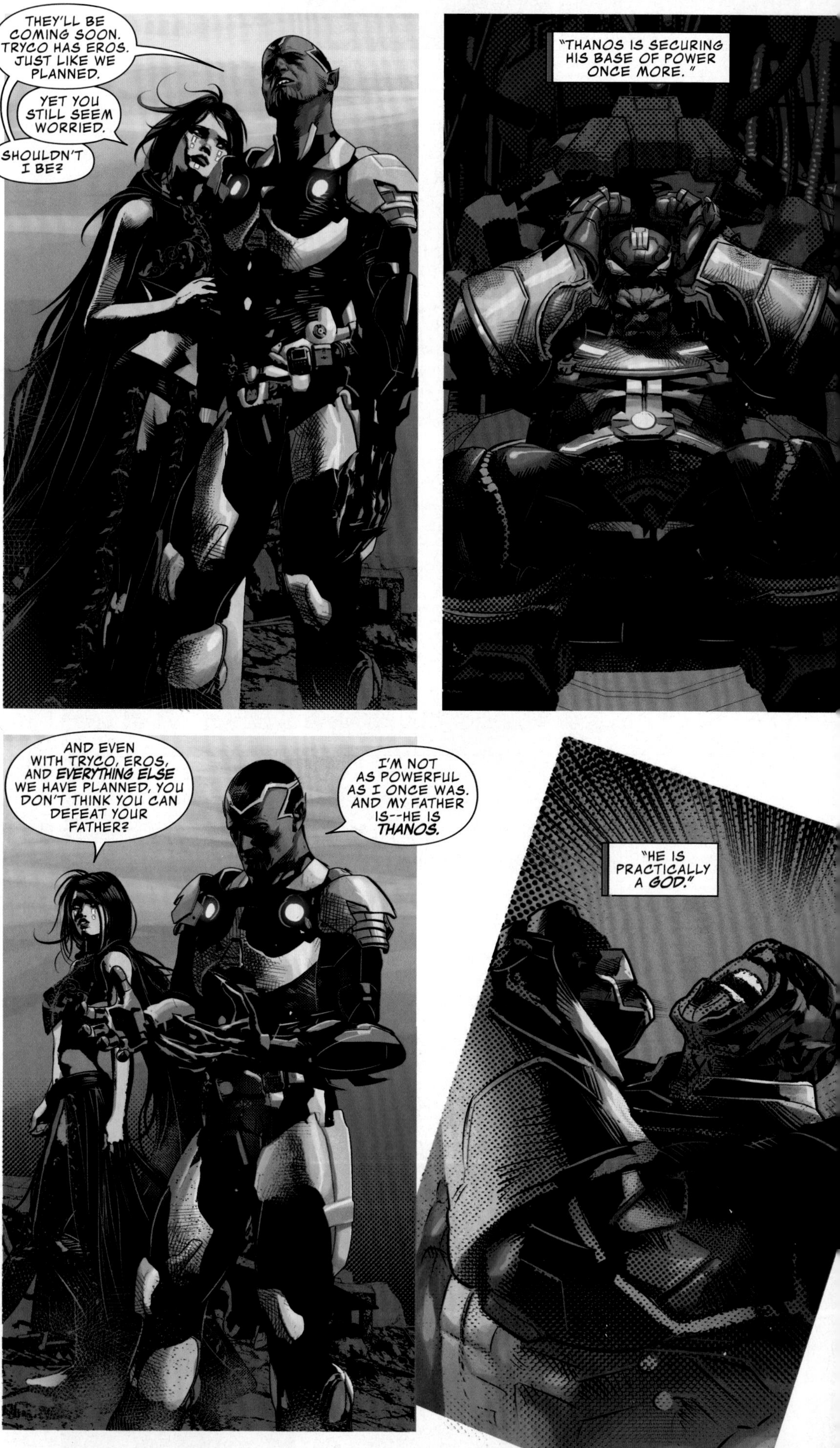
THEY'LL BE COMING SOON. TRYCO HAS EROS. JUST LIKE WE PLANNED.
YET YOU STILL SEEM WORRIED.
SHOULDN'T I BE?
"THANOS IS SECURING HIS BASE OF POWER ONCE MORE."
AND EVEN WITH TRYCO, EROS, AND *EVERYTHING ELSE* WE HAVE PLANNED, YOU DON'T THINK YOU CAN DEFEAT YOUR FATHER?
I'M NOT AS POWERFUL AS I ONCE WAS. AND MY FATHER IS--HE IS *THANOS.*
"HE IS PRACTICALLY A *GOD.*"

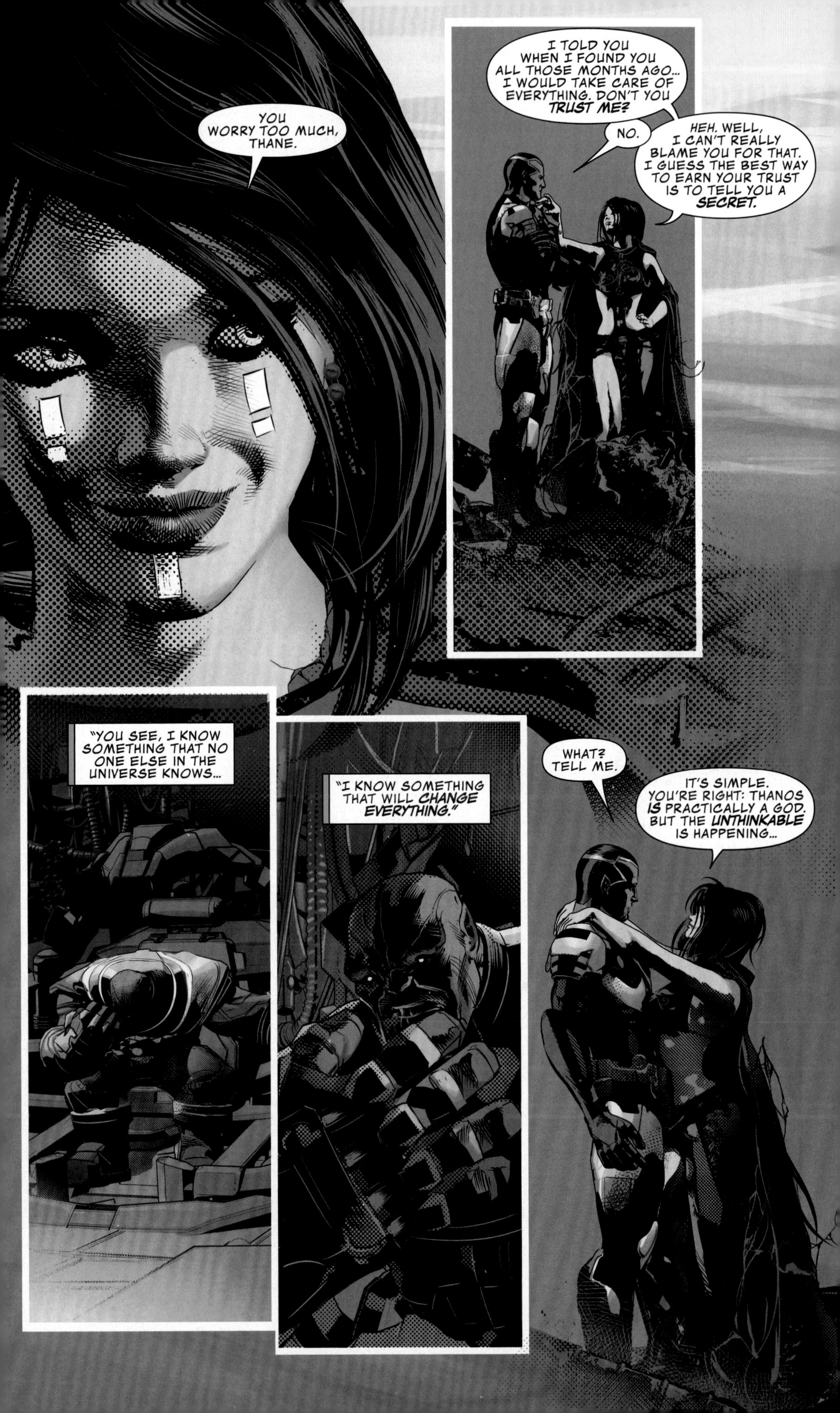
YOU WORRY TOO MUCH, THANE.
I TOLD YOU WHEN I FOUND YOU ALL THOSE MONTHS AGO... I WOULD TAKE CARE OF EVERYTHING. DON'T YOU TRUST ME?
NO.
HEH. WELL, I CAN'T REALLY BLAME YOU FOR THAT. I GUESS THE BEST WAY TO EARN YOUR TRUST IS TO TELL YOU A SECRET.
"YOU SEE, I KNOW SOMETHING THAT NO ONE ELSE IN THE UNIVERSE KNOWS...
"I KNOW SOMETHING THAT WILL CHANGE EVERYTHING."
WHAT? TELL ME.
IT'S SIMPLE. YOU'RE RIGHT: THANOS IS PRACTICALLY A GOD. BUT THE UNTHINKABLE IS HAPPENING...

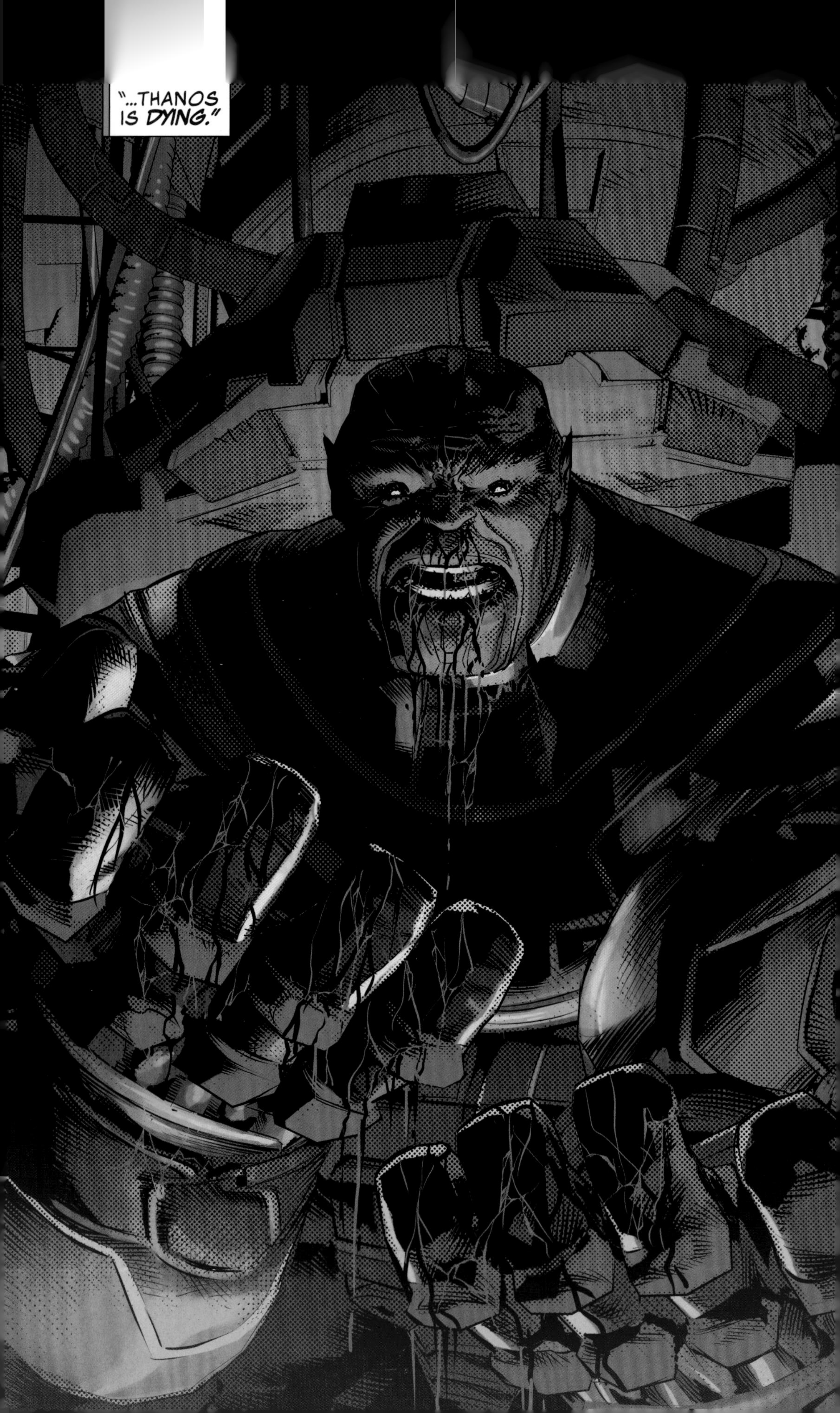
"...THANOS IS DYING."

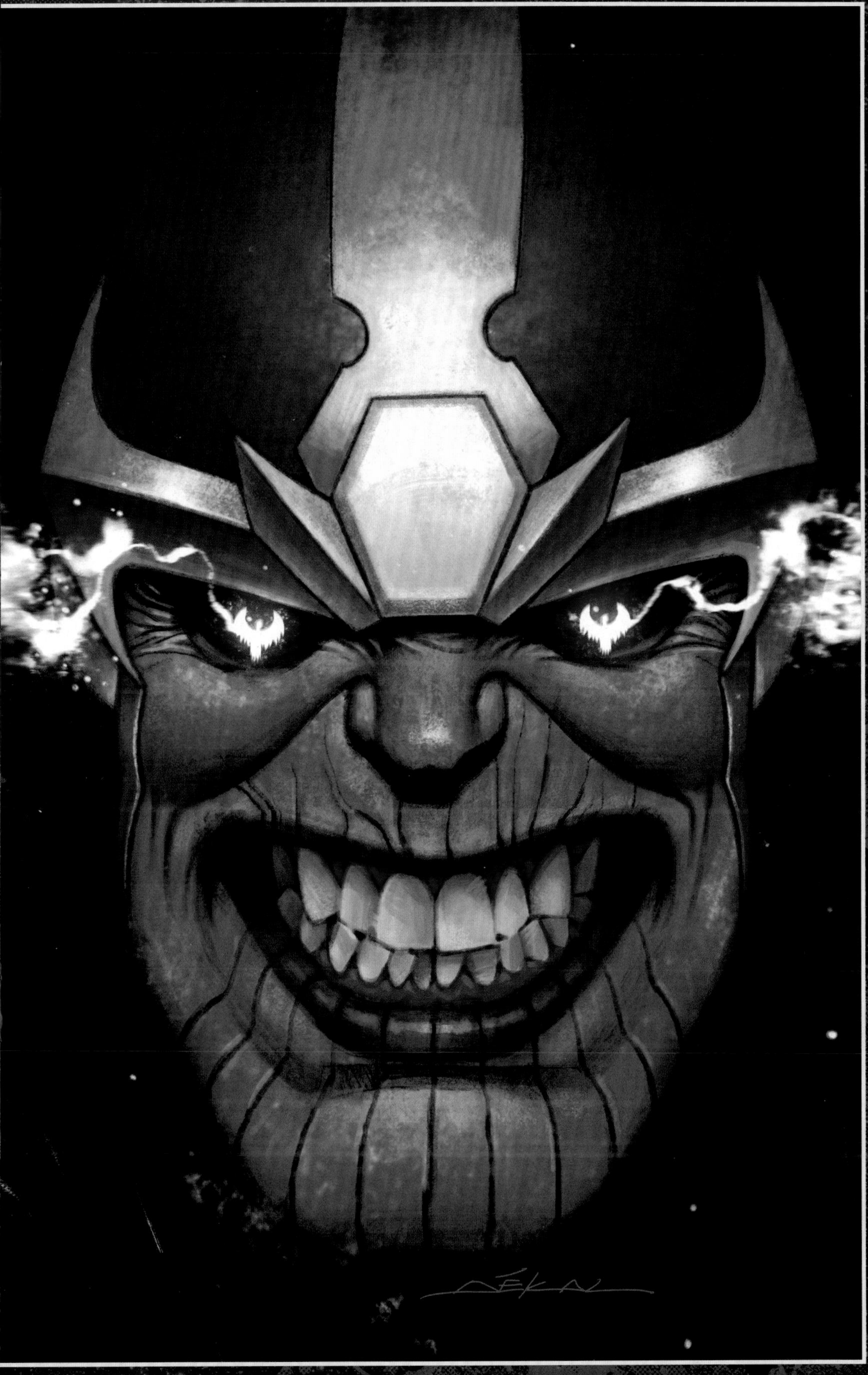

JEFF DEKAL
NO. 1 VARIANT

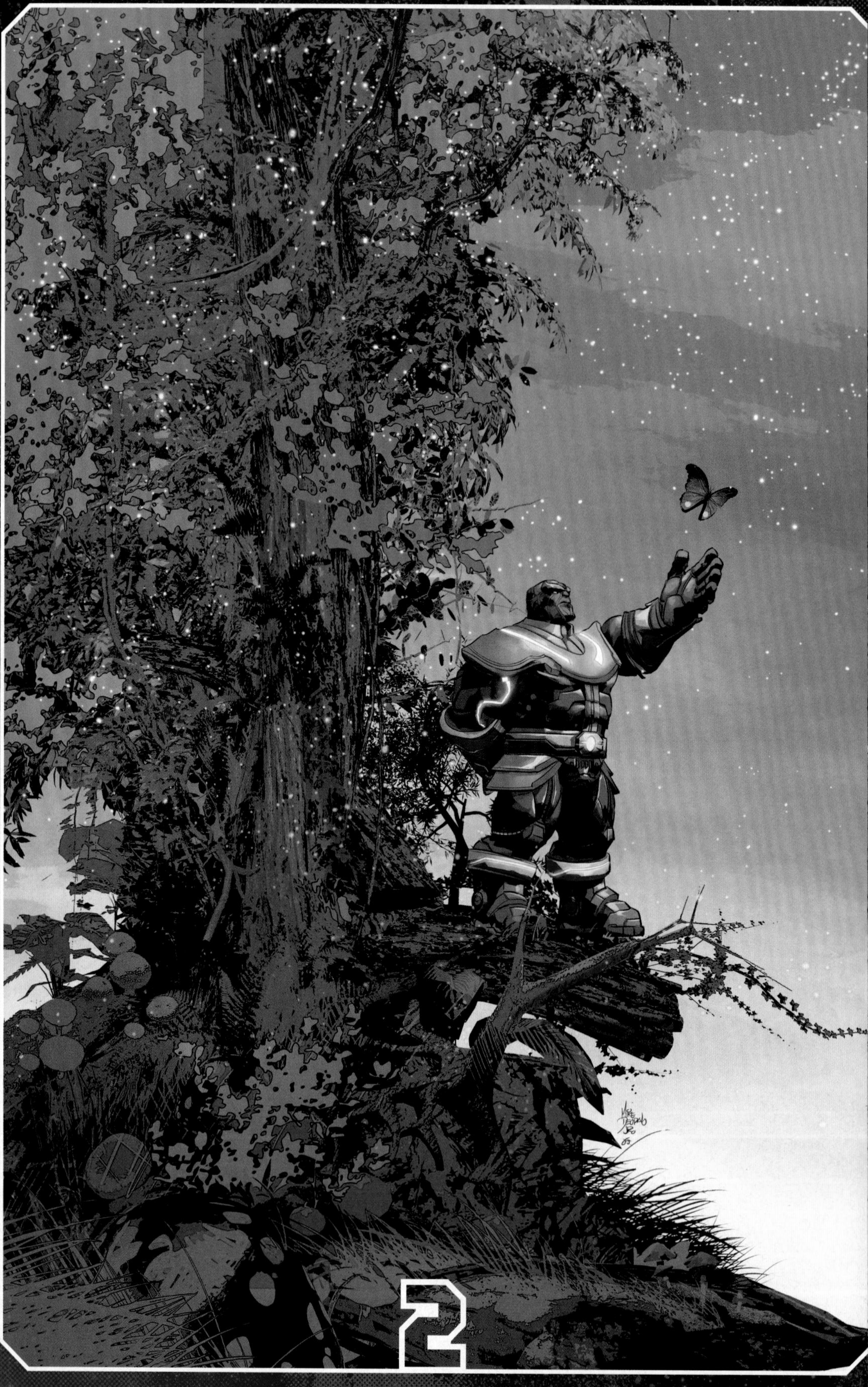
2

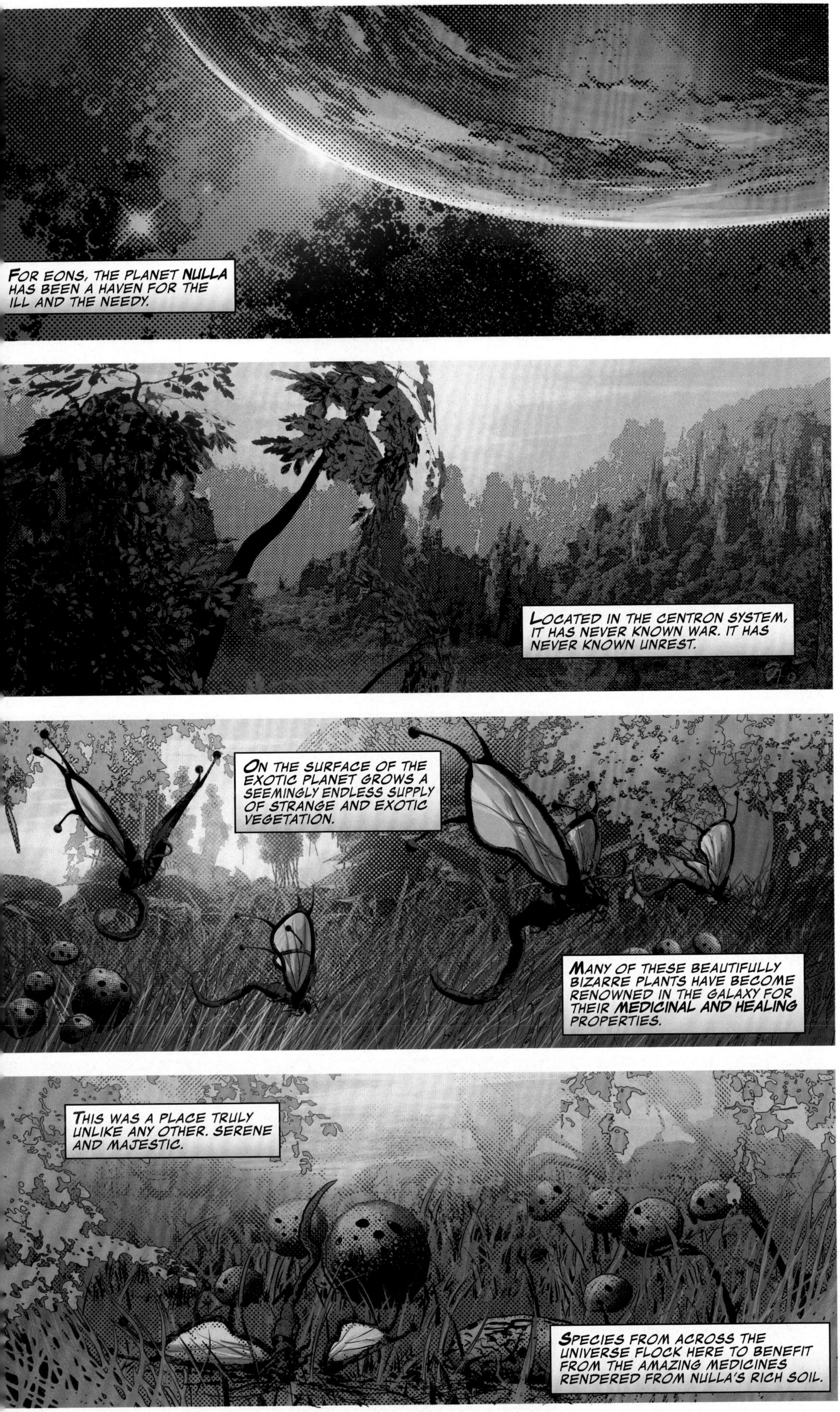
FOR EONS, THE PLANET NULLA HAS BEEN A HAVEN FOR THE ILL AND THE NEEDY.
LOCATED IN THE CENTRON SYSTEM, IT HAS NEVER KNOWN WAR. IT HAS NEVER KNOWN UNREST.
ON THE SURFACE OF THE EXOTIC PLANET GROWS A SEEMINGLY ENDLESS SUPPLY OF STRANGE AND EXOTIC VEGETATION.
MANY OF THESE BEAUTIFULLY BIZARRE PLANTS HAVE BECOME RENOWNED IN THE GALAXY FOR THEIR MEDICINAL AND HEALING PROPERTIES.
THIS WAS A PLACE TRULY UNLIKE ANY OTHER. SERENE AND MAJESTIC.
SPECIES FROM ACROSS THE UNIVERSE FLOCK HERE TO BENEFIT FROM THE AMAZING MEDICINES RENDERED FROM NULLA'S RICH SOIL.

THE NULLANS THEMSELVES ARE AS BEAUTIFUL AS THEIR PLANET. A MONK-LIKE RACE, THEY ARE KIND AND GIVING. THEY ARE HEALERS BY NATURE, LIVING ONLY TO HELP THOSE WHO NEED IT.

NEITHER TECHNOLOGY NOR INDUSTRY MAR THE EXOTIC NULLAN LANDSCAPE. NO POLLUTION FILLS ITS MAGNIFICENT SKIES. THE NULLANS LIVE IN TOTAL HARMONY WITH NATURE.

THEIR VILLAGE IS TENS OF THOUSANDS OF YEARS OLD. A CITADEL OF LEARNING AND HEALING. THIS PLACE IS THE CENTER OF ALL OF THEIR KNOWLEDGE.

HERE, ELDERS PASS ON THEIR KNOWLEDGE AND THE WAYS OF THEIR WORLD'S MEDICINE TO THE YOUNG. FOR THOUSANDS OF YEARS, THIS HAS BEEN THEIR WAY.

AND WHEN THE ELDERS GROW WEAK AND TIRED, THE YOUNG NURSE THEM INTO THE NEXT LIFE. IT IS SAID THEIR SPIRITS ARE THEN ABSORBED INTO THE SOIL TO ONE DAY BE REBORN.

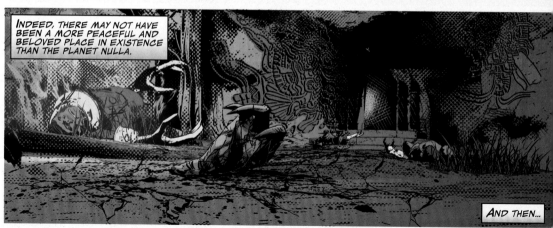

INDEED, THERE MAY NOT HAVE BEEN A MORE PEACEFUL AND BELOVED PLACE IN EXISTENCE THAN THE PLANET NULLA.

AND THEN...

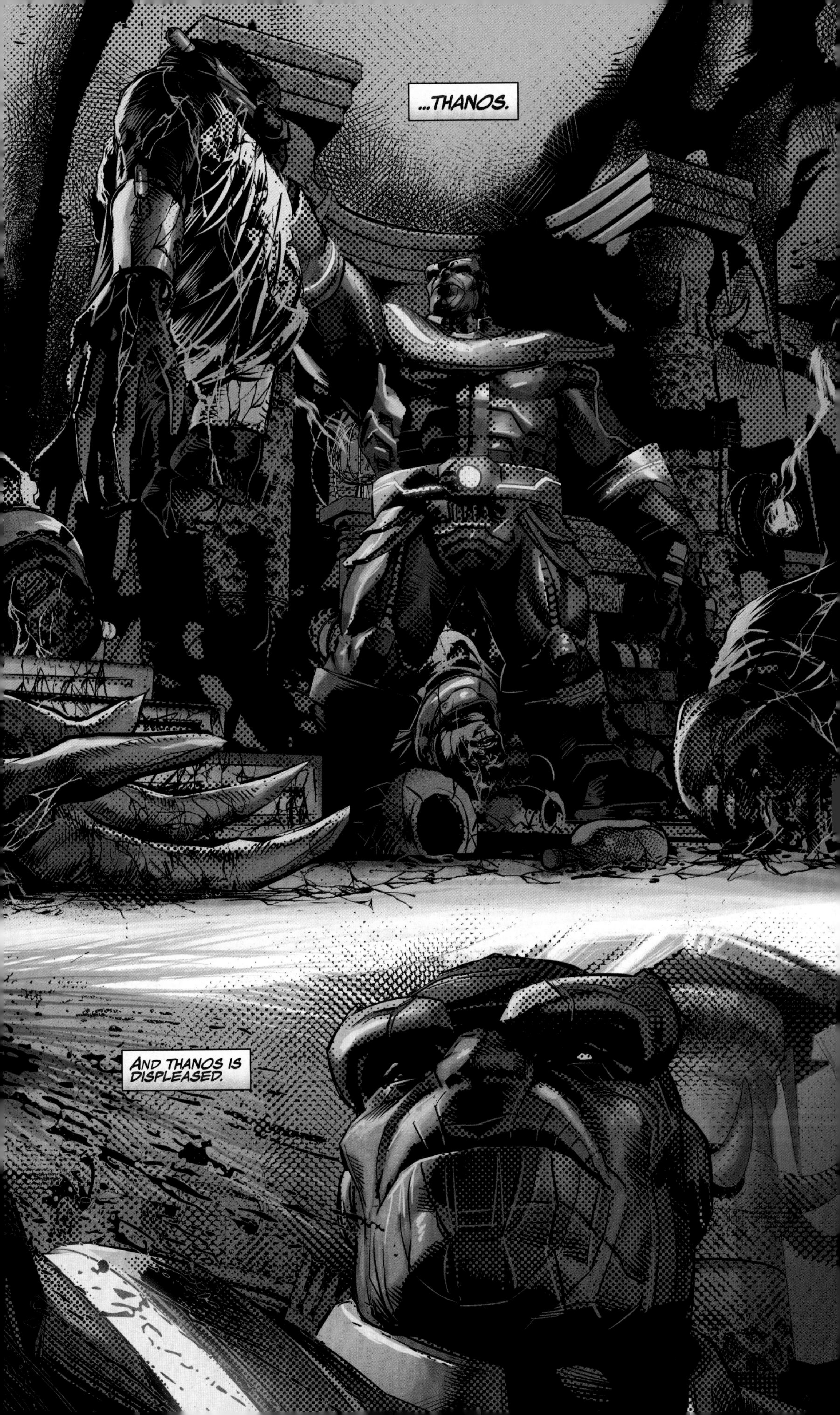
...THANOS.
AND THANOS IS DISPLEASED.

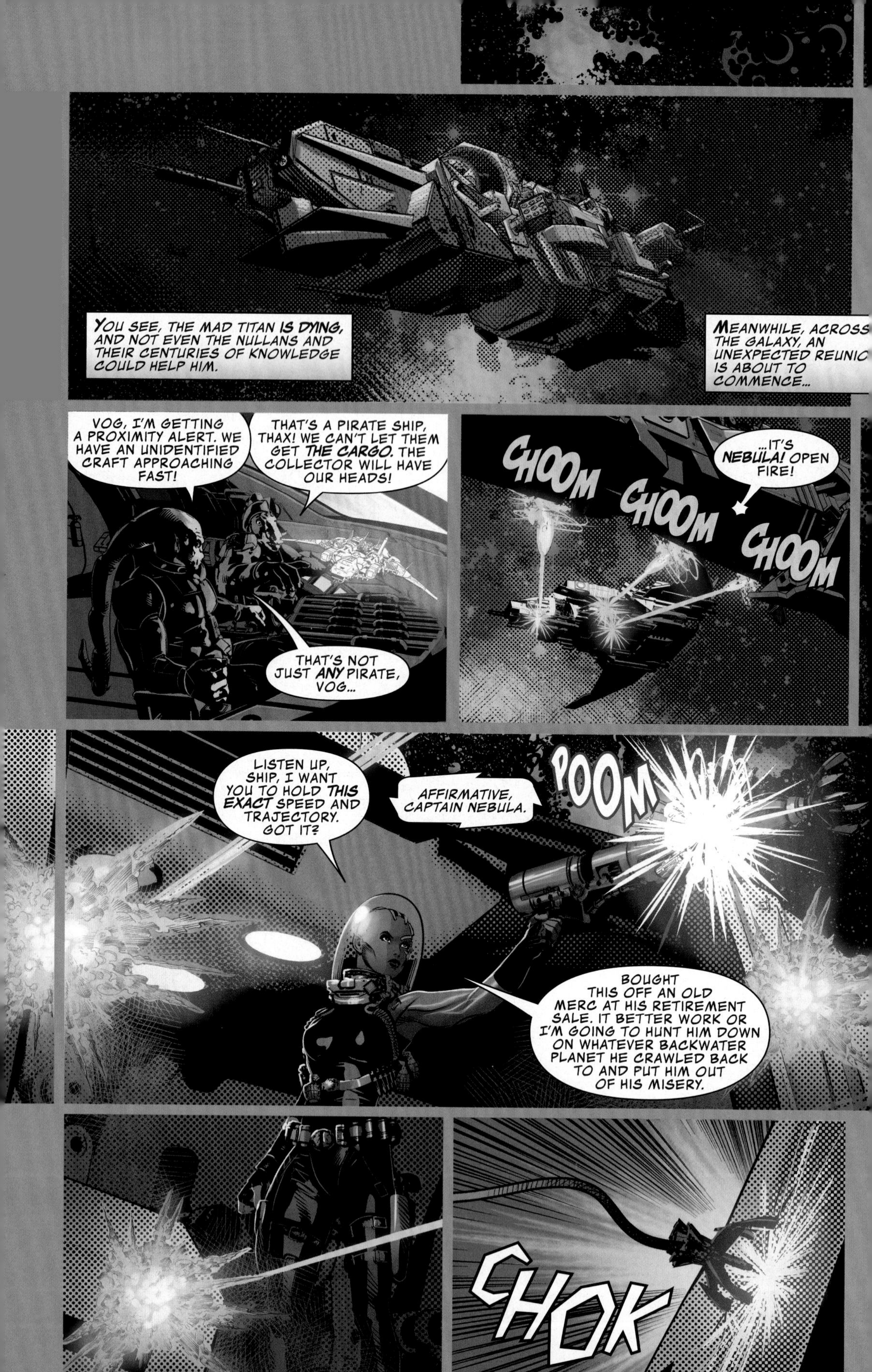

YOU SEE, THE MAD TITAN IS DYING, AND NOT EVEN THE NULLANS AND THEIR CENTURIES OF KNOWLEDGE COULD HELP HIM.
MEANWHILE, ACROSS THE GALAXY, AN UNEXPECTED REUNIC IS ABOUT TO COMMENCE...
VOG, I'M GETTING A PROXIMITY ALERT. WE HAVE AN UNIDENTIFIED CRAFT APPROACHING FAST!
THAT'S A PIRATE SHIP, THAX! WE CAN'T LET THEM GET THE CARGO. THE COLLECTOR WILL HAVE OUR HEADS!
THAT'S NOT JUST ANY PIRATE, VOG...
CHOOM CHOOM CHOOM
...IT'S NEBULA! OPEN FIRE!
LISTEN UP, SHIP, I WANT YOU TO HOLD THIS EXACT SPEED AND TRAJECTORY. GOT IT?
AFFIRMATIVE, CAPTAIN NEBULA.
POOM
BOUGHT THIS OFF AN OLD MERC AT HIS RETIREMENT SALE. IT BETTER WORK OR I'M GOING TO HUNT HIM DOWN ON WHATEVER BACKWATER PLANET HE CRAWLED BACK TO AND PUT HIM OUT OF HIS MISERY.
CHOK

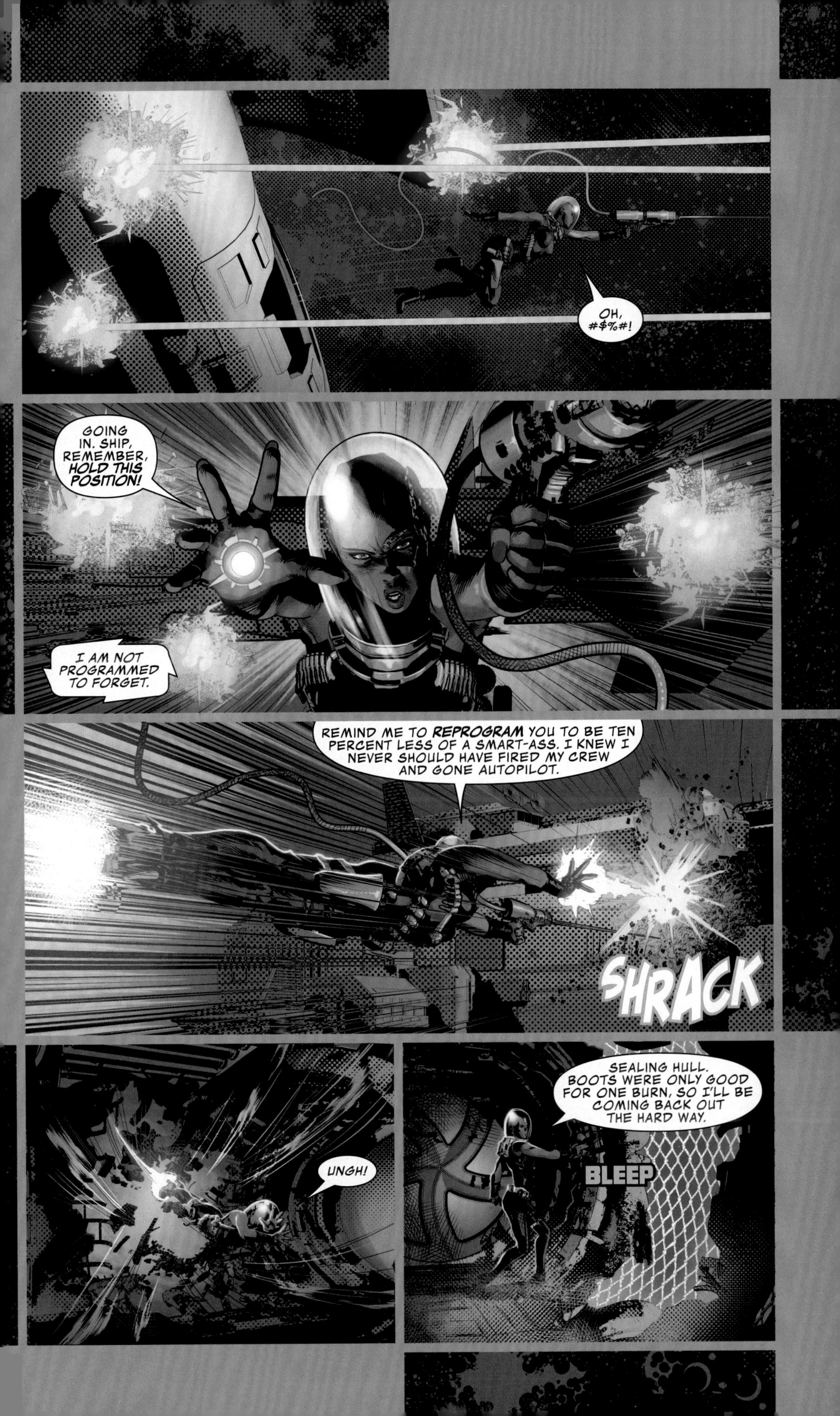
OH, #$%#!
GOING IN. SHIP, REMEMBER, HOLD THIS POSITION!
I AM NOT PROGRAMMED TO FORGET.
REMIND ME TO REPROGRAM YOU TO BE TEN PERCENT LESS OF A SMART-ASS. I KNEW I NEVER SHOULD HAVE FIRED MY CREW AND GONE AUTOPILOT.
SHRACK
UNGH!
SEALING HULL. BOOTS WERE ONLY GOOD FOR ONE BURN, SO I'LL BE COMING BACK OUT THE HARD WAY.
BLEEP

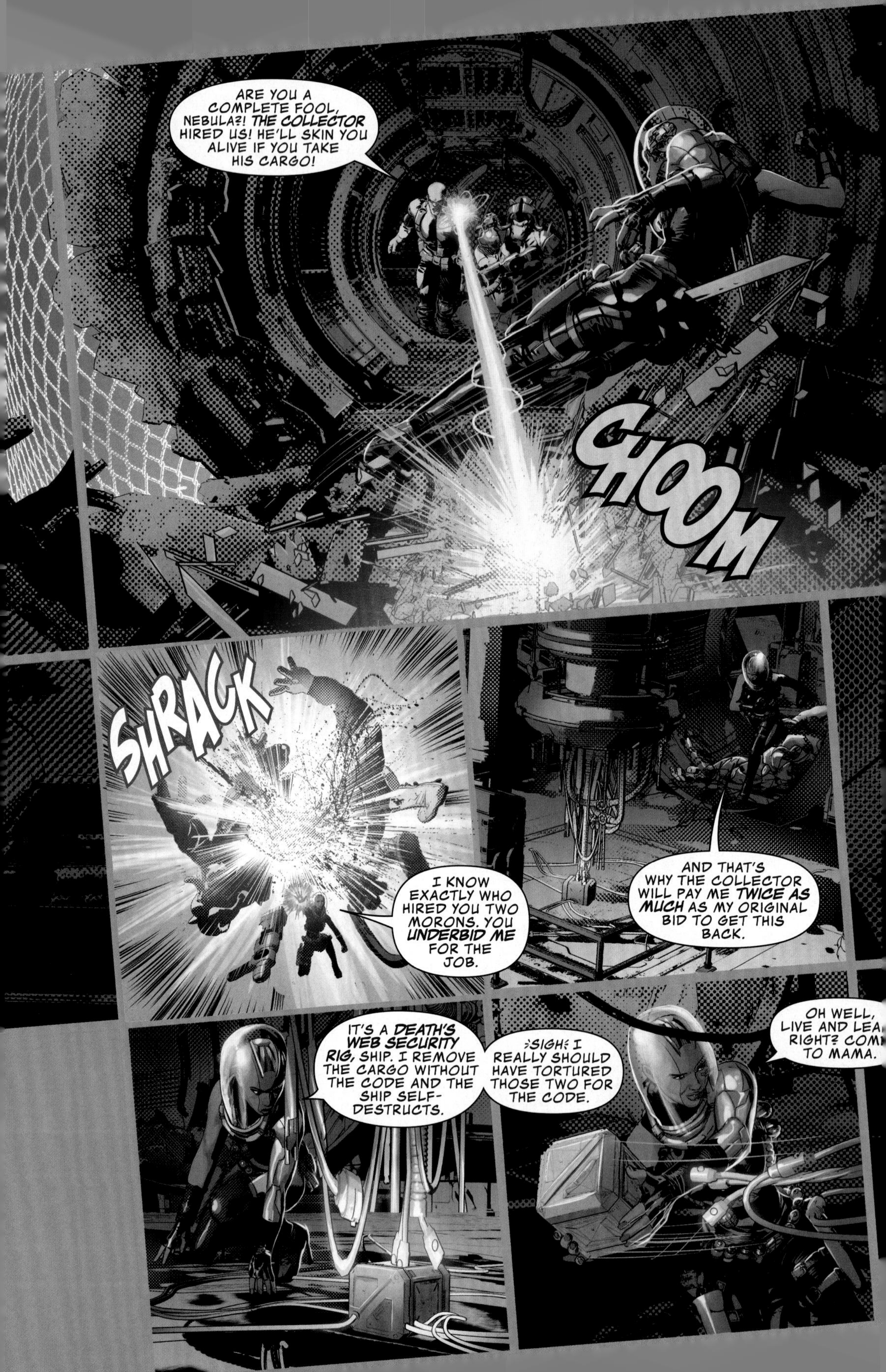
ARE YOU A COMPLETE FOOL, NEBULA?! THE COLLECTOR HIRED US! HE'LL SKIN YOU ALIVE IF YOU TAKE HIS CARGO!
CHOOM
SHRACK
I KNOW EXACTLY WHO HIRED YOU TWO MORONS. YOU UNDERBID ME FOR THE JOB.
AND THAT'S WHY THE COLLECTOR WILL PAY ME TWICE AS MUCH AS MY ORIGINAL BID TO GET THIS BACK.
IT'S A DEATH'S WEB SECURITY RIG, SHIP. I REMOVE THE CARGO WITHOUT THE CODE AND THE SHIP SELF-DESTRUCTS.
SIGH I REALLY SHOULD HAVE TORTURED THOSE TWO FOR THE CODE.
OH WELL, LIVE AND LEA RIGHT? COM TO MAMA.

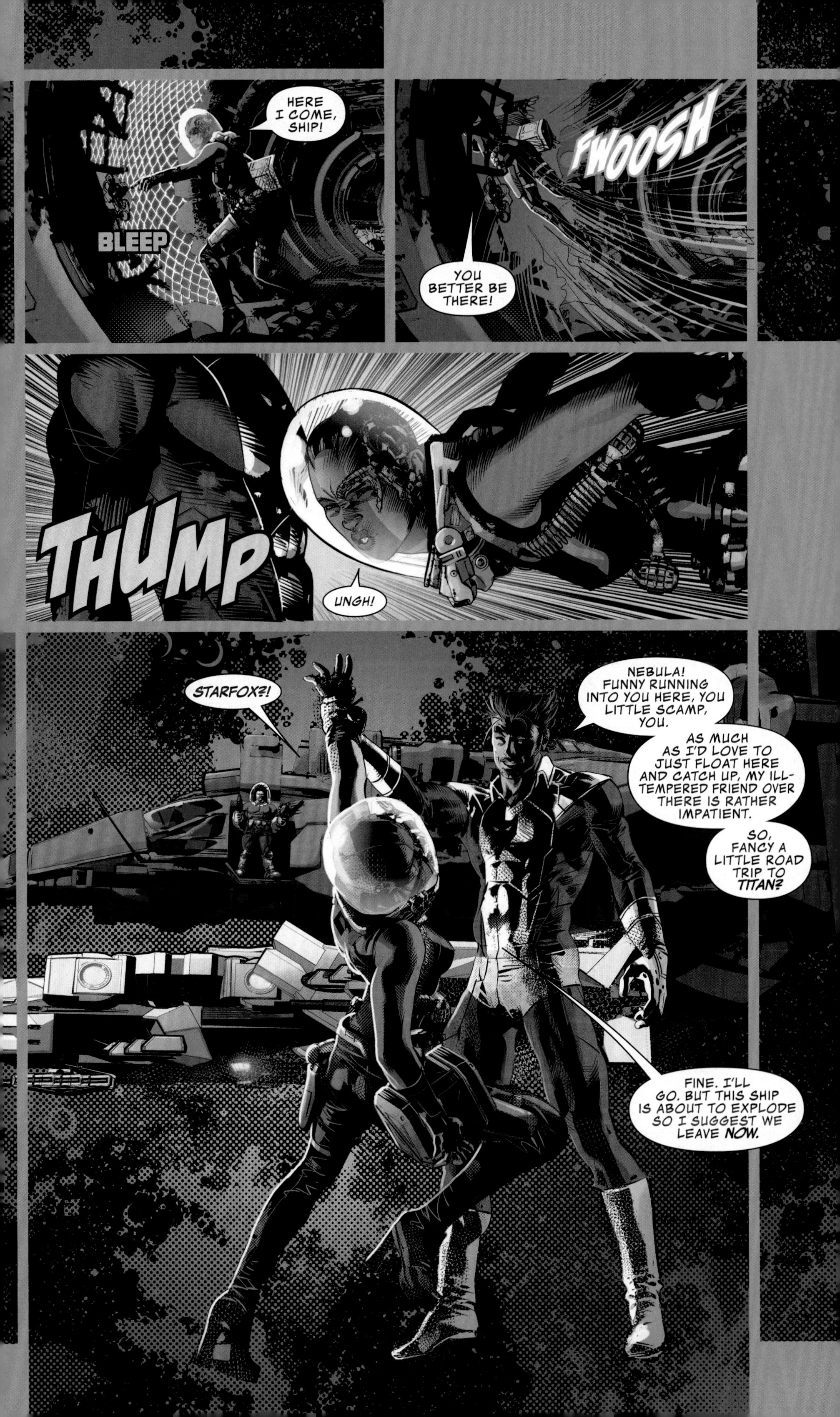
HERE I COME, SHIP!
BLEEP
FWOOSH
YOU BETTER BE THERE!
THUMP
UNGH!
STARFOX?!
NEBULA! FUNNY RUNNING INTO YOU HERE, YOU LITTLE SCAMP, YOU.
AS MUCH AS I'D LOVE TO JUST FLOAT HERE AND CATCH UP, MY ILL-TEMPERED FRIEND OVER THERE IS RATHER IMPATIENT.
SO, FANCY A LITTLE ROAD TRIP TO TITAN?
FINE. I'LL GO. BUT THIS SHIP IS ABOUT TO EXPLODE SO I SUGGEST WE LEAVE NOW.

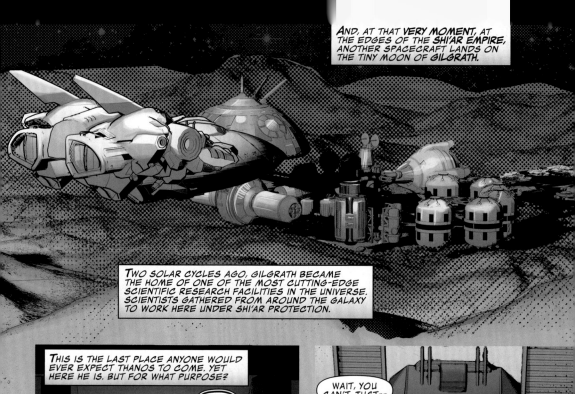

AND, AT THAT *VERY MOMENT*, AT THE EDGES OF THE *SHI'AR EMPIRE*, ANOTHER SPACECRAFT LANDS ON THE TINY MOON OF *GILGRATH*.

TWO SOLAR CYCLES AGO, GILGRATH BECAME THE HOME OF ONE OF THE MOST CUTTING-EDGE SCIENTIFIC RESEARCH FACILITIES IN THE UNIVERSE. SCIENTISTS GATHERED FROM AROUND THE GALAXY TO WORK HERE UNDER SHI'AR PROTECTION.

THIS IS THE LAST PLACE ANYONE WOULD EVER EXPECT THANOS TO COME. YET HERE HE IS. BUT FOR WHAT PURPOSE?

STAY HERE.

WAIT, YOU CAN'T JUST-- *ARRRGH!*

SHRACK

YES. I CAN.

THANOS!

HELLO, FATHER.

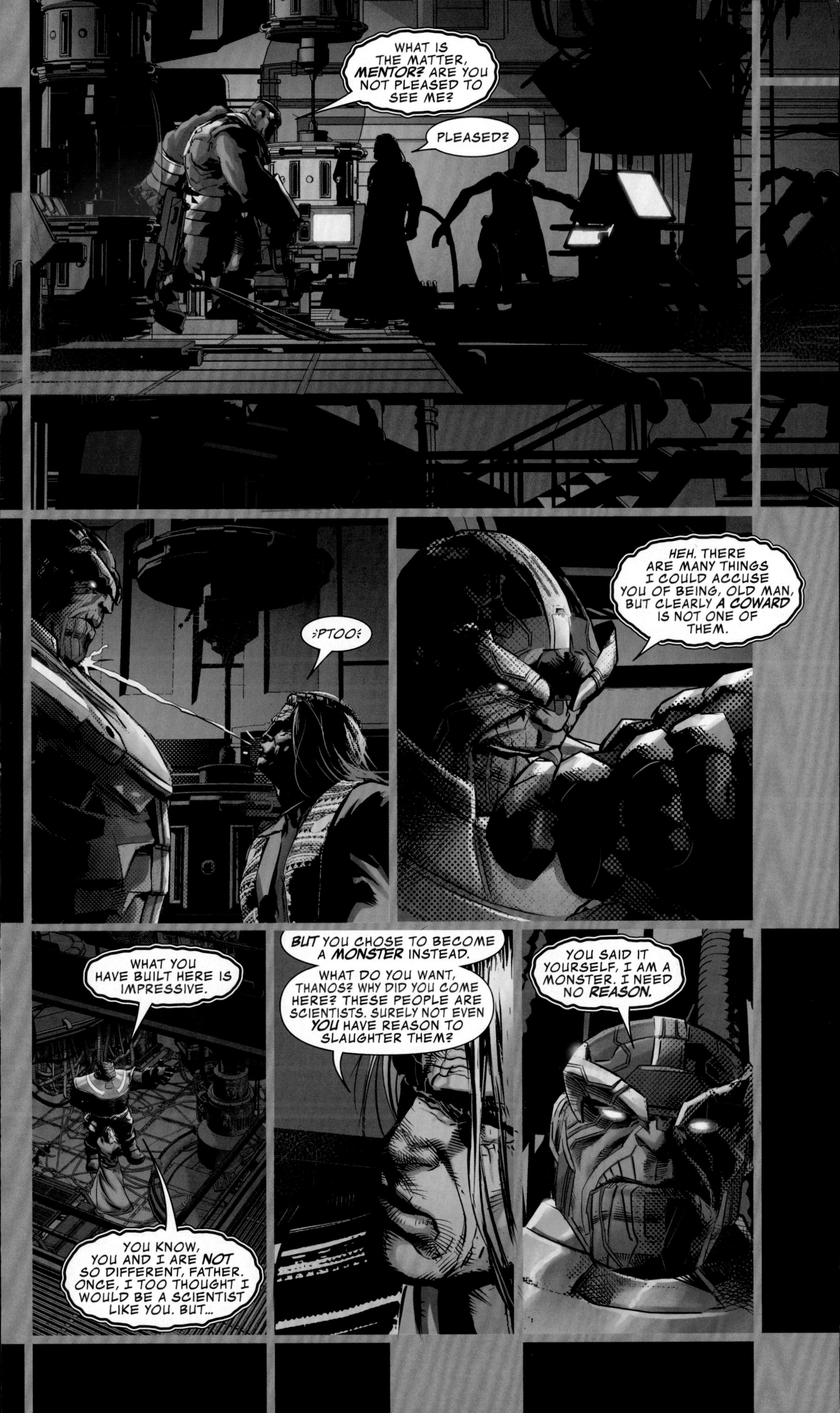
WHAT IS THE MATTER, MENTOR? ARE YOU NOT PLEASED TO SEE ME?
PLEASED?
PTOO
HEH. THERE ARE MANY THINGS I COULD ACCUSE YOU OF BEING, OLD MAN, BUT CLEARLY A COWARD IS NOT ONE OF THEM.
WHAT YOU HAVE BUILT HERE IS IMPRESSIVE.
YOU KNOW, YOU AND I ARE NOT SO DIFFERENT, FATHER. ONCE, I TOO THOUGHT I WOULD BE A SCIENTIST LIKE YOU. BUT...
BUT YOU CHOSE TO BECOME A MONSTER INSTEAD.
WHAT DO YOU WANT, THANOS? WHY DID YOU COME HERE? THESE PEOPLE ARE SCIENTISTS. SURELY NOT EVEN YOU HAVE REASON TO SLAUGHTER THEM?
YOU SAID IT YOURSELF, I AM A MONSTER. I NEED NO REASON.

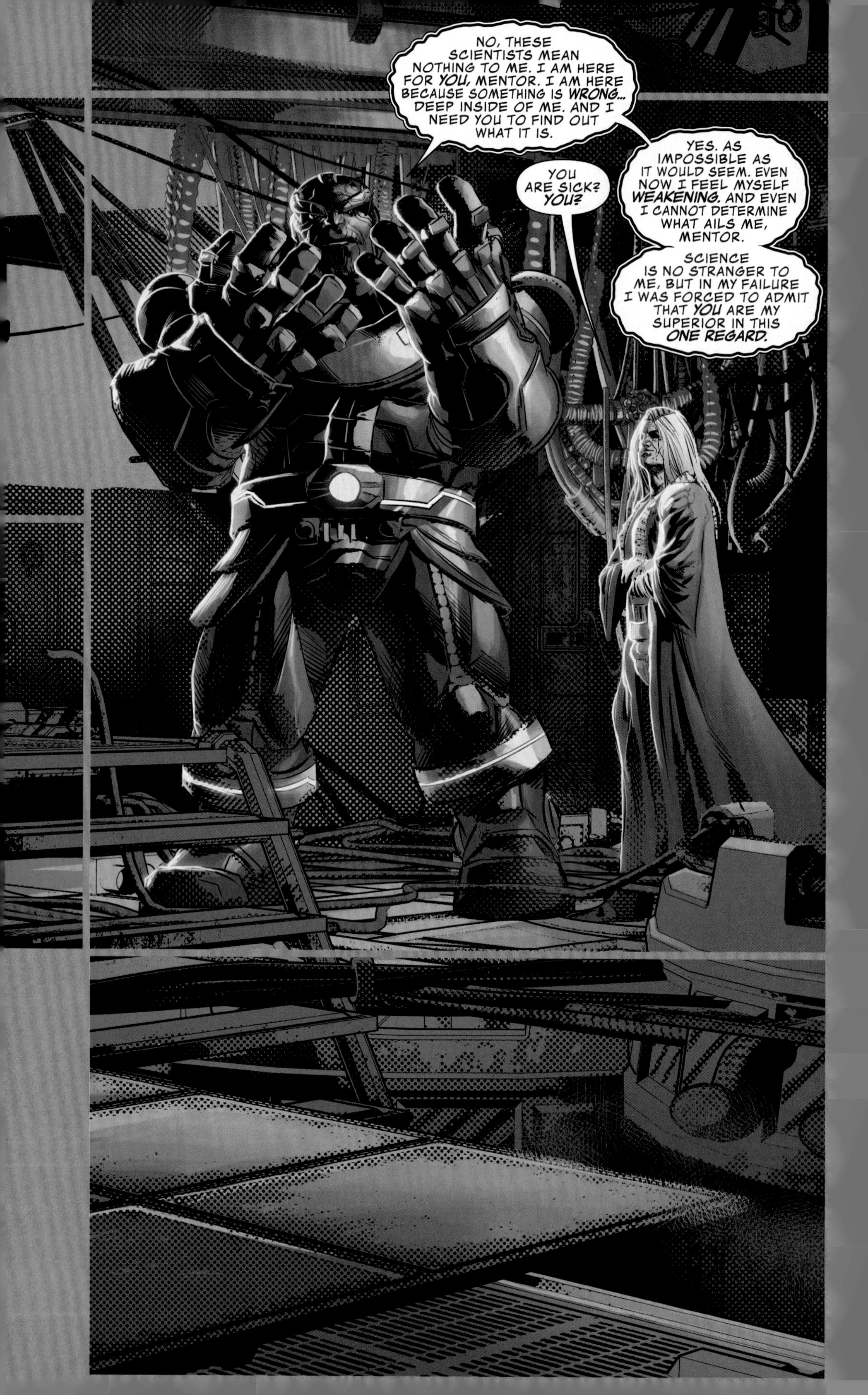
NO, THESE SCIENTISTS MEAN NOTHING TO ME. I AM HERE FOR YOU, MENTOR. I AM HERE BECAUSE SOMETHING IS WRONG... DEEP INSIDE OF ME. AND I NEED YOU TO FIND OUT WHAT IT IS.
YOU ARE SICK? YOU?
YES. AS IMPOSSIBLE AS IT WOULD SEEM. EVEN NOW I FEEL MYSELF WEAKENING. AND EVEN I CANNOT DETERMINE WHAT AILS ME, MENTOR.
SCIENCE IS NO STRANGER TO ME, BUT IN MY FAILURE I WAS FORCED TO ADMIT THAT YOU ARE MY SUPERIOR IN THIS ONE REGARD.

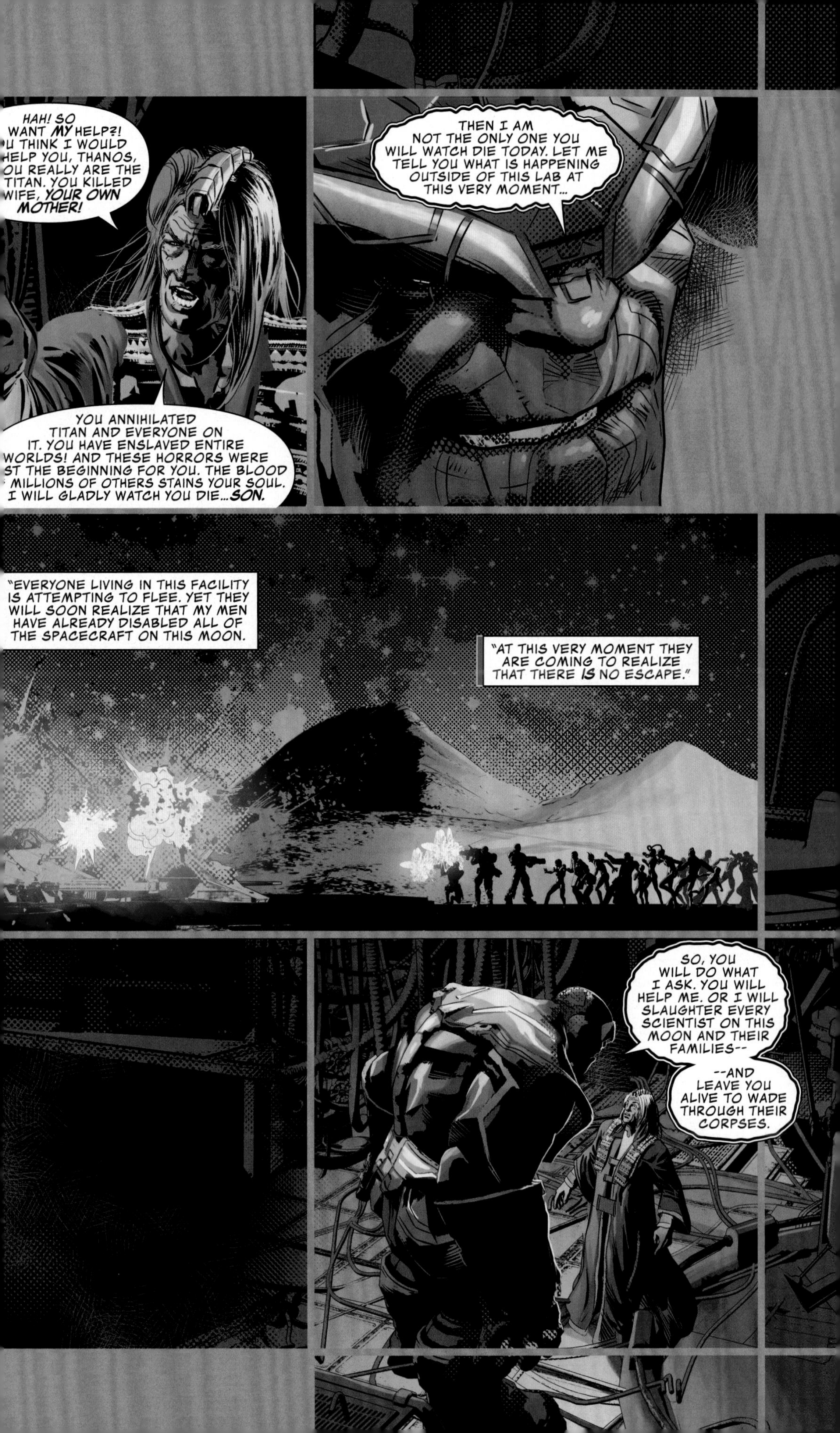
HAH! SO
WANT MY HELP?!
U THINK I WOULD
HELP YOU, THANOS,
OU REALLY ARE THE
TITAN. YOU KILLED
WIFE, YOUR OWN
MOTHER!
YOU ANNIHILATED TITAN AND EVERYONE ON IT. YOU HAVE ENSLAVED ENTIRE WORLDS! AND THESE HORRORS WERE ST THE BEGINNING FOR YOU. THE BLOOD MILLIONS OF OTHERS STAINS YOUR SOUL. I WILL GLADLY WATCH YOU DIE...SON.
THEN I AM NOT THE ONLY ONE YOU WILL WATCH DIE TODAY. LET ME TELL YOU WHAT IS HAPPENING OUTSIDE OF THIS LAB AT THIS VERY MOMENT...
"EVERYONE LIVING IN THIS FACILITY IS ATTEMPTING TO FLEE. YET THEY WILL SOON REALIZE THAT MY MEN HAVE ALREADY DISABLED ALL OF THE SPACECRAFT ON THIS MOON.
"AT THIS VERY MOMENT THEY ARE COMING TO REALIZE THAT THERE IS NO ESCAPE."
SO, YOU WILL DO WHAT I ASK. YOU WILL HELP ME. OR I WILL SLAUGHTER EVERY SCIENTIST ON THIS MOON AND THEIR FAMILIES--
--AND LEAVE YOU ALIVE TO WADE THROUGH THEIR CORPSES.

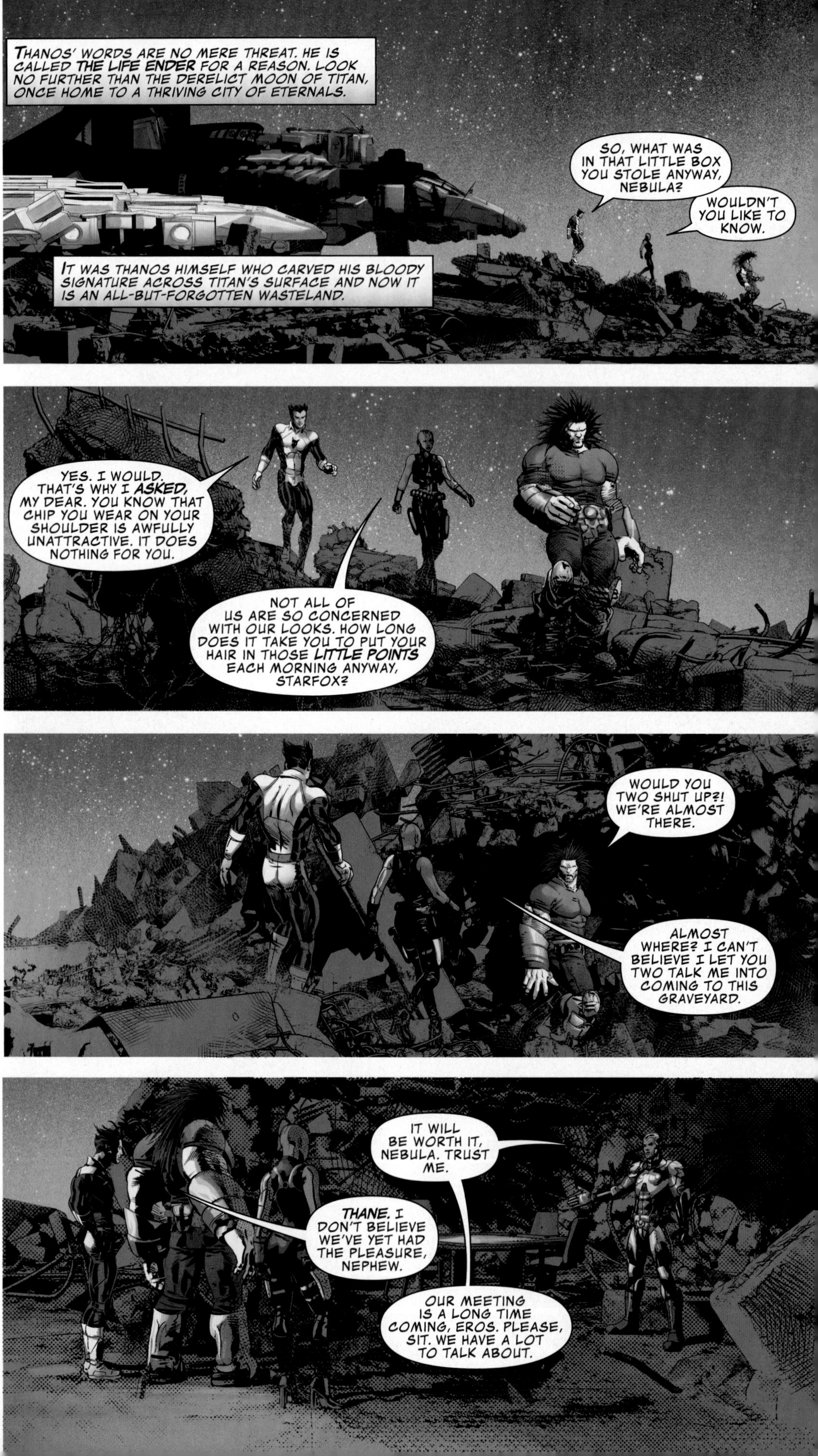
THANOS' WORDS ARE NO MERE THREAT. HE IS CALLED **THE LIFE ENDER** FOR A REASON. LOOK NO FURTHER THAN THE DERELICT MOON OF TITAN, ONCE HOME TO A THRIVING CITY OF ETERNALS.
SO, WHAT WAS IN THAT LITTLE BOX YOU STOLE ANYWAY, NEBULA?
WOULDN'T YOU LIKE TO KNOW.
IT WAS THANOS HIMSELF WHO CARVED HIS BLOODY SIGNATURE ACROSS TITAN'S SURFACE AND NOW IT IS AN ALL-BUT-FORGOTTEN WASTELAND.
YES. I WOULD. THAT'S WHY I *ASKED,* MY DEAR. YOU KNOW THAT CHIP YOU WEAR ON YOUR SHOULDER IS AWFULLY UNATTRACTIVE. IT DOES NOTHING FOR YOU.
NOT ALL OF US ARE SO CONCERNED WITH OUR LOOKS. HOW LONG DOES IT TAKE YOU TO PUT YOUR HAIR IN THOSE ***LITTLE POINTS*** EACH MORNING ANYWAY, STARFOX?
WOULD YOU TWO SHUT UP?! WE'RE ALMOST THERE.
ALMOST WHERE? I CAN'T BELIEVE I LET YOU TWO TALK ME INTO COMING TO THIS GRAVEYARD.
IT WILL BE WORTH IT, NEBULA. TRUST ME.
THANE. I DON'T BELIEVE WE'VE YET HAD THE PLEASURE, NEPHEW.
OUR MEETING IS A LONG TIME COMING, EROS. PLEASE, SIT. WE HAVE A LOT TO TALK ABOUT.

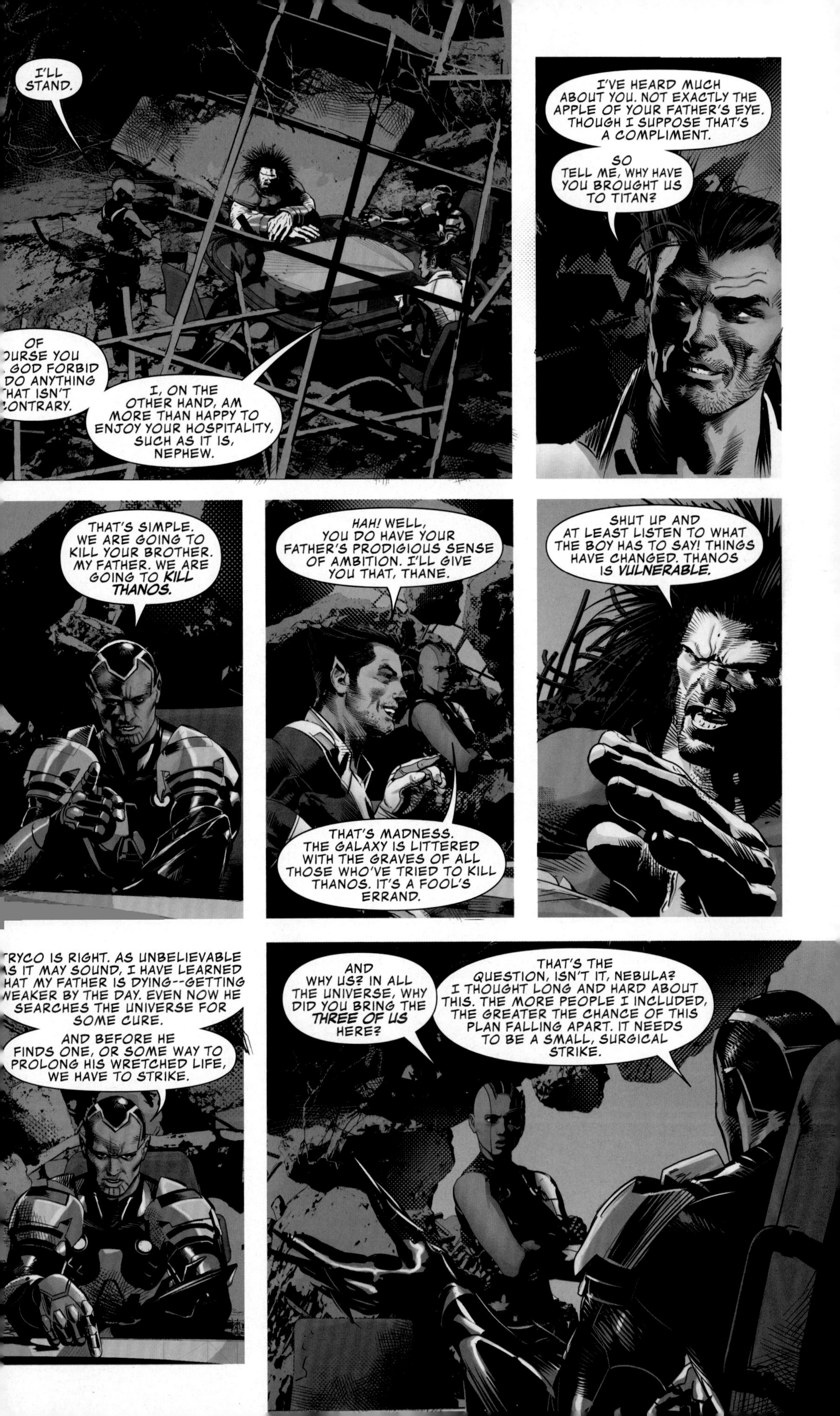
I'LL STAND.
OF COURSE YOU ... GOD FORBID DO ANYTHING THAT ISN'T CONTRARY.
I, ON THE OTHER HAND, AM MORE THAN HAPPY TO ENJOY YOUR HOSPITALITY, SUCH AS IT IS, NEPHEW.
I'VE HEARD MUCH ABOUT YOU. NOT EXACTLY THE APPLE OF YOUR FATHER'S EYE. THOUGH I SUPPOSE THAT'S A COMPLIMENT.
SO TELL ME, WHY HAVE YOU BROUGHT US TO TITAN?
THAT'S SIMPLE. WE ARE GOING TO KILL YOUR BROTHER. MY FATHER. WE ARE GOING TO *KILL THANOS.*
HAH! WELL, YOU DO HAVE YOUR FATHER'S PRODIGIOUS SENSE OF AMBITION. I'LL GIVE YOU THAT, THANE.
THAT'S MADNESS. THE GALAXY IS LITTERED WITH THE GRAVES OF ALL THOSE WHO'VE TRIED TO KILL THANOS. IT'S A FOOL'S ERRAND.
SHUT UP AND AT LEAST LISTEN TO WHAT THE BOY HAS TO SAY! THINGS HAVE CHANGED. THANOS IS *VULNERABLE.*
TRYCO IS RIGHT. AS UNBELIEVABLE AS IT MAY SOUND, I HAVE LEARNED THAT MY FATHER IS DYING--GETTING WEAKER BY THE DAY. EVEN NOW HE SEARCHES THE UNIVERSE FOR SOME CURE.
AND BEFORE HE FINDS ONE, OR SOME WAY TO PROLONG HIS WRETCHED LIFE, WE HAVE TO STRIKE.
AND WHY US? IN ALL THE UNIVERSE, WHY DID YOU BRING THE *THREE OF US* HERE?
THAT'S THE QUESTION, ISN'T IT, NEBULA? I THOUGHT LONG AND HARD ABOUT THIS. THE MORE PEOPLE I INCLUDED, THE GREATER THE CHANCE OF THIS PLAN FALLING APART. IT NEEDS TO BE A SMALL, SURGICAL STRIKE.

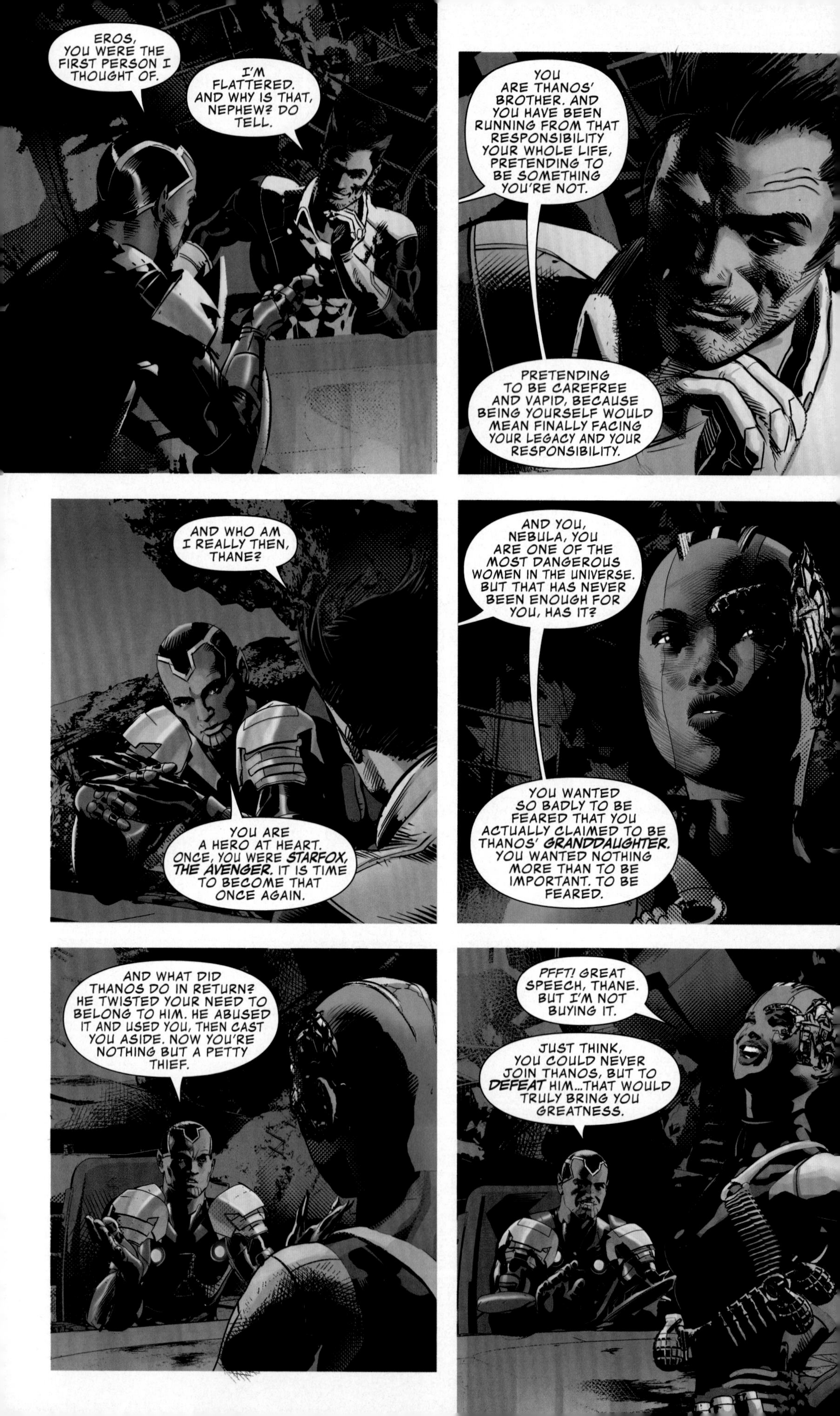
EROS, YOU WERE THE FIRST PERSON I THOUGHT OF.
I'M FLATTERED. AND WHY IS THAT, NEPHEW? DO TELL.
YOU ARE THANOS' BROTHER. AND YOU HAVE BEEN RUNNING FROM THAT RESPONSIBILITY YOUR WHOLE LIFE, PRETENDING TO BE SOMETHING YOU'RE NOT.
PRETENDING TO BE CAREFREE AND VAPID, BECAUSE BEING YOURSELF WOULD MEAN FINALLY FACING YOUR LEGACY AND YOUR RESPONSIBILITY.
AND WHO AM I REALLY THEN, THANE?
YOU ARE A HERO AT HEART. ONCE, YOU WERE STARFOX, THE AVENGER. IT IS TIME TO BECOME THAT ONCE AGAIN.
AND YOU, NEBULA, YOU ARE ONE OF THE MOST DANGEROUS WOMEN IN THE UNIVERSE. BUT THAT HAS NEVER BEEN ENOUGH FOR YOU, HAS IT?
YOU WANTED SO BADLY TO BE FEARED THAT YOU ACTUALLY CLAIMED TO BE THANOS' GRANDDAUGHTER. YOU WANTED NOTHING MORE THAN TO BE IMPORTANT. TO BE FEARED.
AND WHAT DID THANOS DO IN RETURN? HE TWISTED YOUR NEED TO BELONG TO HIM. HE ABUSED IT AND USED YOU, THEN CAST YOU ASIDE. NOW YOU'RE NOTHING BUT A PETTY THIEF.
PFFT! GREAT SPEECH, THANE. BUT I'M NOT BUYING IT.
JUST THINK, YOU COULD NEVER JOIN THANOS, BUT TO DEFEAT HIM...THAT WOULD TRULY BRING YOU GREATNESS.

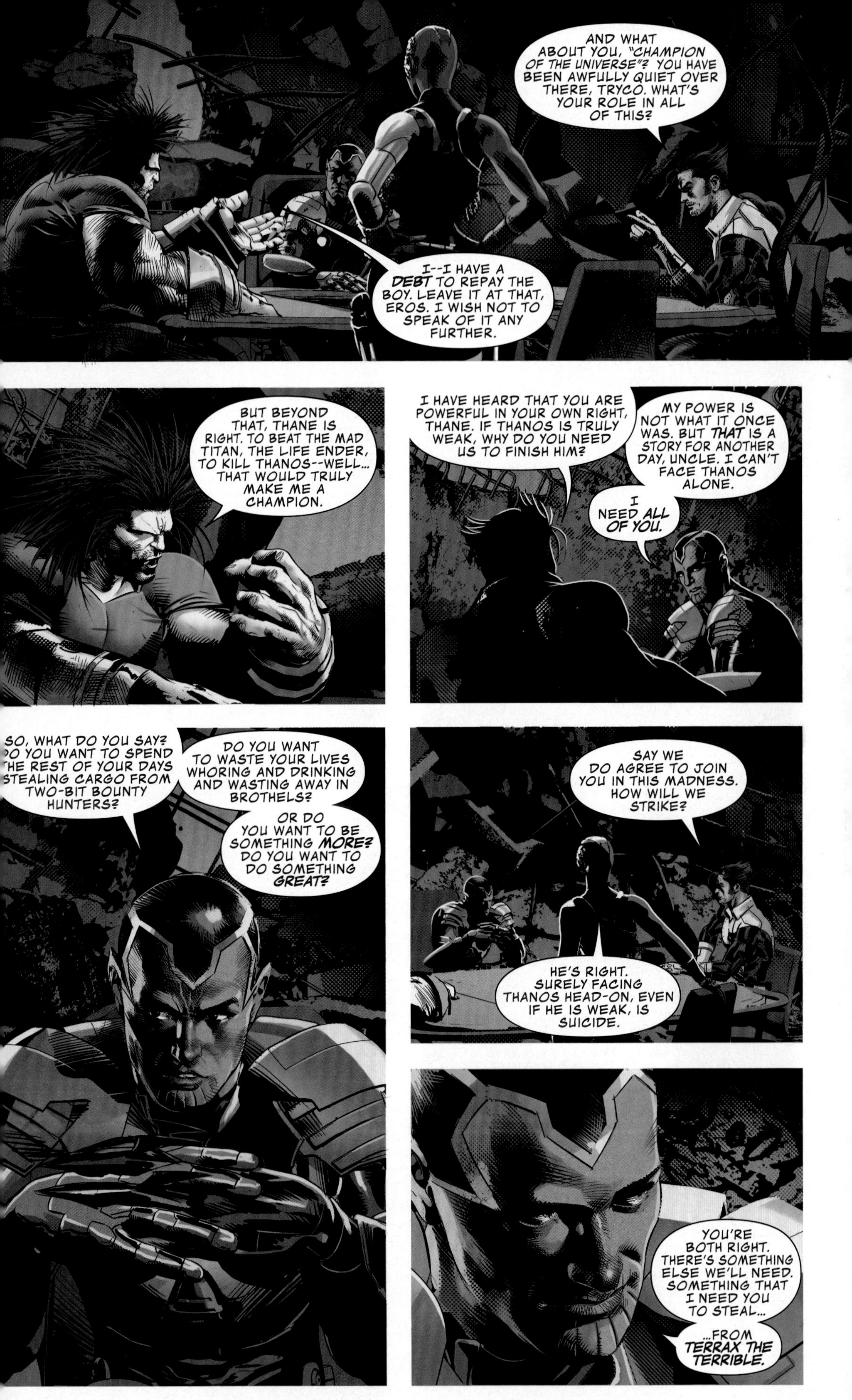
AND WHAT ABOUT YOU, "CHAMPION OF THE UNIVERSE"? YOU HAVE BEEN AWFULLY QUIET OVER THERE, TRYCO. WHAT'S YOUR ROLE IN ALL OF THIS?
I--I HAVE A DEBT TO REPAY THE BOY. LEAVE IT AT THAT, EROS. I WISH NOT TO SPEAK OF IT ANY FURTHER.
BUT BEYOND THAT, THANE IS RIGHT. TO BEAT THE MAD TITAN, THE LIFE ENDER, TO KILL THANOS--WELL... THAT WOULD TRULY MAKE ME A CHAMPION.
I HAVE HEARD THAT YOU ARE POWERFUL IN YOUR OWN RIGHT, THANE. IF THANOS IS TRULY WEAK, WHY DO YOU NEED US TO FINISH HIM?
MY POWER IS NOT WHAT IT ONCE WAS. BUT THAT IS A STORY FOR ANOTHER DAY, UNCLE. I CAN'T FACE THANOS ALONE.
I NEED ALL OF YOU.
SO, WHAT DO YOU SAY? DO YOU WANT TO SPEND THE REST OF YOUR DAYS STEALING CARGO FROM TWO-BIT BOUNTY HUNTERS?
DO YOU WANT TO WASTE YOUR LIVES WHORING AND DRINKING AND WASTING AWAY IN BROTHELS?
OR DO YOU WANT TO BE SOMETHING MORE? DO YOU WANT TO DO SOMETHING GREAT?
SAY WE DO AGREE TO JOIN YOU IN THIS MADNESS. HOW WILL WE STRIKE?
HE'S RIGHT. SURELY FACING THANOS HEAD-ON, EVEN IF HE IS WEAK, IS SUICIDE.
YOU'RE BOTH RIGHT. THERE'S SOMETHING ELSE WE'LL NEED. SOMETHING THAT I NEED YOU TO STEAL...
...FROM TERRAX THE TERRIBLE.

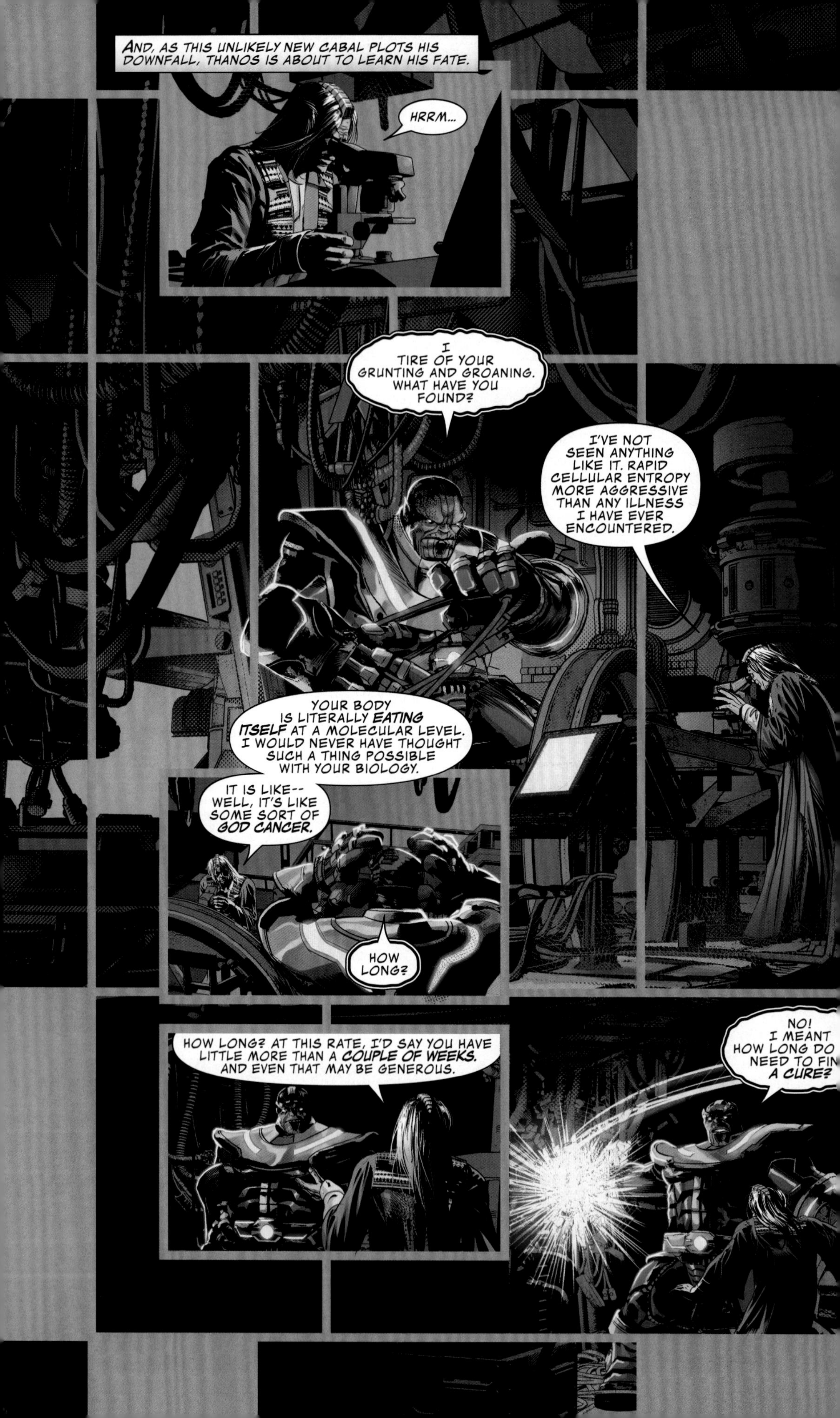
AND, AS THIS UNLIKELY NEW CABAL PLOTS HIS DOWNFALL, THANOS IS ABOUT TO LEARN HIS FATE.
HRRM...
I TIRE OF YOUR GRUNTING AND GROANING. WHAT HAVE YOU FOUND?
I'VE NOT SEEN ANYTHING LIKE IT. RAPID CELLULAR ENTROPY MORE AGGRESSIVE THAN ANY ILLNESS I HAVE EVER ENCOUNTERED.
YOUR BODY IS LITERALLY EATING ITSELF AT A MOLECULAR LEVEL. I WOULD NEVER HAVE THOUGHT SUCH A THING POSSIBLE WITH YOUR BIOLOGY.
IT IS LIKE-- WELL, IT'S LIKE SOME SORT OF GOD CANCER.
HOW LONG?
HOW LONG? AT THIS RATE, I'D SAY YOU HAVE LITTLE MORE THAN A COUPLE OF WEEKS. AND EVEN THAT MAY BE GENEROUS.
NO! I MEANT HOW LONG DO NEED TO FIN A CURE?

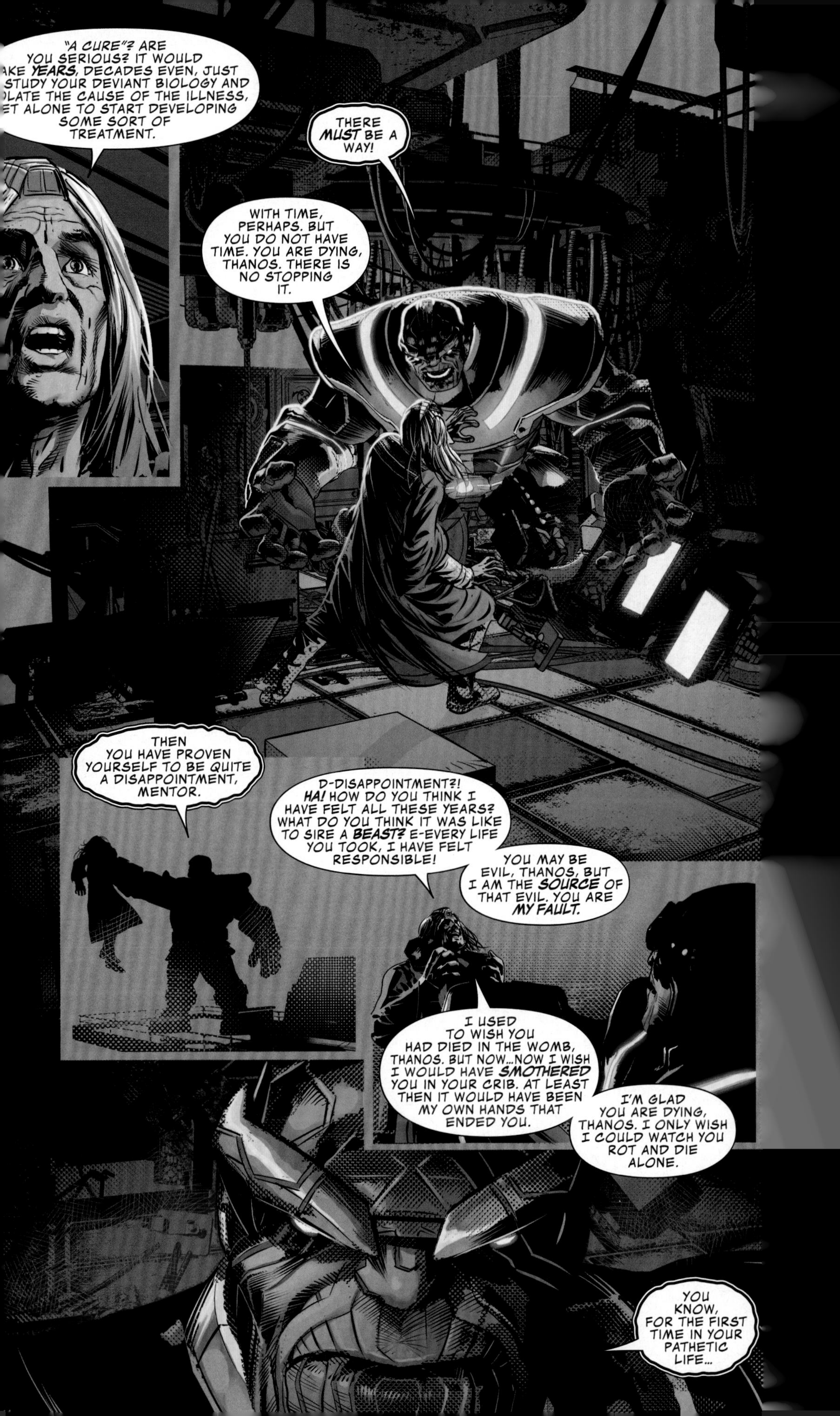

"A CURE"? ARE YOU SERIOUS? IT WOULD AKE YEARS, DECADES EVEN, JUST STUDY YOUR DEVIANT BIOLOGY AND OLATE THE CAUSE OF THE ILLNESS, ET ALONE TO START DEVELOPING SOME SORT OF TREATMENT.
THERE MUST BE A WAY!
WITH TIME, PERHAPS. BUT YOU DO NOT HAVE TIME. YOU ARE DYING, THANOS. THERE IS NO STOPPING IT.
THEN YOU HAVE PROVEN YOURSELF TO BE QUITE A DISAPPOINTMENT, MENTOR.
D-DISAPPOINTMENT?! HA! HOW DO YOU THINK I HAVE FELT ALL THESE YEARS? WHAT DO YOU THINK IT WAS LIKE TO SIRE A BEAST? E-EVERY LIFE YOU TOOK, I HAVE FELT RESPONSIBLE!
YOU MAY BE EVIL, THANOS, BUT I AM THE SOURCE OF THAT EVIL. YOU ARE MY FAULT.
I USED TO WISH YOU HAD DIED IN THE WOMB, THANOS. BUT NOW...NOW I WISH I WOULD HAVE SMOTHERED YOU IN YOUR CRIB. AT LEAST THEN IT WOULD HAVE BEEN MY OWN HANDS THAT ENDED YOU.
I'M GLAD YOU ARE DYING, THANOS. I ONLY WISH I COULD WATCH YOU ROT AND DIE ALONE.
YOU KNOW, FOR THE FIRST TIME IN YOUR PATHETIC LIFE...

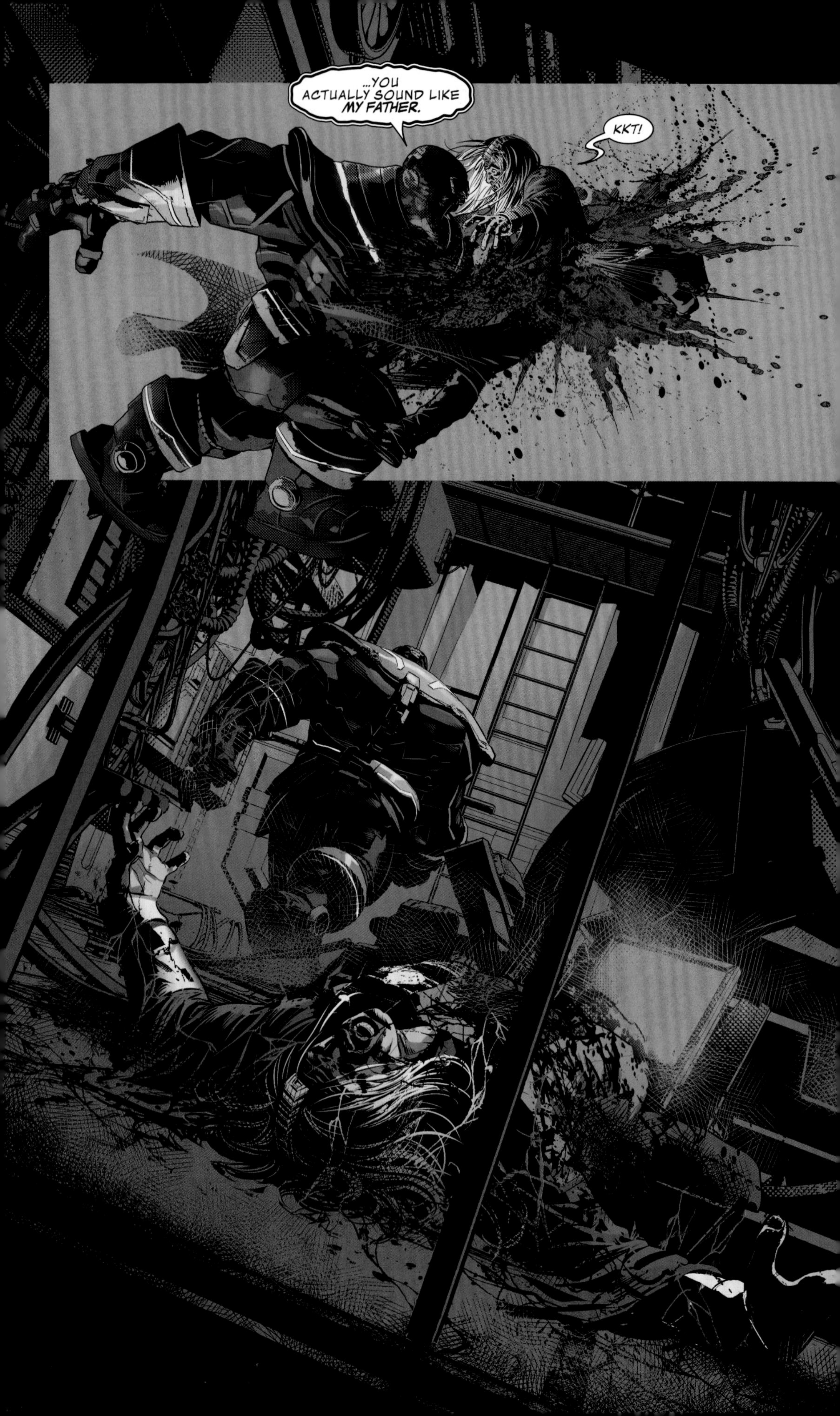
...YOU ACTUALLY SOUND LIKE MY FATHER.
KKT!

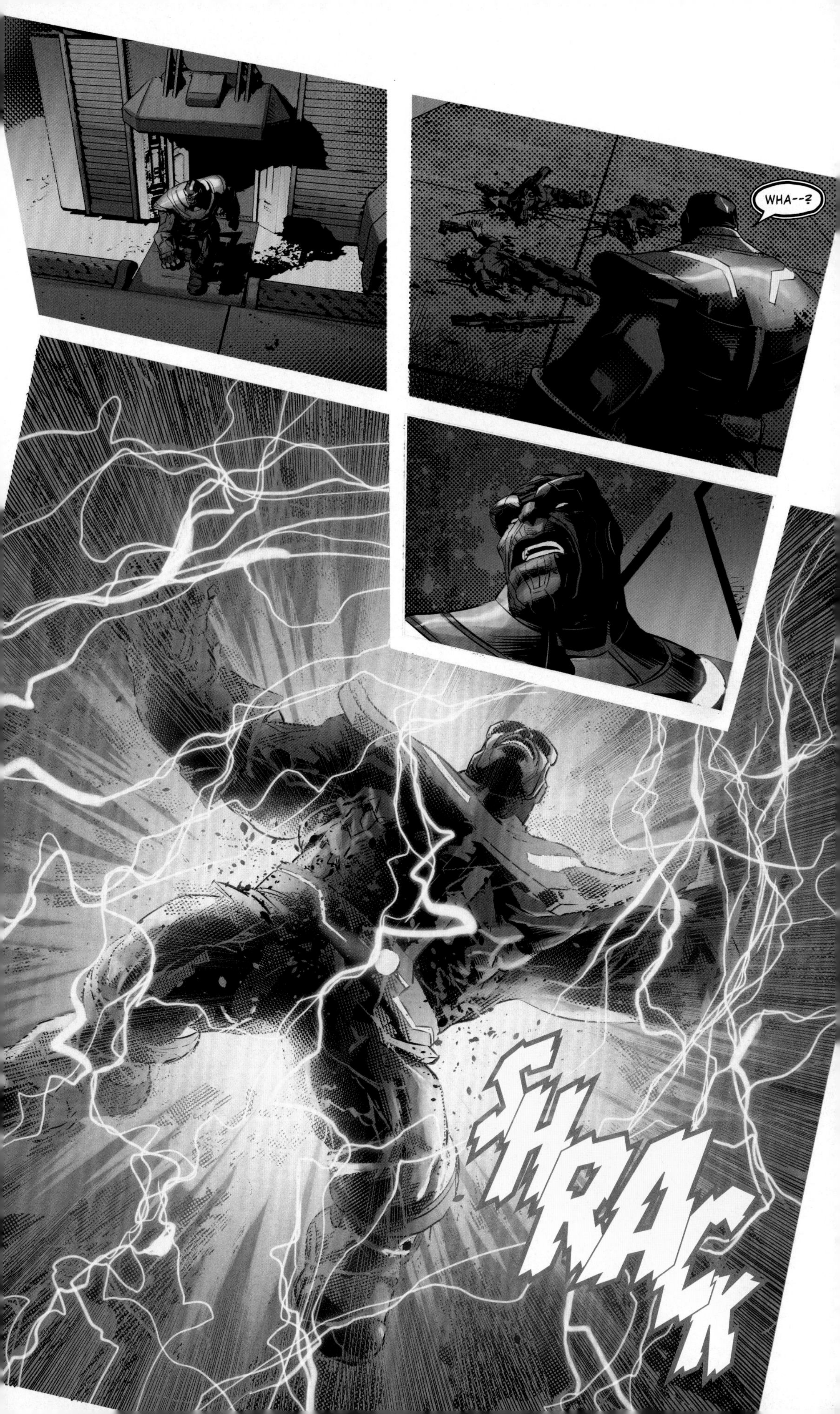
WHA--?
FRAK

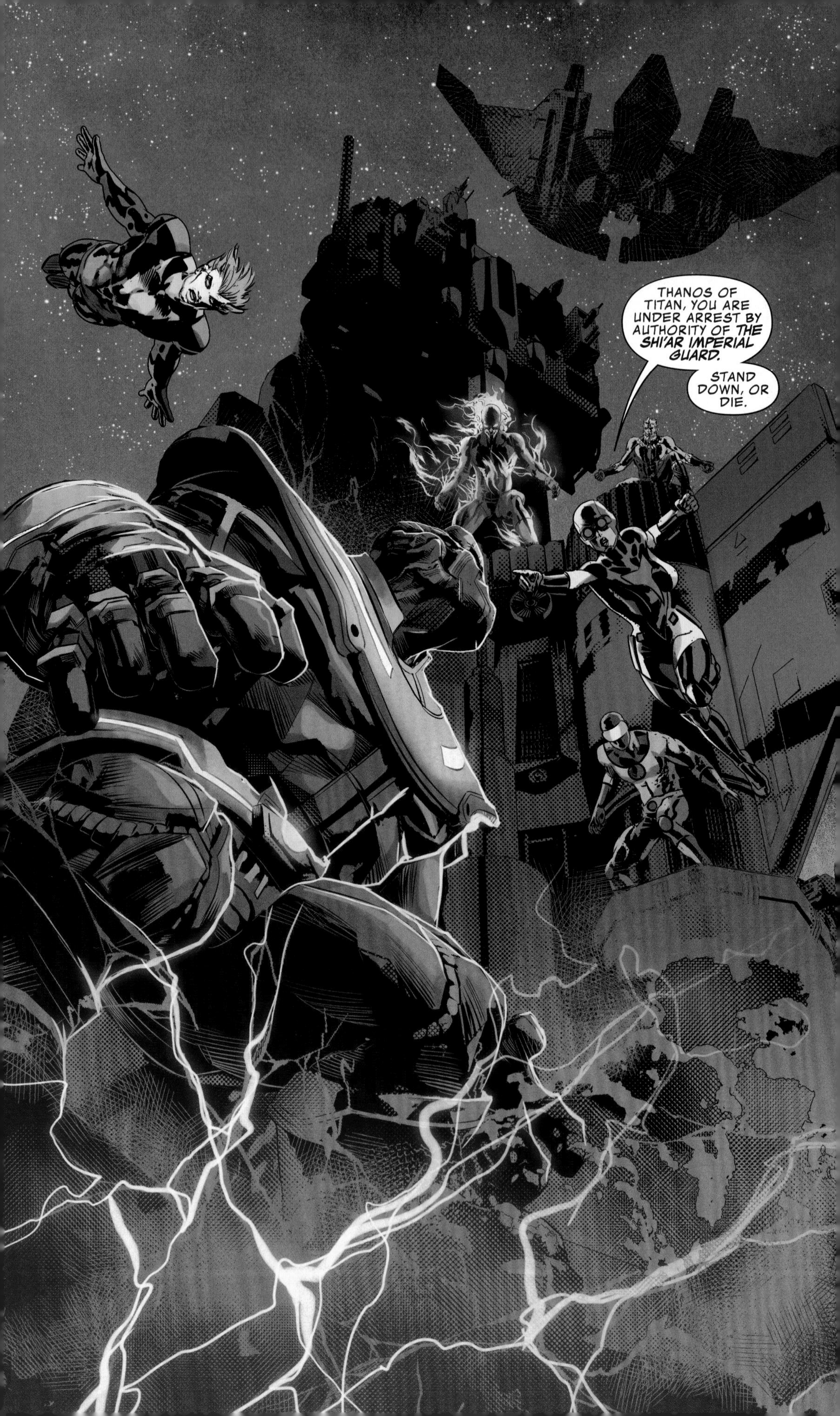
THANOS OF TITAN, YOU ARE UNDER ARREST BY AUTHORITY OF THE SHI'AR IMPERIAL GUARD.
STAND DOWN, OR DIE.

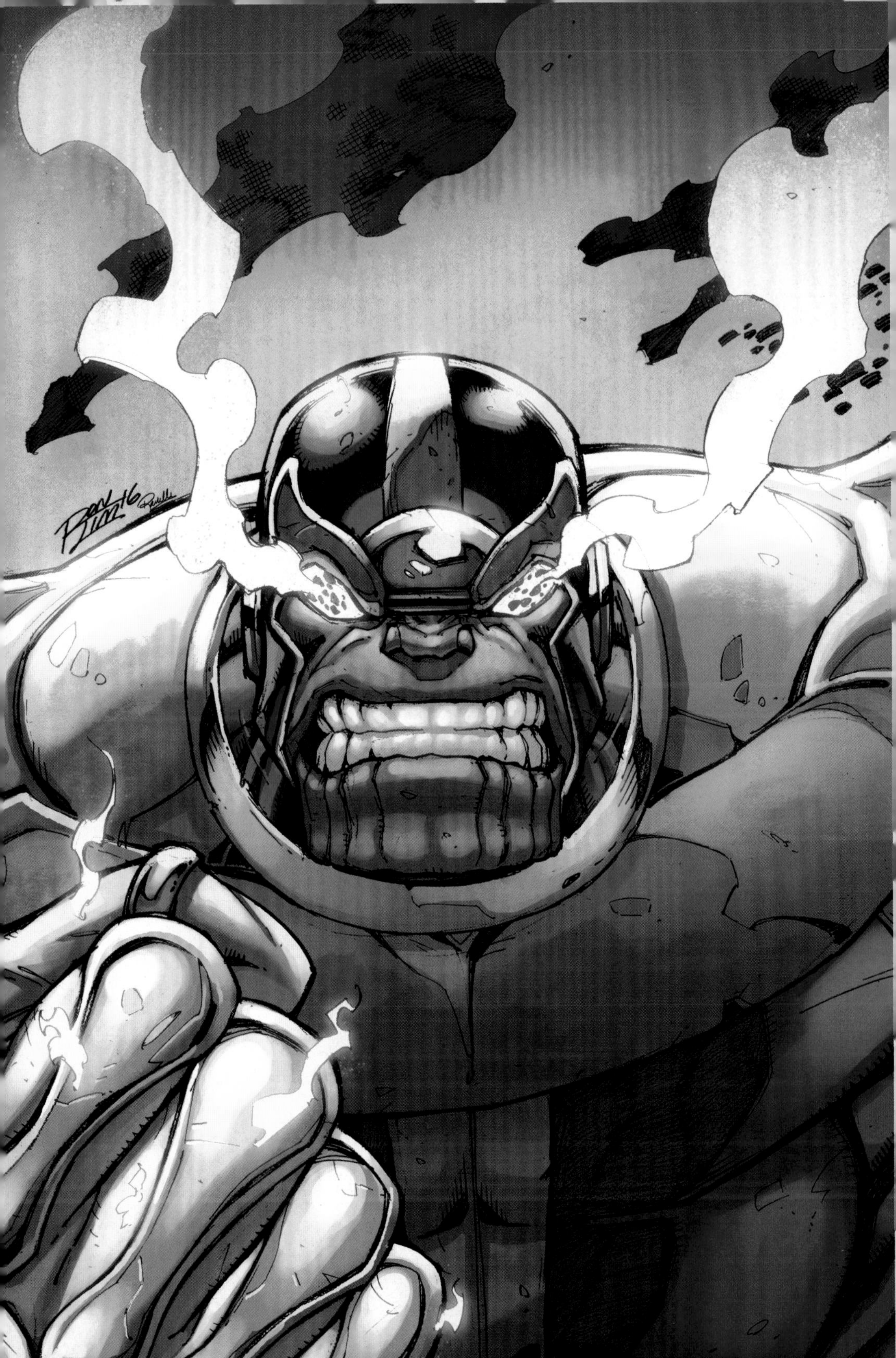

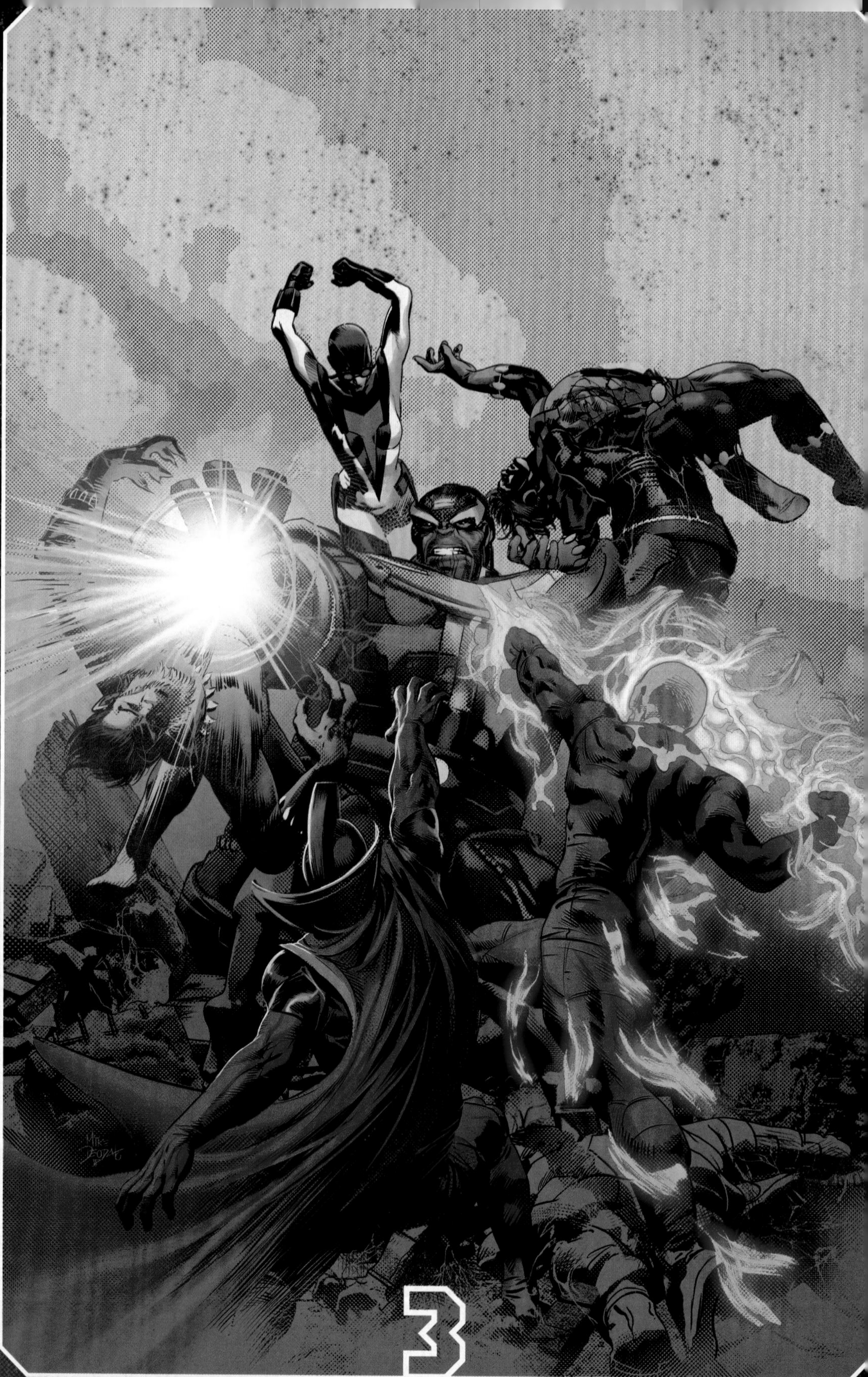
3

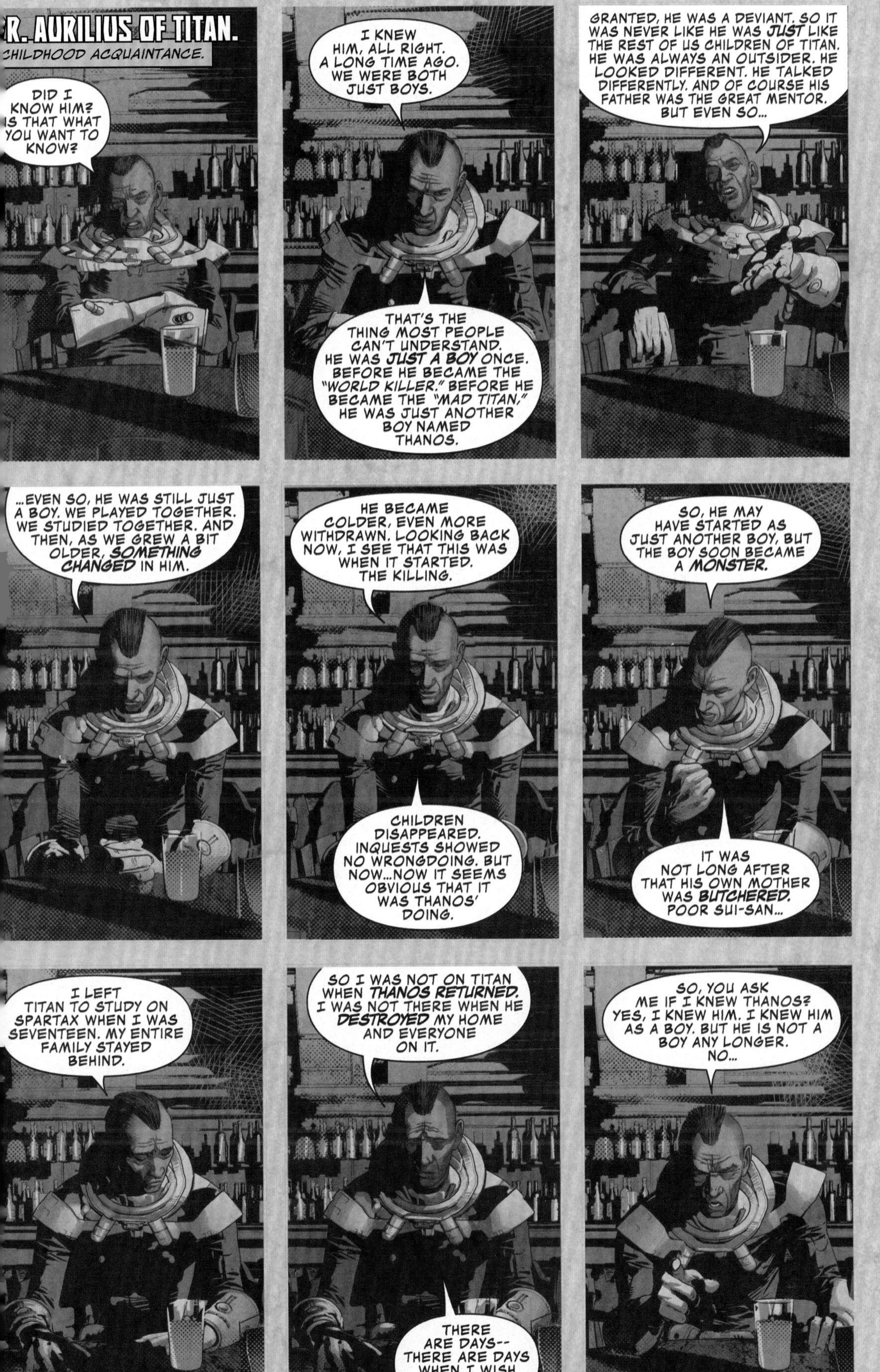
R. AURILIUS OF TITAN.
CHILDHOOD ACQUAINTANCE.
DID I KNOW HIM? IS THAT WHAT YOU WANT TO KNOW?
I KNEW HIM, ALL RIGHT. A LONG TIME AGO. WE WERE BOTH JUST BOYS.
THAT'S THE THING MOST PEOPLE CAN'T UNDERSTAND. HE WAS JUST A BOY ONCE. BEFORE HE BECAME THE "WORLD KILLER." BEFORE HE BECAME THE "MAD TITAN," HE WAS JUST ANOTHER BOY NAMED THANOS.
GRANTED, HE WAS A DEVIANT. SO IT WAS NEVER LIKE HE WAS JUST LIKE THE REST OF US CHILDREN OF TITAN. HE WAS ALWAYS AN OUTSIDER. HE LOOKED DIFFERENT. HE TALKED DIFFERENTLY. AND OF COURSE HIS FATHER WAS THE GREAT MENTOR. BUT EVEN SO...
...EVEN SO, HE WAS STILL JUST A BOY. WE PLAYED TOGETHER. WE STUDIED TOGETHER. AND THEN, AS WE GREW A BIT OLDER, SOMETHING CHANGED IN HIM.
HE BECAME COLDER, EVEN MORE WITHDRAWN. LOOKING BACK NOW, I SEE THAT THIS WAS WHEN IT STARTED. THE KILLING.
CHILDREN DISAPPEARED. INQUESTS SHOWED NO WRONGDOING. BUT NOW...NOW IT SEEMS OBVIOUS THAT IT WAS THANOS' DOING.
SO, HE MAY HAVE STARTED AS JUST ANOTHER BOY, BUT THE BOY SOON BECAME A MONSTER.
IT WAS NOT LONG AFTER THAT HIS OWN MOTHER WAS BUTCHERED. POOR SUI-SAN...
I LEFT TITAN TO STUDY ON SPARTAX WHEN I WAS SEVENTEEN. MY ENTIRE FAMILY STAYED BEHIND.
SO I WAS NOT ON TITAN WHEN THANOS RETURNED. I WAS NOT THERE WHEN HE DESTROYED MY HOME AND EVERYONE ON IT.
THERE ARE DAYS-- THERE ARE DAYS WHEN I WISH THAT I HAD BEEN.
SO, YOU ASK ME IF I KNEW THANOS? YES, I KNEW HIM. I KNEW HIM AS A BOY. BUT HE IS NOT A BOY ANY LONGER. NO...

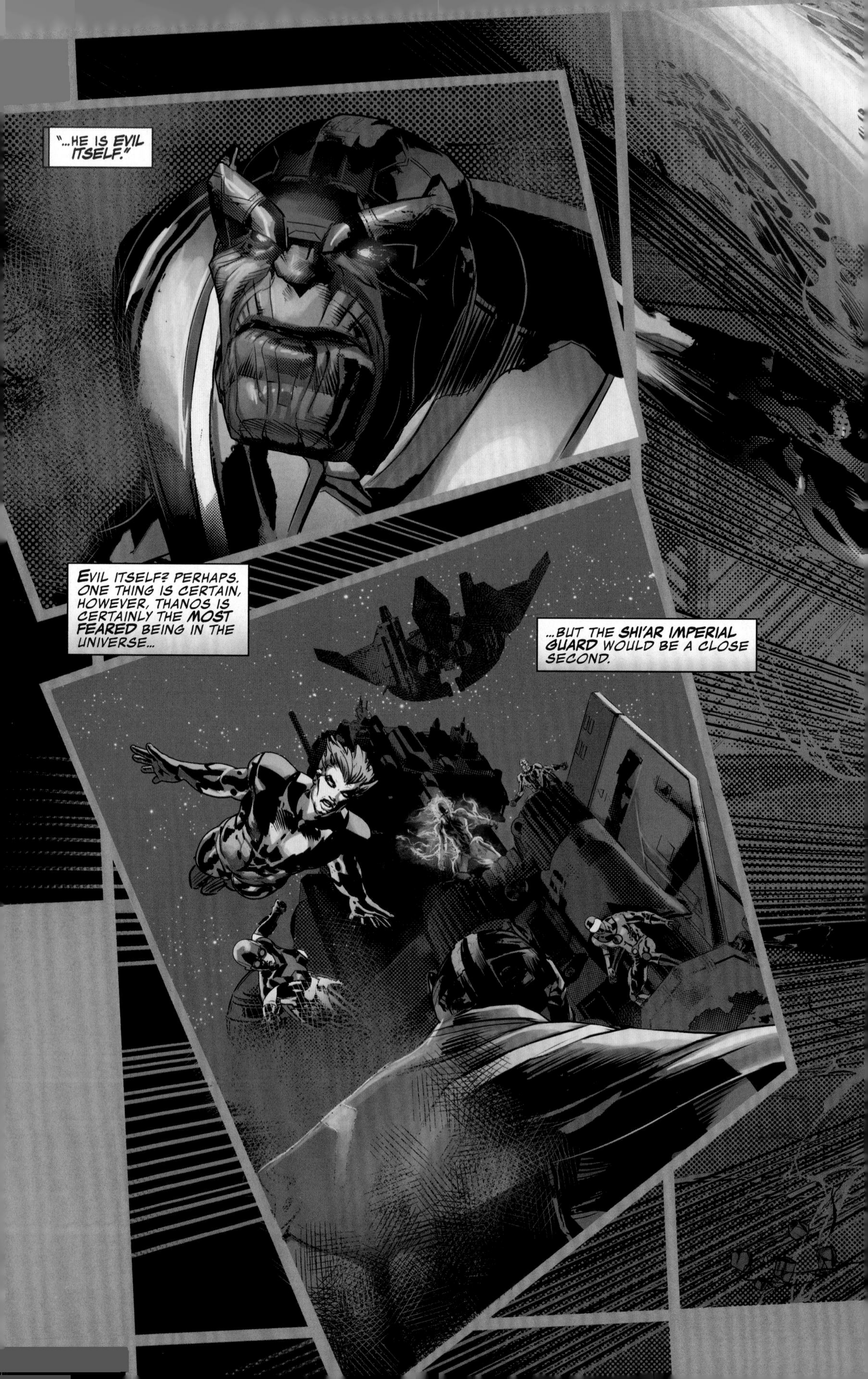
"...HE IS EVIL ITSELF."
EVIL ITSELF? PERHAPS. ONE THING IS CERTAIN, HOWEVER, THANOS IS CERTAINLY THE MOST FEARED BEING IN THE UNIVERSE...
...BUT THE SHI'AR IMPERIAL GUARD WOULD BE A CLOSE SECOND.

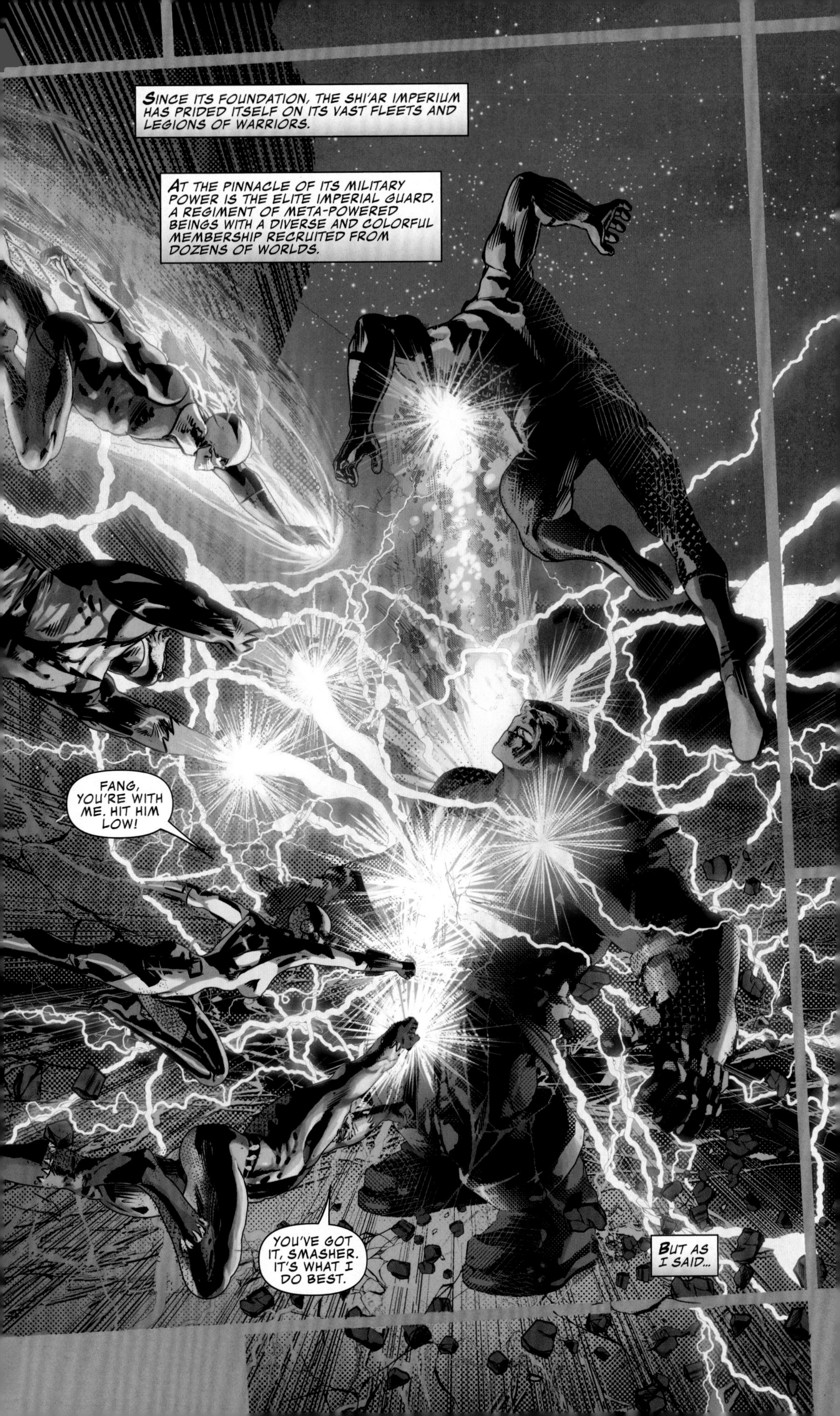
SINCE ITS FOUNDATION, THE SHI'AR IMPERIUM HAS PRIDED ITSELF ON ITS VAST FLEETS AND LEGIONS OF WARRIORS.
AT THE PINNACLE OF ITS MILITARY POWER IS THE ELITE IMPERIAL GUARD. A REGIMENT OF META-POWERED BEINGS WITH A DIVERSE AND COLORFUL MEMBERSHIP RECRUITED FROM DOZENS OF WORLDS.
FANG, YOU'RE WITH ME. HIT HIM LOW!
YOU'VE GOT IT, SMASHER. IT'S WHAT I DO BEST.
BUT AS I SAID...

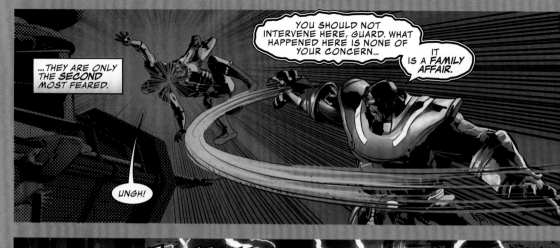

...THEY ARE ONLY THE **SECOND** MOST FEARED.

YOU SHOULD NOT INTERVENE HERE, GUARD. WHAT HAPPENED HERE IS NONE OF YOUR CONCERN...

IT IS A **FAMILY** AFFAIR.

UNGH!

SHRACK

WRONG, MAD TITAN! THIS MOON IS IN SHI'AR SPACE. THIS RESEARCH FACILITY IS UNDER OUR PROTECTION!

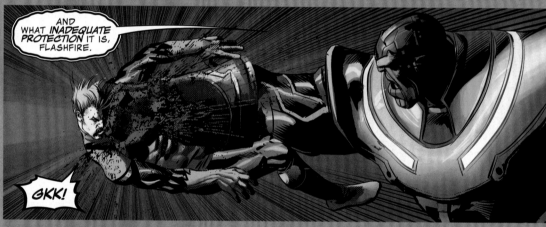

AND WHAT **INADEQUATE PROTECTION** IT IS, FLASHFIRE.

GKK!

I'LL GIVE YOU ALL ONE CHANCE TO RETREAT. ONE CHANCE TO SAVE YOURSELVES.

H-HERE'S THE THING, THANOS...

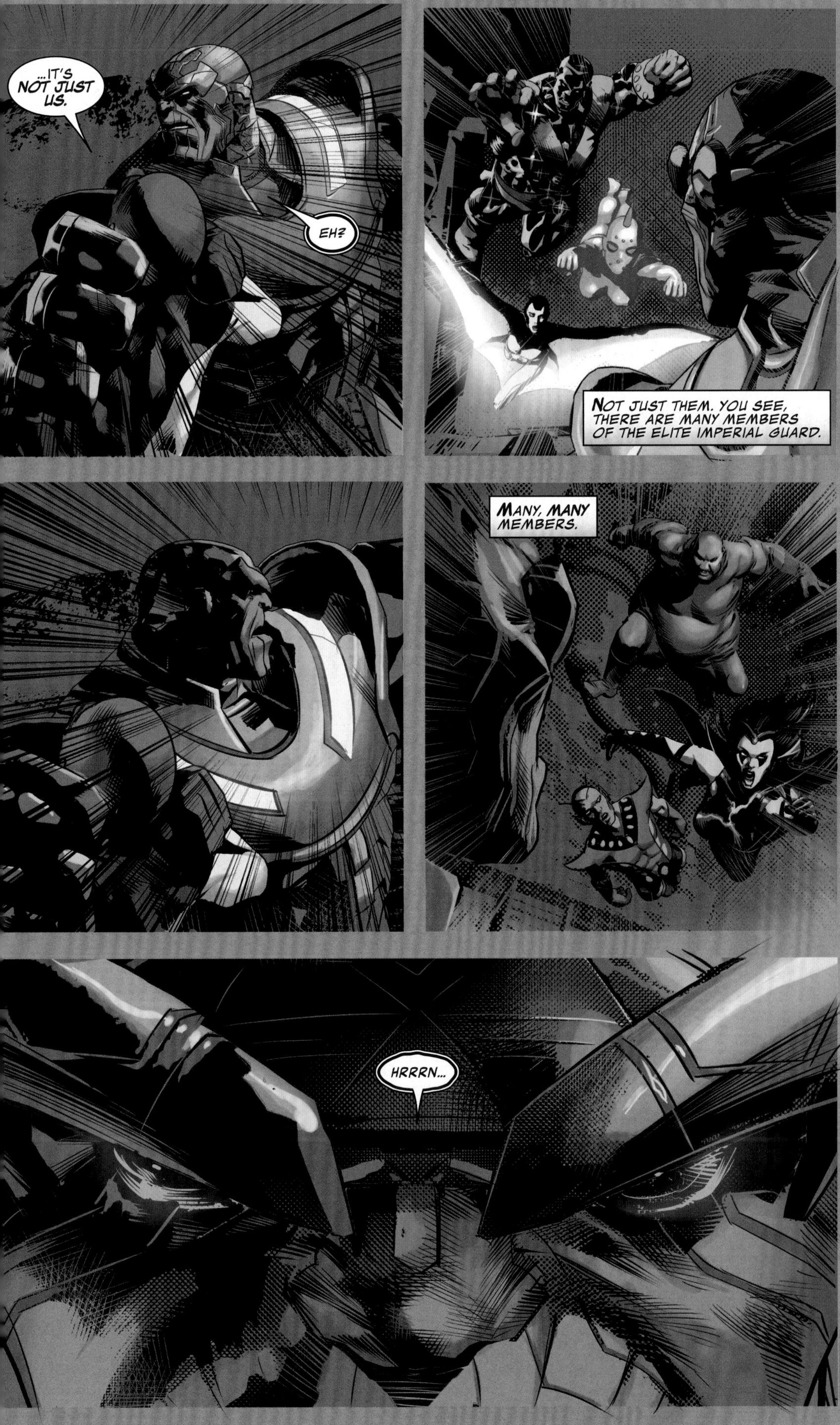
...IT'S NOT JUST US.
EH?
NOT JUST THEM. YOU SEE, THERE ARE MANY MEMBERS OF THE ELITE IMPERIAL GUARD.
MANY, MANY MEMBERS.
HRRRN...

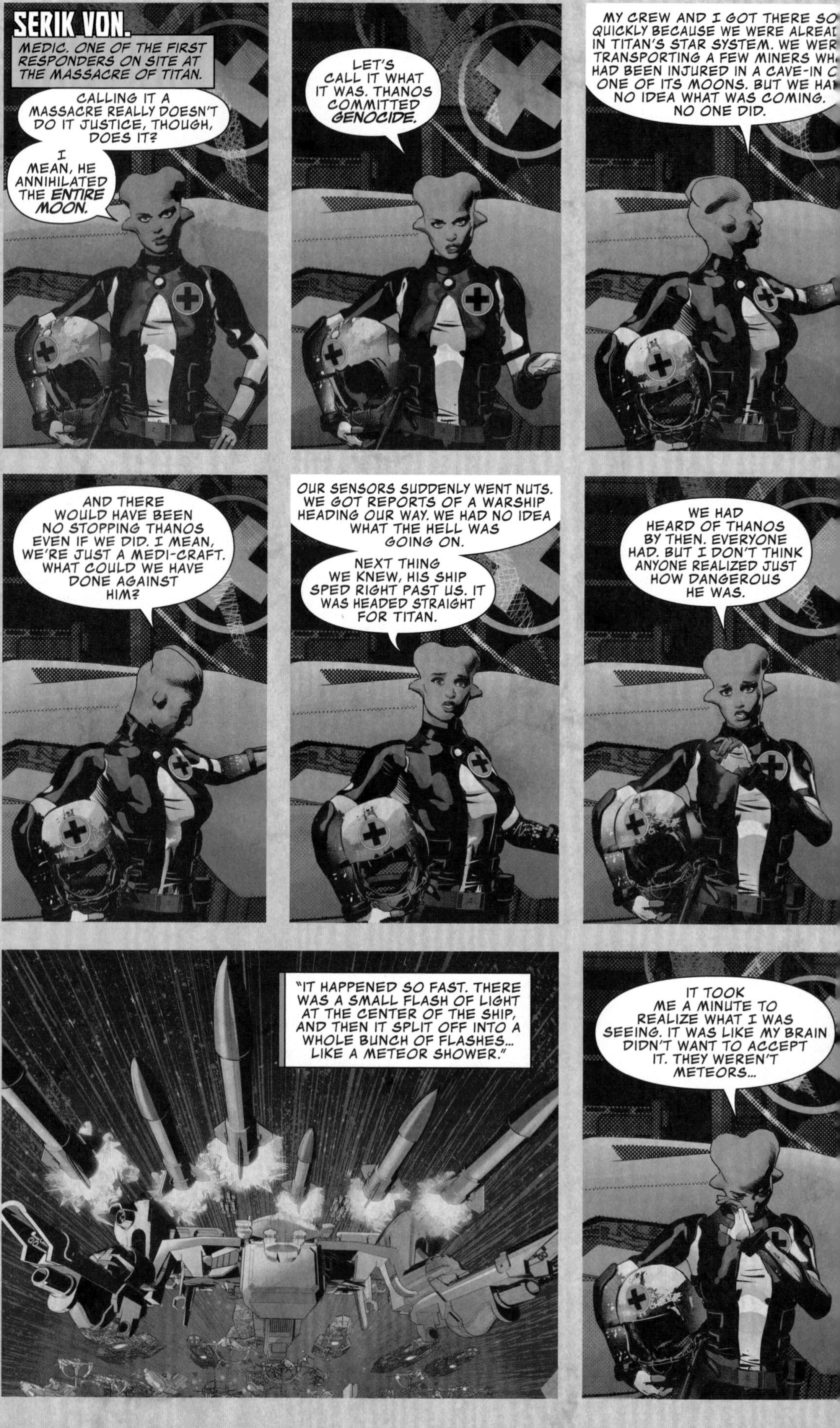
SERIK VON.
MEDIC. ONE OF THE FIRST RESPONDERS ON SITE AT THE MASSACRE OF TITAN.
CALLING IT A MASSACRE REALLY DOESN'T DO IT JUSTICE, THOUGH, DOES IT?
I MEAN, HE ANNIHILATED THE ENTIRE MOON.
LET'S CALL IT WHAT IT WAS. THANOS COMMITTED GENOCIDE.
MY CREW AND I GOT THERE SO QUICKLY BECAUSE WE WERE ALREA IN TITAN'S STAR SYSTEM. WE WER TRANSPORTING A FEW MINERS WH HAD BEEN INJURED IN A CAVE-IN O ONE OF ITS MOONS. BUT WE HA NO IDEA WHAT WAS COMING. NO ONE DID.
AND THERE WOULD HAVE BEEN NO STOPPING THANOS EVEN IF WE DID. I MEAN, WE'RE JUST A MEDI-CRAFT. WHAT COULD WE HAVE DONE AGAINST HIM?
OUR SENSORS SUDDENLY WENT NUTS. WE GOT REPORTS OF A WARSHIP HEADING OUR WAY. WE HAD NO IDEA WHAT THE HELL WAS GOING ON.
NEXT THING WE KNEW, HIS SHIP SPED RIGHT PAST US. IT WAS HEADED STRAIGHT FOR TITAN.
WE HAD HEARD OF THANOS BY THEN. EVERYONE HAD. BUT I DON'T THINK ANYONE REALIZED JUST HOW DANGEROUS HE WAS.
"IT HAPPENED SO FAST. THERE WAS A SMALL FLASH OF LIGHT AT THE CENTER OF THE SHIP, AND THEN IT SPLIT OFF INTO A WHOLE BUNCH OF FLASHES... LIKE A METEOR SHOWER."
IT TOOK ME A MINUTE TO REALIZE WHAT I WAS SEEING. IT WAS LIKE MY BRAIN DIDN'T WANT TO ACCEPT IT. THEY WEREN'T METEORS...

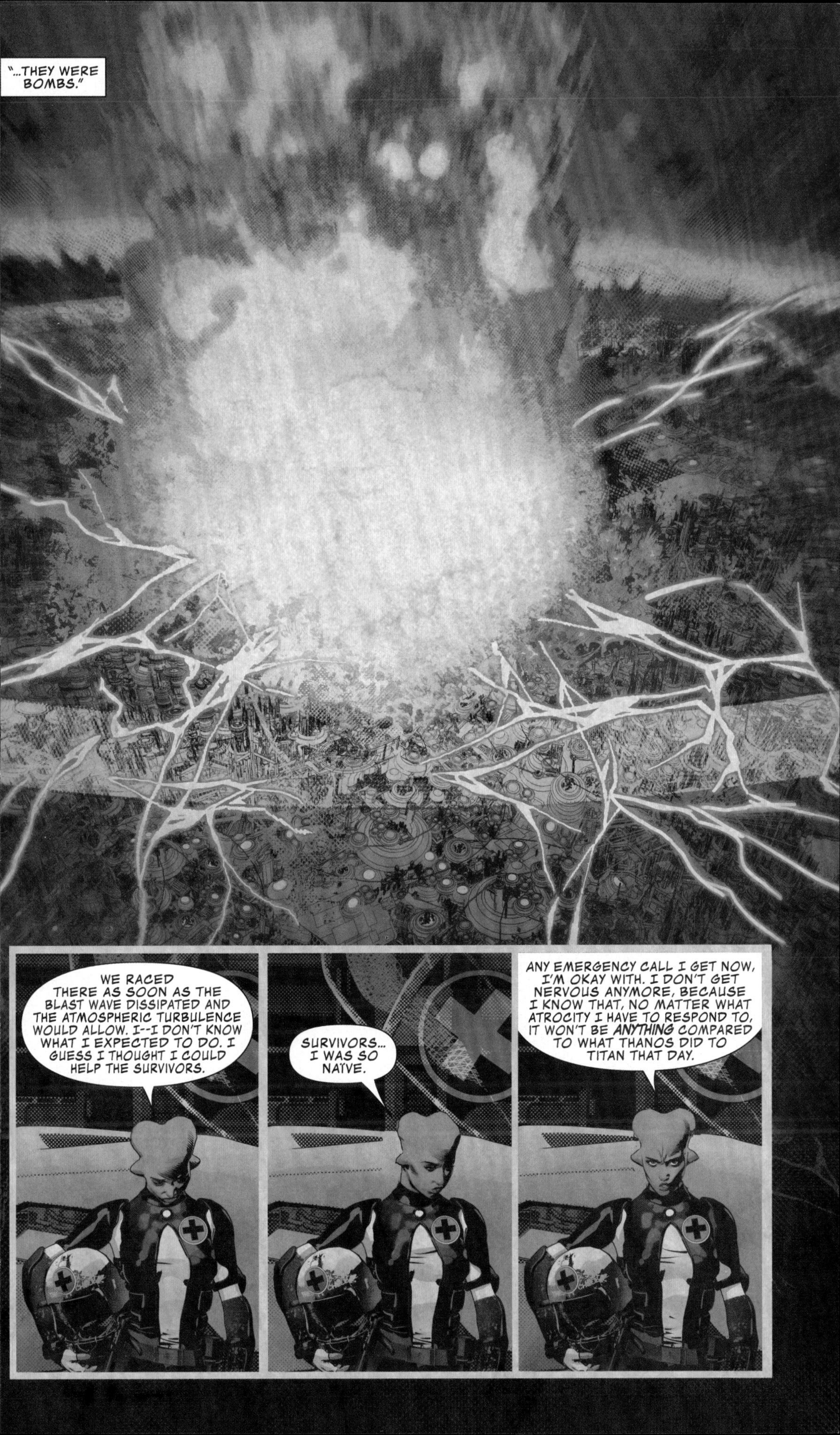
"...THEY WERE BOMBS."
WE RACED THERE AS SOON AS THE BLAST WAVE DISSIPATED AND THE ATMOSPHERIC TURBULENCE WOULD ALLOW. I--I DON'T KNOW WHAT I EXPECTED TO DO. I GUESS I THOUGHT I COULD HELP THE SURVIVORS.
SURVIVORS... I WAS SO NAÏVE.
ANY EMERGENCY CALL I GET NOW, I'M OKAY WITH. I DON'T GET NERVOUS ANYMORE, BECAUSE I KNOW THAT, NO MATTER WHAT ATROCITY I HAVE TO RESPOND TO, IT WON'T BE *ANYTHING* COMPARED TO WHAT THANOS DID TO TITAN THAT DAY.

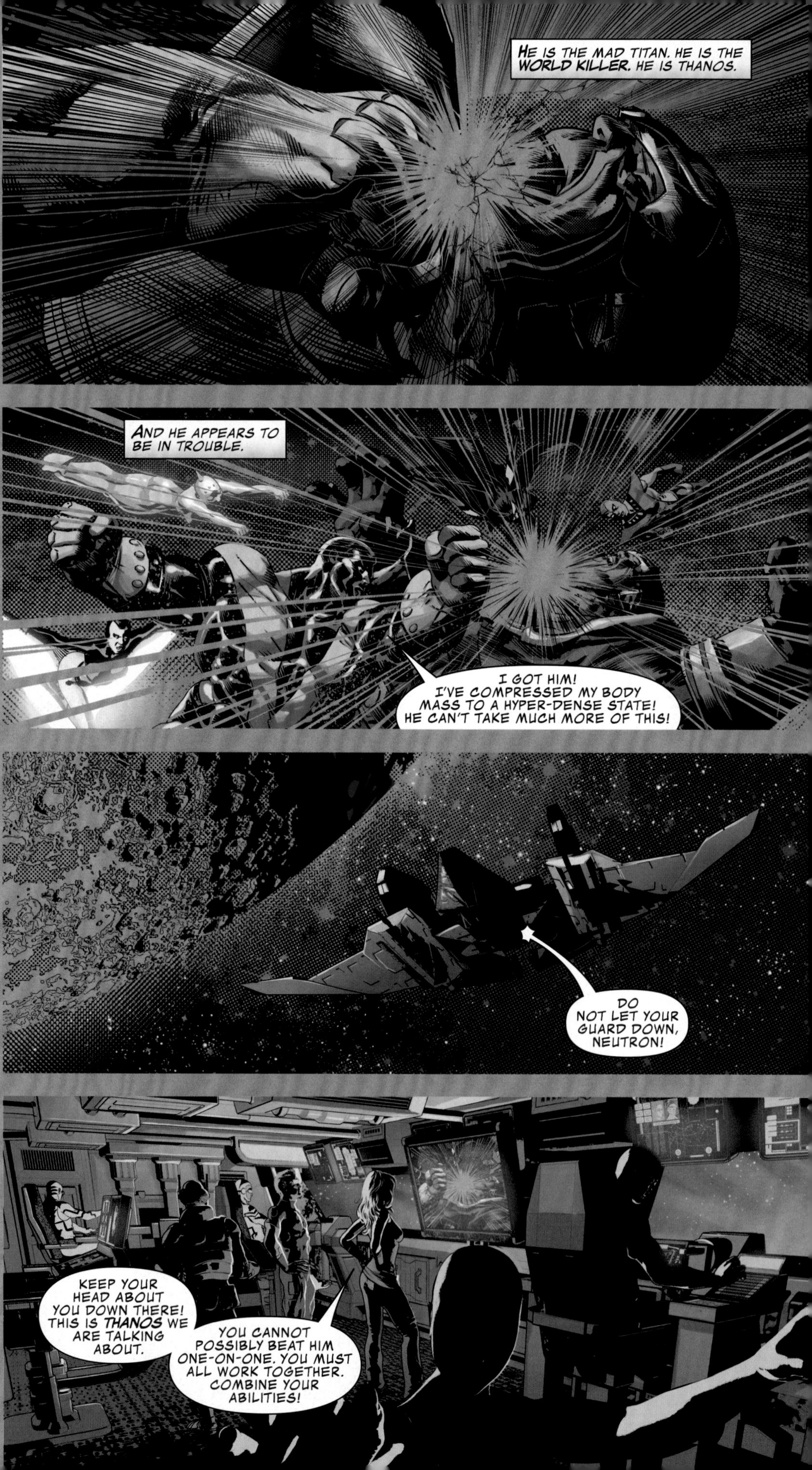
HE IS THE MAD TITAN. HE IS THE WORLD KILLER. HE IS THANOS.
AND HE APPEARS TO BE IN TROUBLE.
I GOT HIM! I'VE COMPRESSED MY BODY MASS TO A HYPER-DENSE STATE! HE CAN'T TAKE MUCH MORE OF THIS!
DO NOT LET YOUR GUARD DOWN, NEUTRON!
KEEP YOUR HEAD ABOUT YOU DOWN THERE! THIS IS THANOS WE ARE TALKING ABOUT.
YOU CANNOT POSSIBLY BEAT HIM ONE-ON-ONE. YOU MUST ALL WORK TOGETHER. COMBINE YOUR ABILITIES!

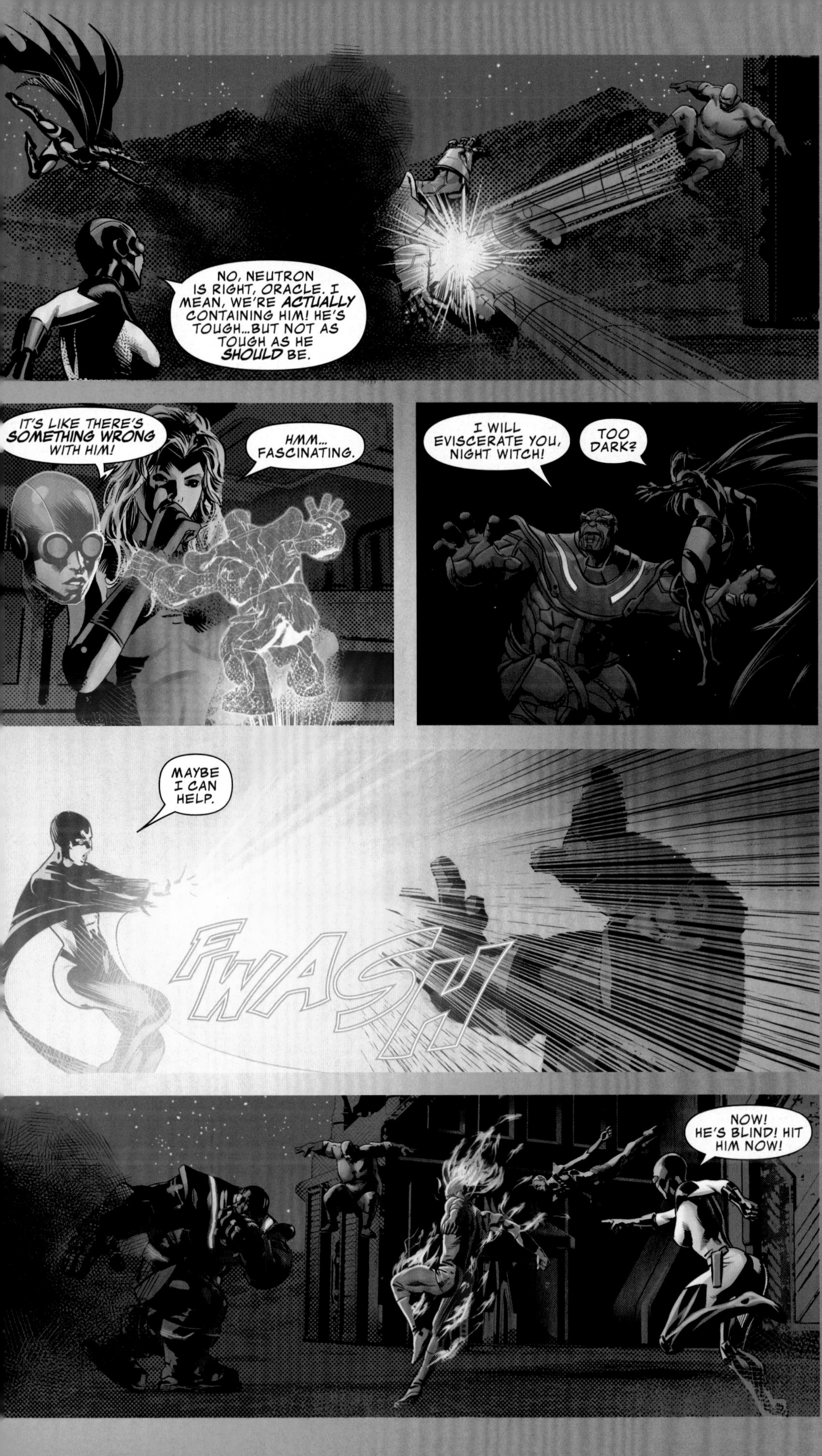
NO, NEUTRON IS RIGHT, ORACLE. I MEAN, WE'RE ACTUALLY CONTAINING HIM! HE'S TOUGH...BUT NOT AS TOUGH AS HE SHOULD BE.
IT'S LIKE THERE'S SOMETHING WRONG WITH HIM!
HMM... FASCINATING.
I WILL EVISCERATE YOU, NIGHT WITCH!
TOO DARK?
MAYBE I CAN HELP.
FWASH
NOW! HE'S BLIND! HIT HIM NOW!

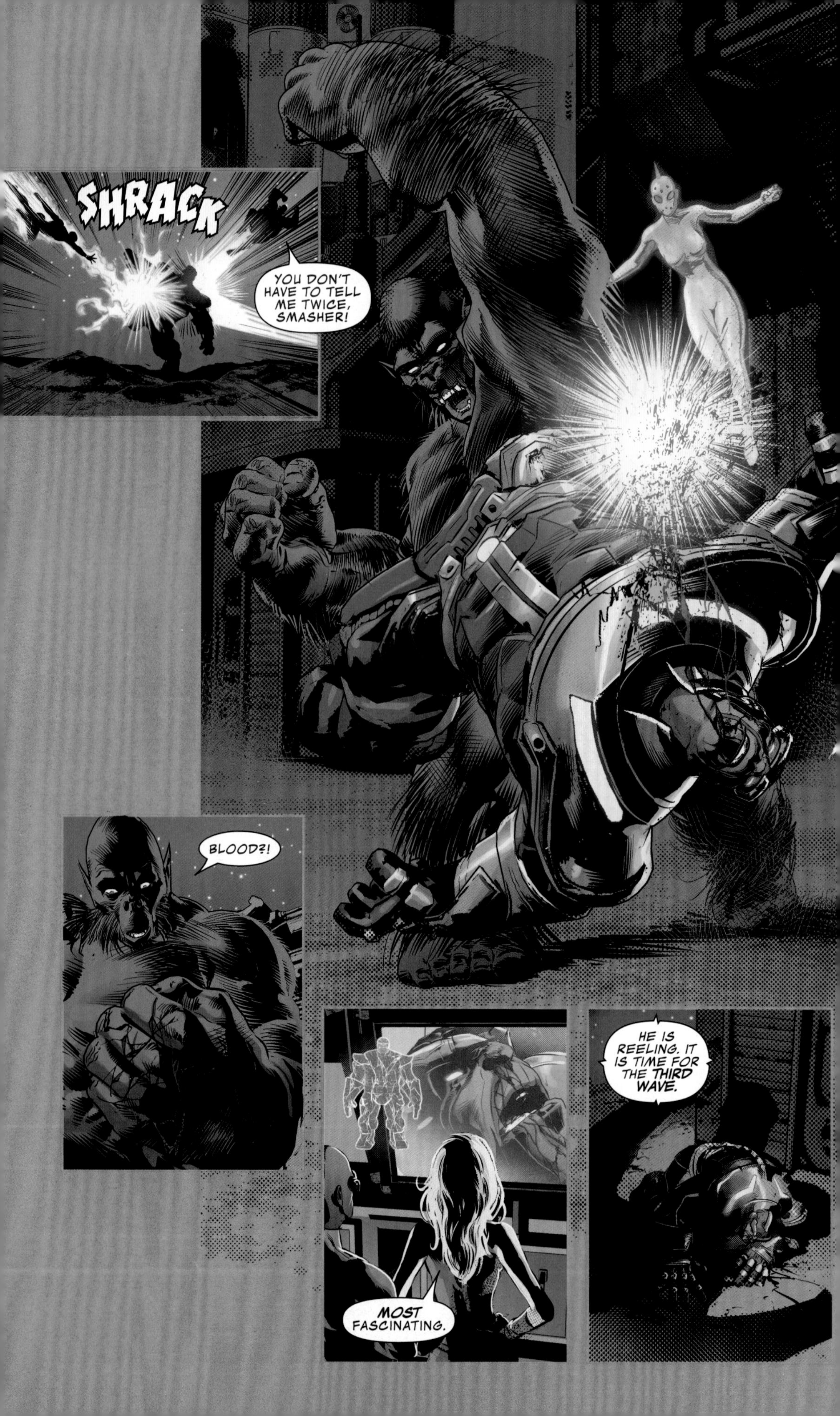
SHRACK
YOU DON'T HAVE TO TELL ME TWICE, SMASHER!
BLOOD?!
MOST FASCINATING.
HE IS REELING. IT IS TIME FOR THE THIRD WAVE.

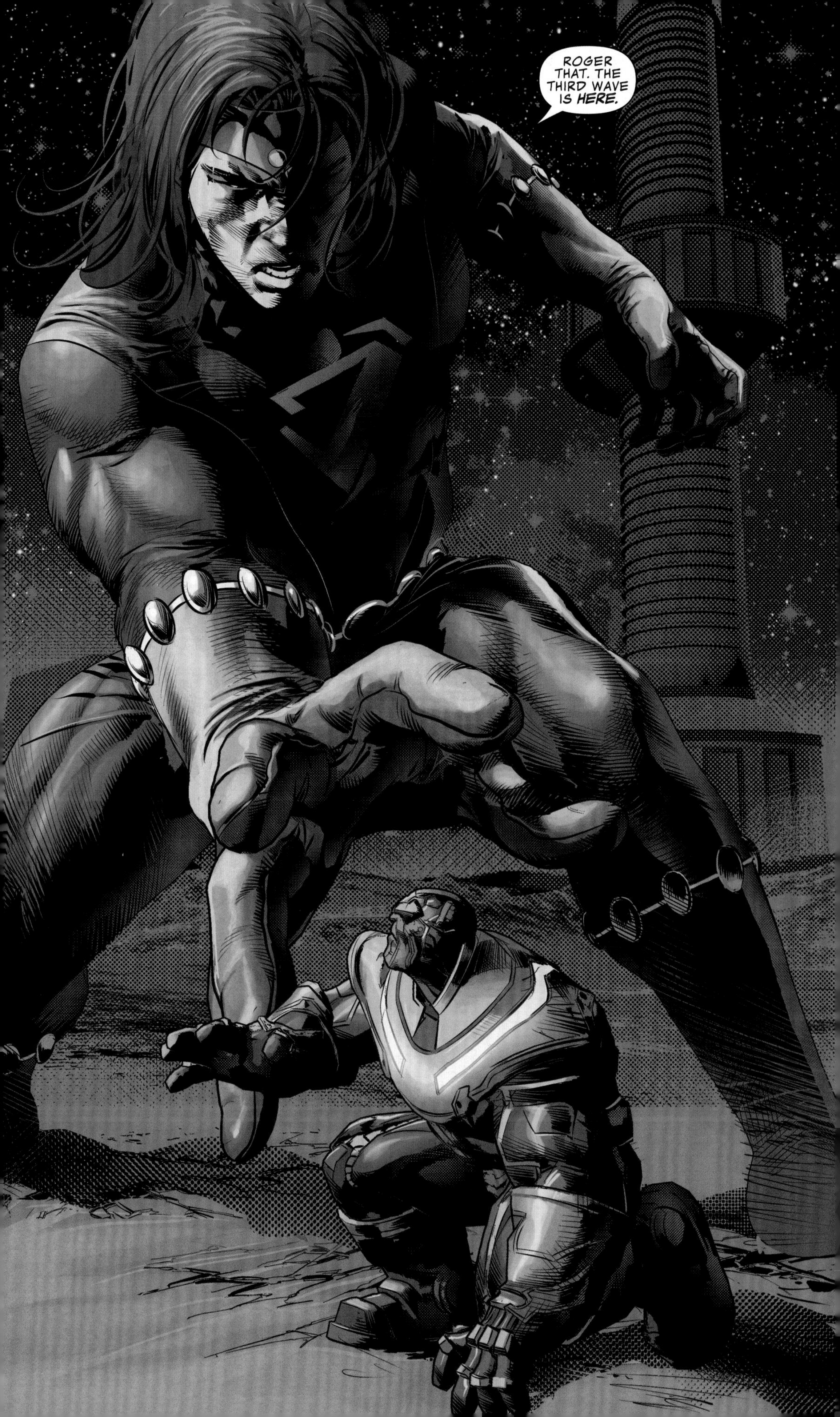
ROGER THAT. THE THIRD WAVE IS HERE.

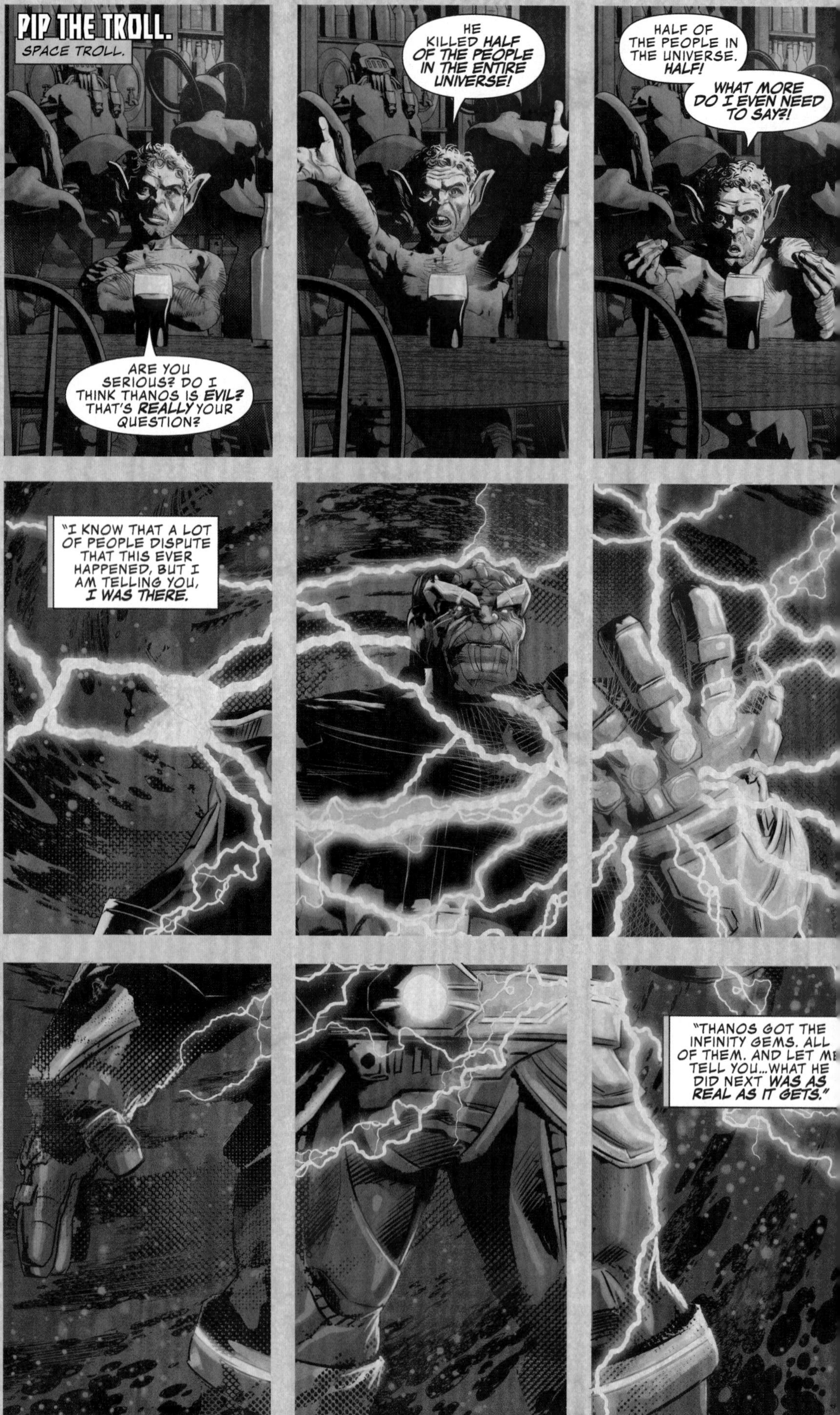
PIP THE TROLL.
SPACE TROLL.
ARE YOU SERIOUS? DO I THINK THANOS IS EVIL? THAT'S REALLY YOUR QUESTION?
HE KILLED HALF OF THE PEOPLE IN THE ENTIRE UNIVERSE!
HALF OF THE PEOPLE IN THE UNIVERSE. HALF!
WHAT MORE DO I EVEN NEED TO SAY?!
"I KNOW THAT A LOT OF PEOPLE DISPUTE THAT THIS EVER HAPPENED, BUT I AM TELLING YOU, I WAS THERE.
"THANOS GOT THE INFINITY GEMS. ALL OF THEM. AND LET ME TELL YOU...WHAT HE DID NEXT WAS AS REAL AS IT GETS."

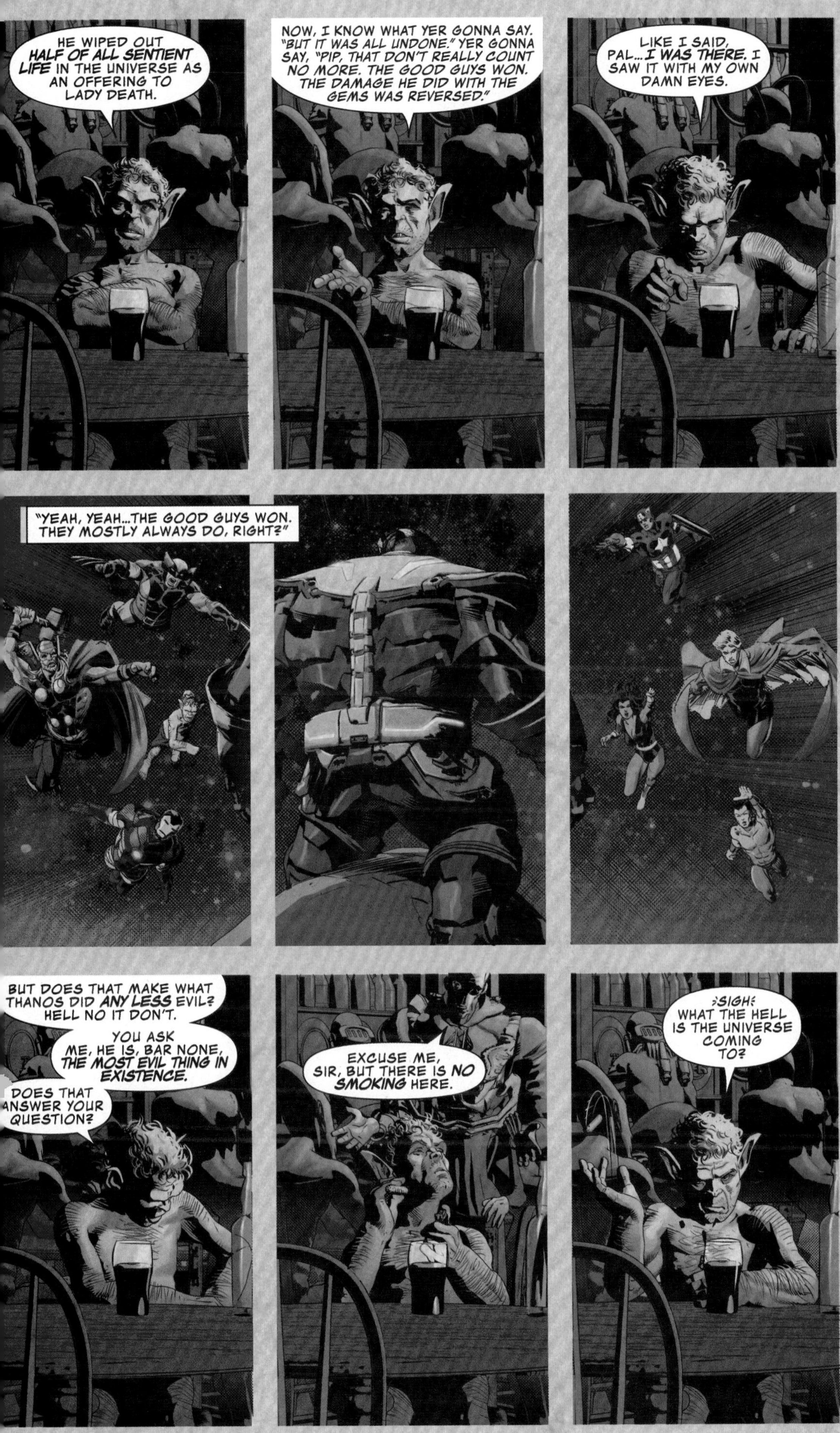
HE WIPED OUT HALF OF ALL SENTIENT LIFE IN THE UNIVERSE AS AN OFFERING TO LADY DEATH.
NOW, I KNOW WHAT YER GONNA SAY. "BUT IT WAS ALL UNDONE." YER GONNA SAY, "PIP, THAT DON'T REALLY COUNT NO MORE. THE GOOD GUYS WON. THE DAMAGE HE DID WITH THE GEMS WAS REVERSED."
LIKE I SAID, PAL... I WAS THERE. I SAW IT WITH MY OWN DAMN EYES.
"YEAH, YEAH... THE GOOD GUYS WON. THEY MOSTLY ALWAYS DO, RIGHT?"
BUT DOES THAT MAKE WHAT THANOS DID ANY LESS EVIL? HELL NO IT DON'T.
YOU ASK ME, HE IS, BAR NONE, THE MOST EVIL THING IN EXISTENCE.
DOES THAT ANSWER YOUR QUESTION?
EXCUSE ME, SIR, BUT THERE IS NO SMOKING HERE.
SIGH
WHAT THE HELL IS THE UNIVERSE COMING TO?

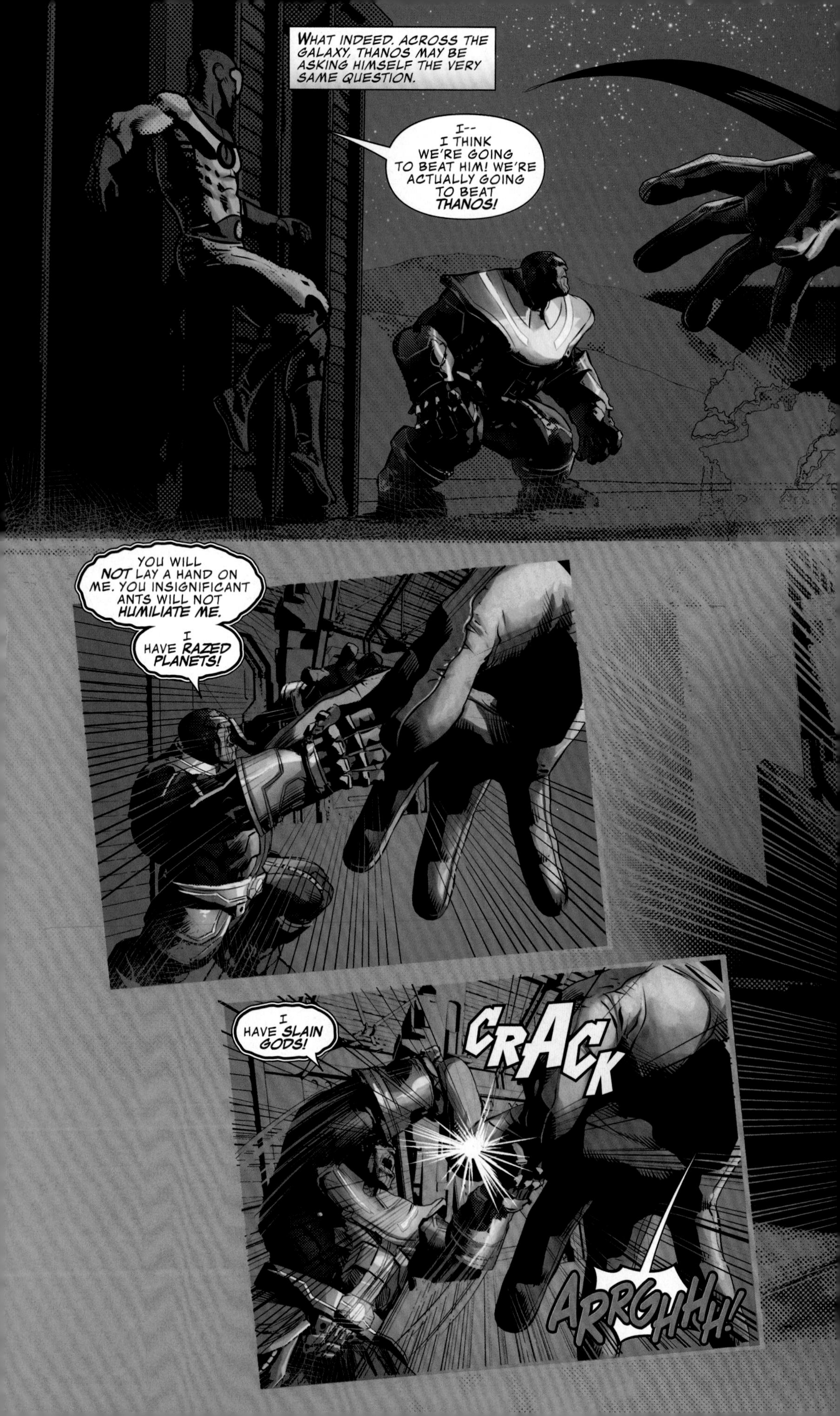
WHAT INDEED. ACROSS THE GALAXY, THANOS MAY BE ASKING HIMSELF THE VERY SAME QUESTION.
I-- I THINK WE'RE GOING TO BEAT HIM! WE'RE ACTUALLY GOING TO BEAT THANOS!
YOU WILL NOT LAY A HAND ON ME. YOU INSIGNIFICANT ANTS WILL NOT HUMILIATE ME.
I HAVE RAZED PLANETS!
I HAVE SLAIN GODS!
CRACK
ARRGHHH!

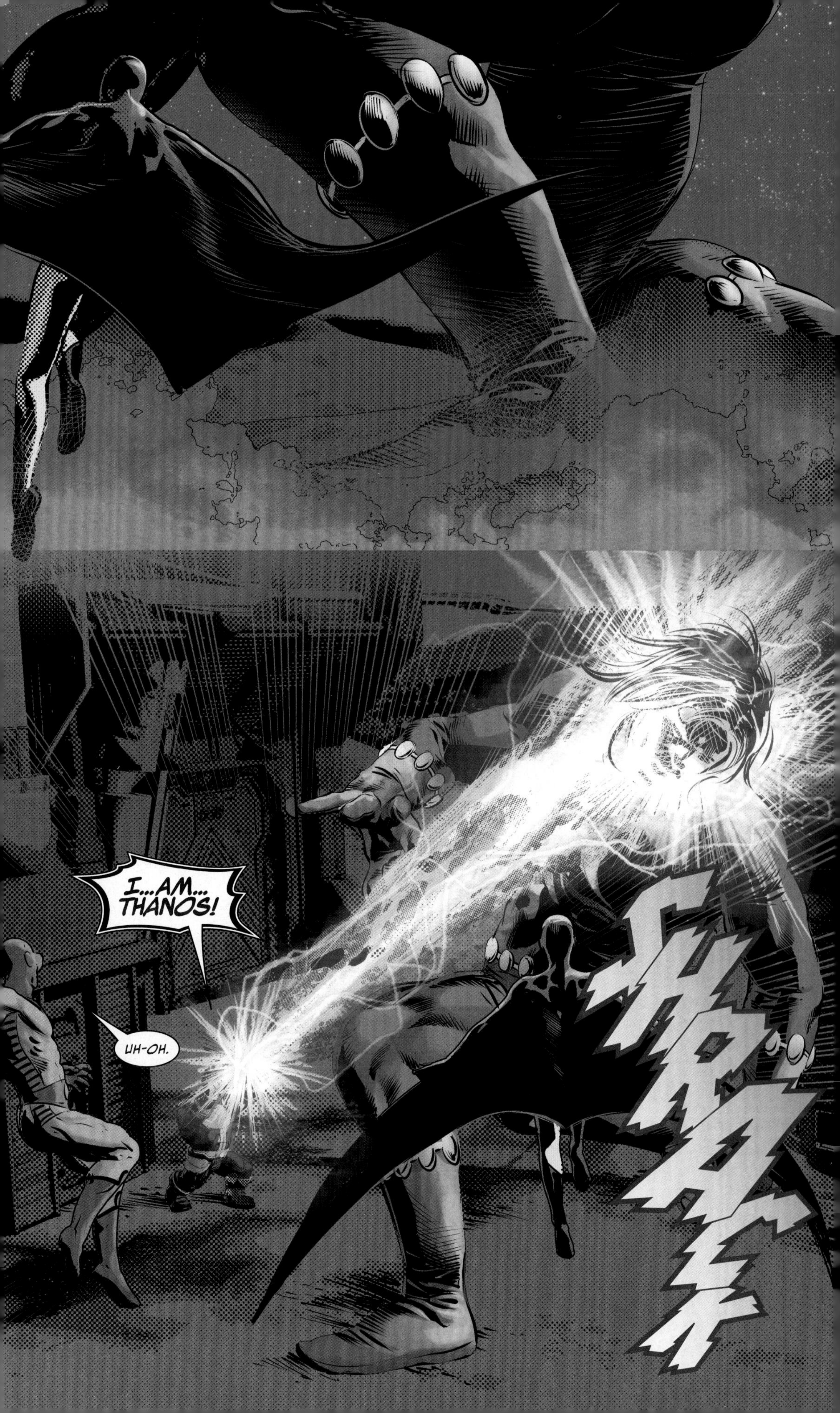
I...AM... THANOS!
UH-OH.
SKRAKK

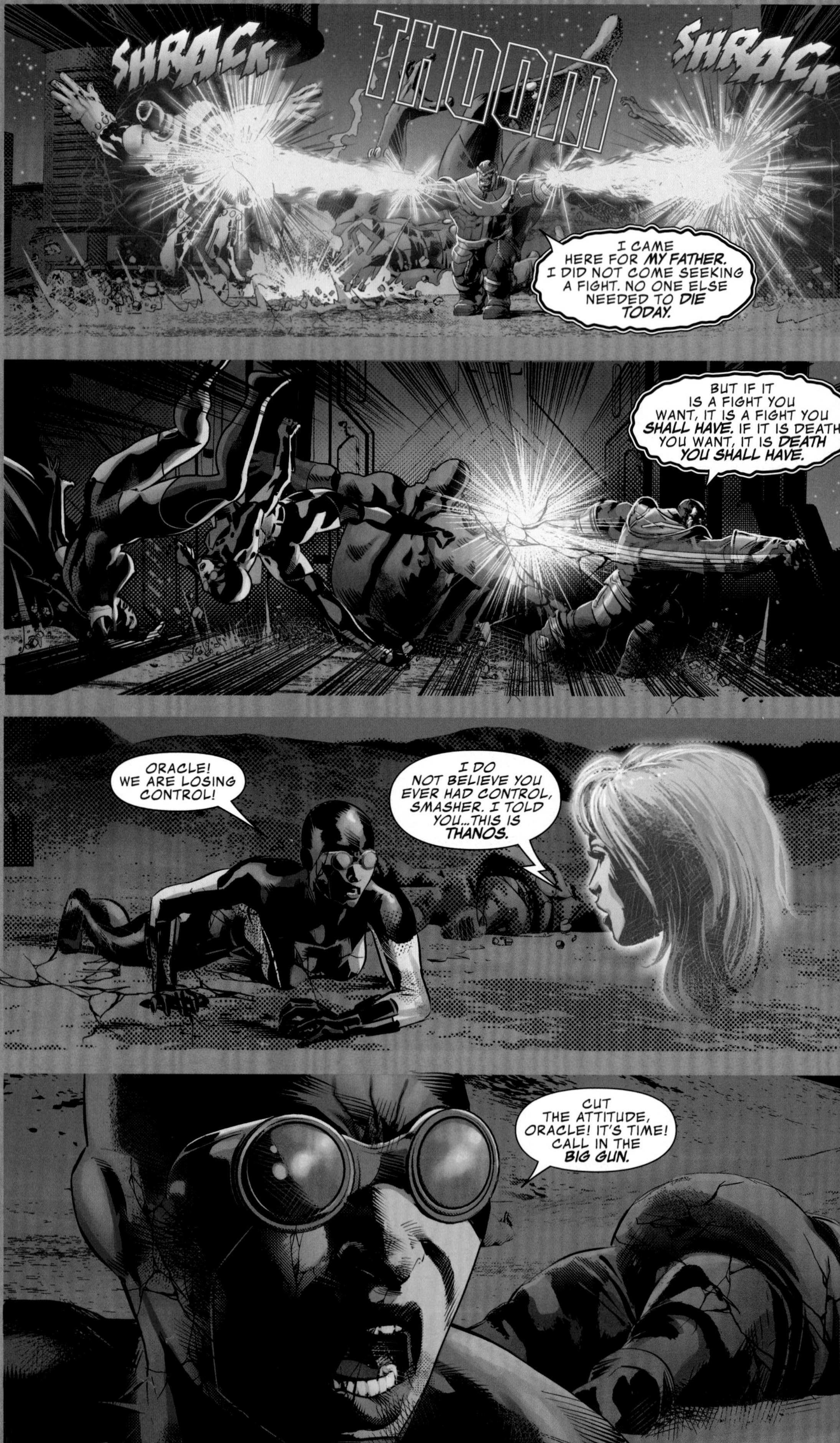
SHRACK
THOOM
SHRACK
I CAME HERE FOR MY FATHER. I DID NOT COME SEEKING A FIGHT. NO ONE ELSE NEEDED TO DIE TODAY.
BUT IF IT IS A FIGHT YOU WANT, IT IS A FIGHT YOU SHALL HAVE. IF IT IS DEATH YOU WANT, IT IS DEATH YOU SHALL HAVE.
ORACLE! WE ARE LOSING CONTROL!
I DO NOT BELIEVE YOU EVER HAD CONTROL, SMASHER. I TOLD YOU...THIS IS THANOS.
CUT THE ATTITUDE, ORACLE! IT'S TIME! CALL IN THE BIG GUN.

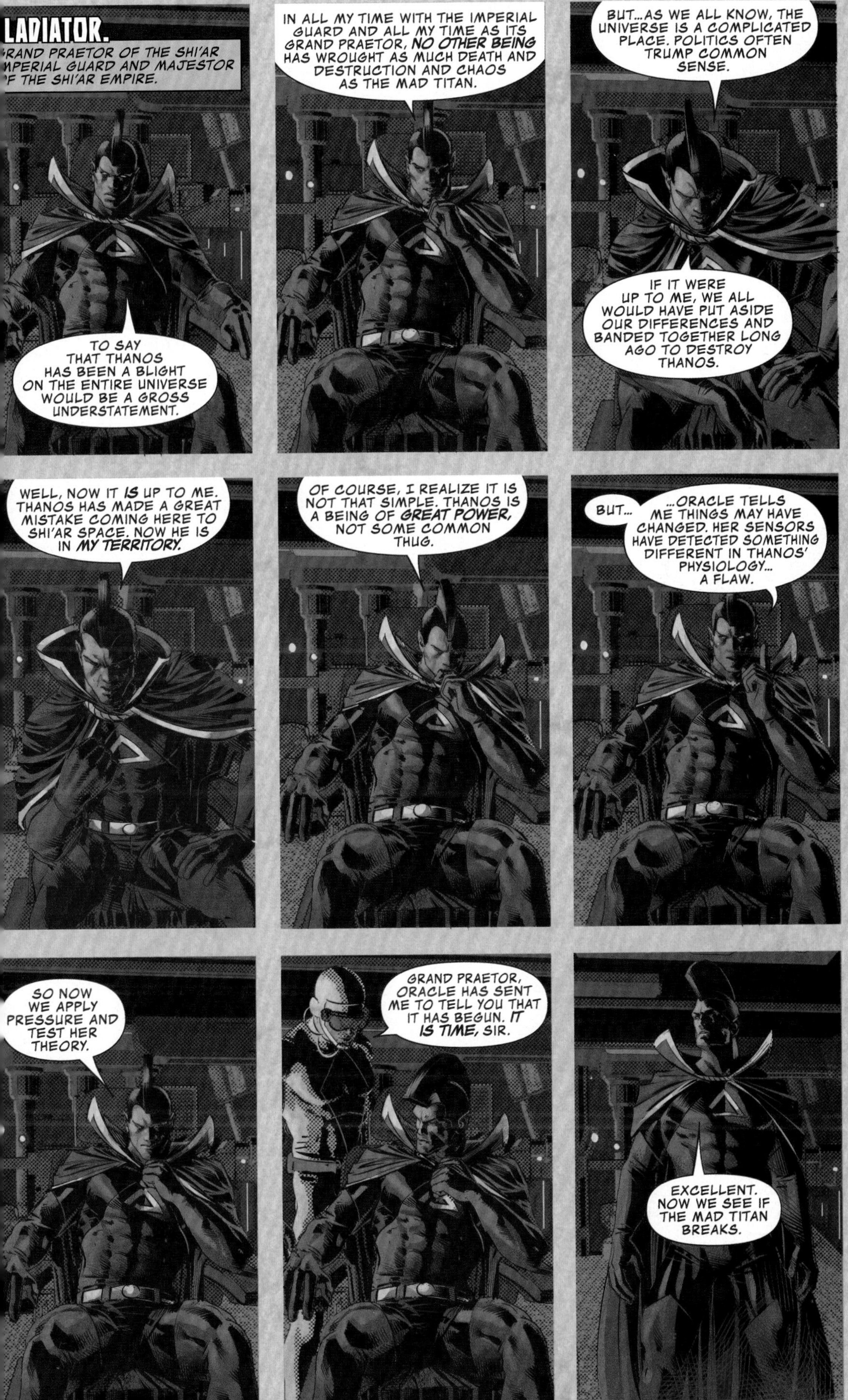
LADIATOR.
RAND PRAETOR OF THE SHI'AR MPERIAL GUARD AND MAJESTOR F THE SHI'AR EMPIRE.
TO SAY THAT THANOS HAS BEEN A BLIGHT ON THE ENTIRE UNIVERSE WOULD BE A GROSS UNDERSTATEMENT.
IN ALL MY TIME WITH THE IMPERIAL GUARD AND ALL MY TIME AS ITS GRAND PRAETOR, NO OTHER BEING HAS WROUGHT AS MUCH DEATH AND DESTRUCTION AND CHAOS AS THE MAD TITAN.
BUT...AS WE ALL KNOW, THE UNIVERSE IS A COMPLICATED PLACE. POLITICS OFTEN TRUMP COMMON SENSE.
IF IT WERE UP TO ME, WE ALL WOULD HAVE PUT ASIDE OUR DIFFERENCES AND BANDED TOGETHER LONG AGO TO DESTROY THANOS.
WELL, NOW IT IS UP TO ME. THANOS HAS MADE A GREAT MISTAKE COMING HERE TO SHI'AR SPACE. NOW HE IS IN MY TERRITORY.
OF COURSE, I REALIZE IT IS NOT THAT SIMPLE. THANOS IS A BEING OF GREAT POWER, NOT SOME COMMON THUG.
BUT...
...ORACLE TELLS ME THINGS MAY HAVE CHANGED. HER SENSORS HAVE DETECTED SOMETHING DIFFERENT IN THANOS' PHYSIOLOGY... A FLAW.
SO NOW WE APPLY PRESSURE AND TEST HER THEORY.
GRAND PRAETOR, ORACLE HAS SENT ME TO TELL YOU THAT IT HAS BEGUN. IT IS TIME, SIR.
EXCELLENT. NOW WE SEE IF THE MAD TITAN BREAKS.

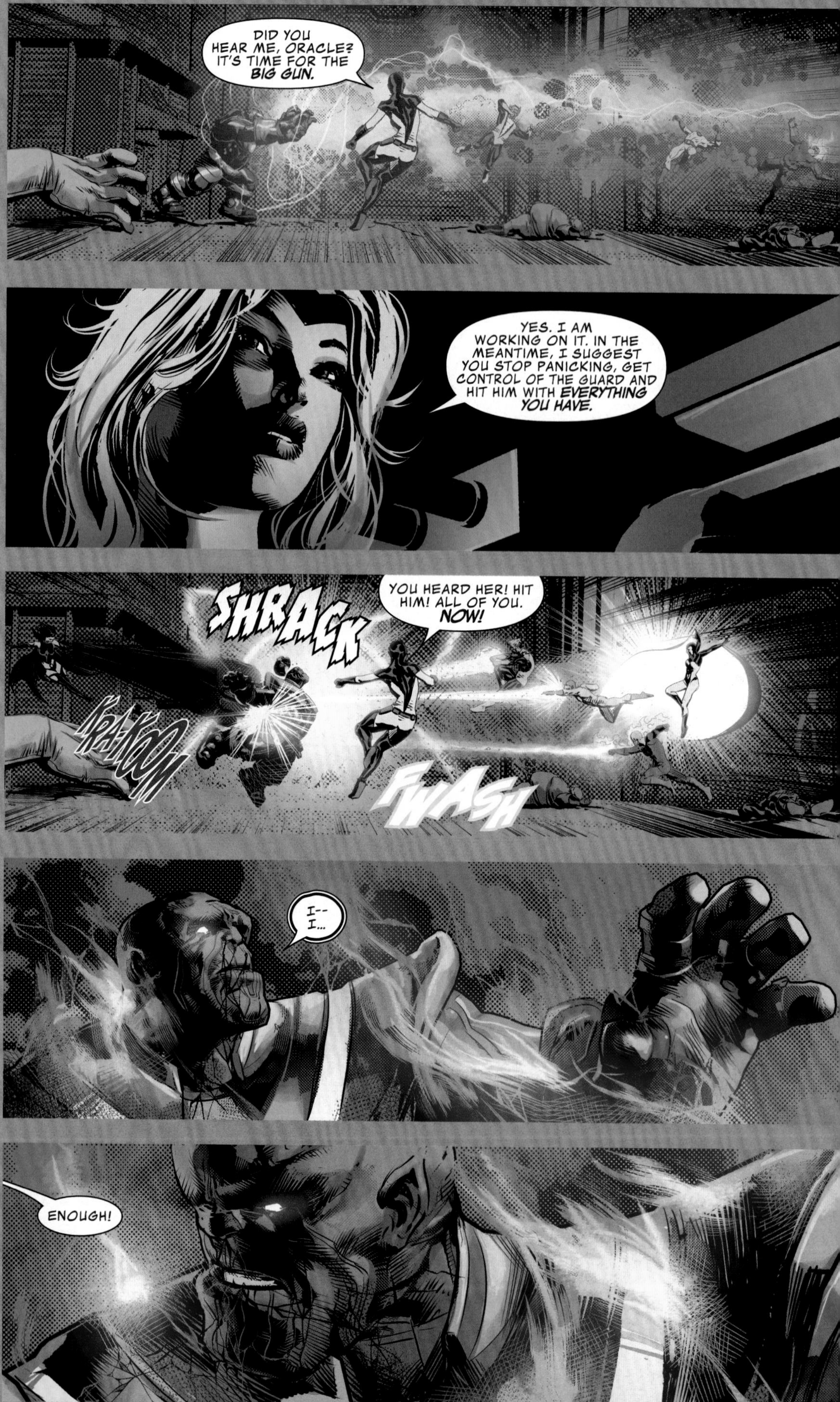
DID YOU HEAR ME, ORACLE? IT'S TIME FOR THE BIG GUN.
YES. I AM WORKING ON IT. IN THE MEANTIME, I SUGGEST YOU STOP PANICKING, GET CONTROL OF THE GUARD AND HIT HIM WITH EVERYTHING YOU HAVE.
SHRACK
YOU HEARD HER! HIT HIM! ALL OF YOU. NOW!
KRA-KOOM
FWASH
I-- I...
ENOUGH!

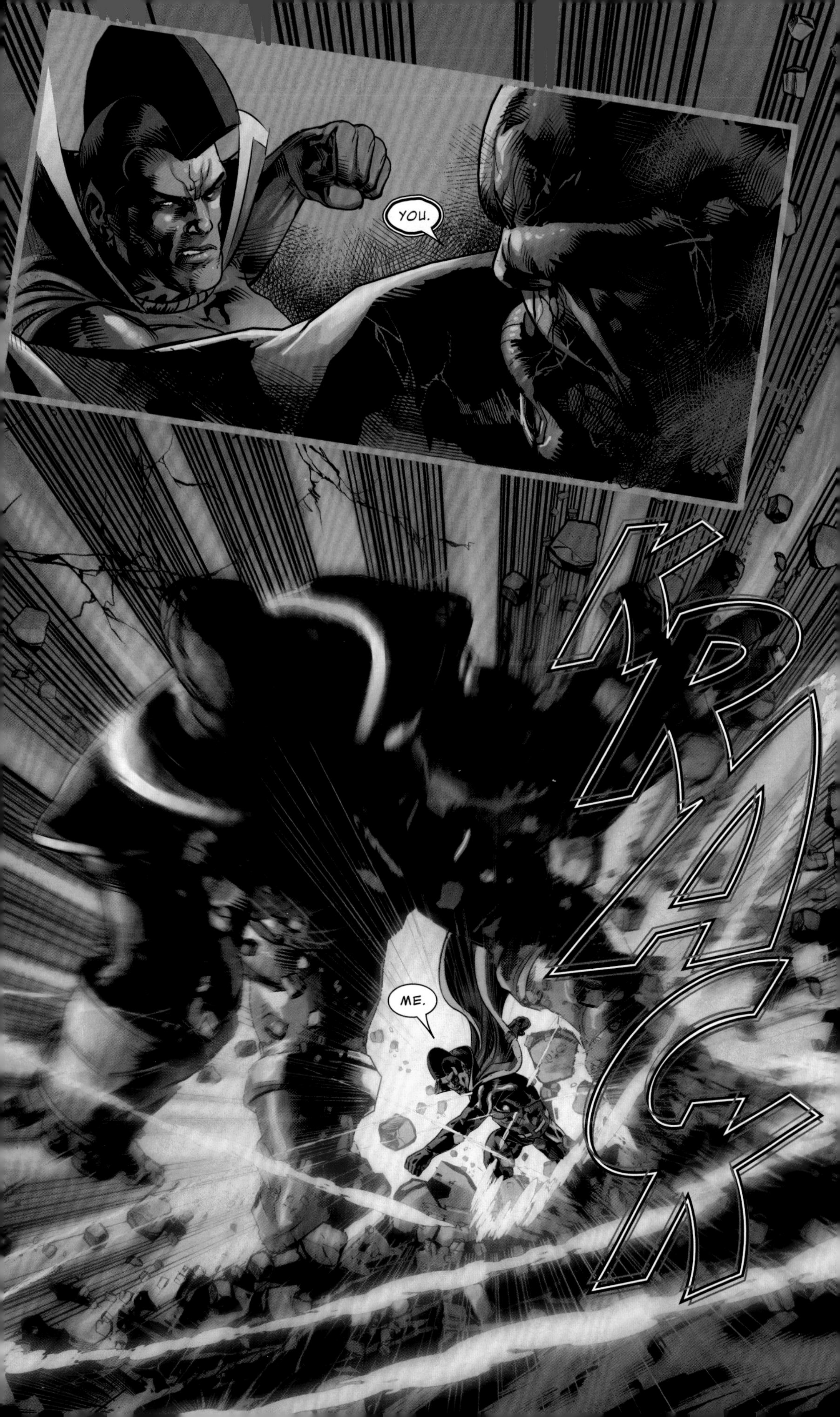
YOU.
KRAKOOM
ME.

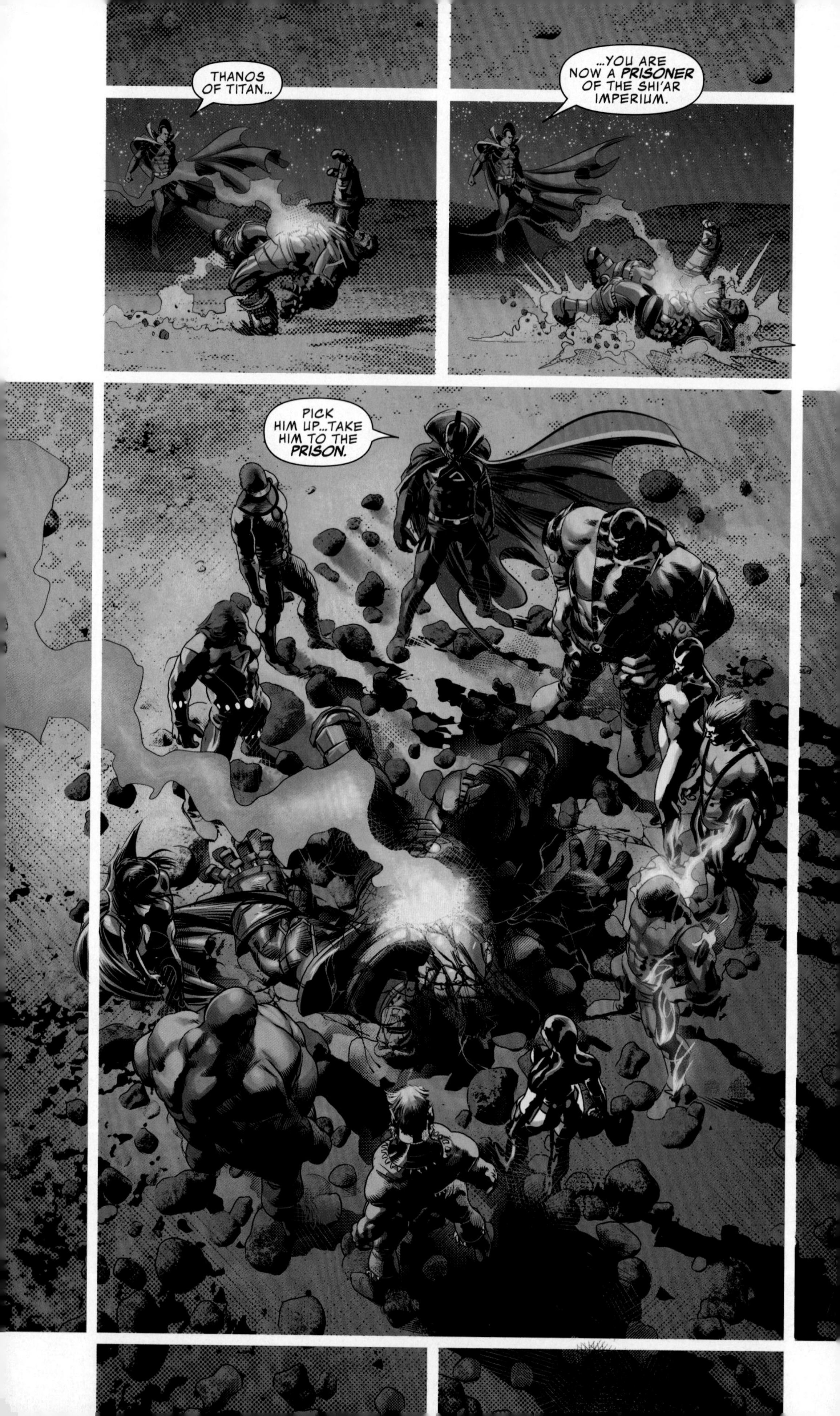
THANOS OF TITAN...
...YOU ARE NOW A PRISONER OF THE SHI'AR IMPERIUM.
PICK HIM UP...TAKE HIM TO THE PRISON.

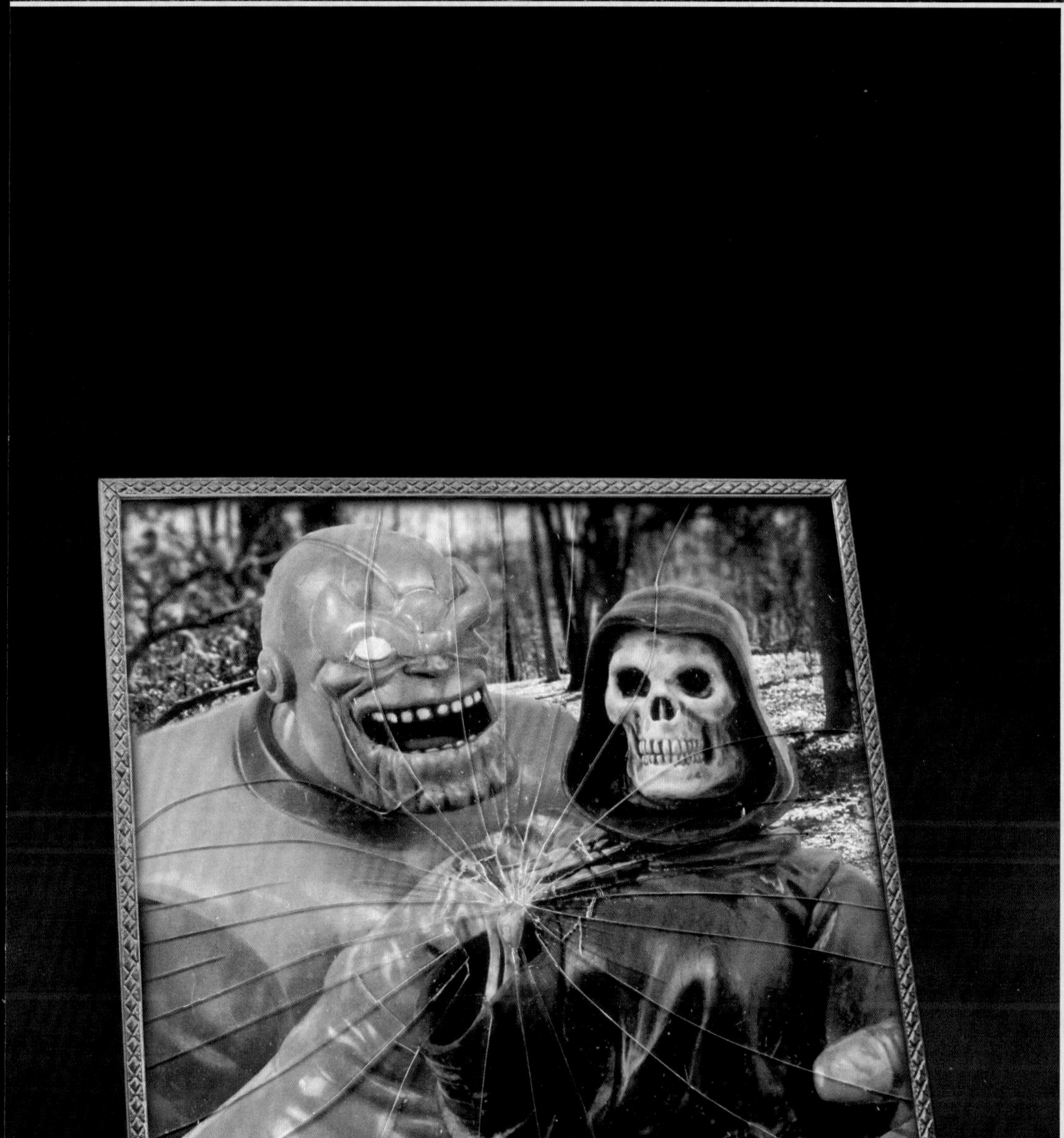

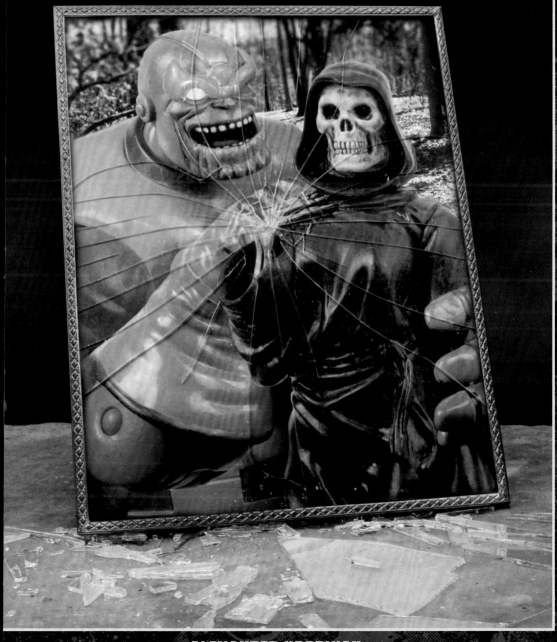

ALEXANDER KROPINAK

NO. 1 TOY VARIANT

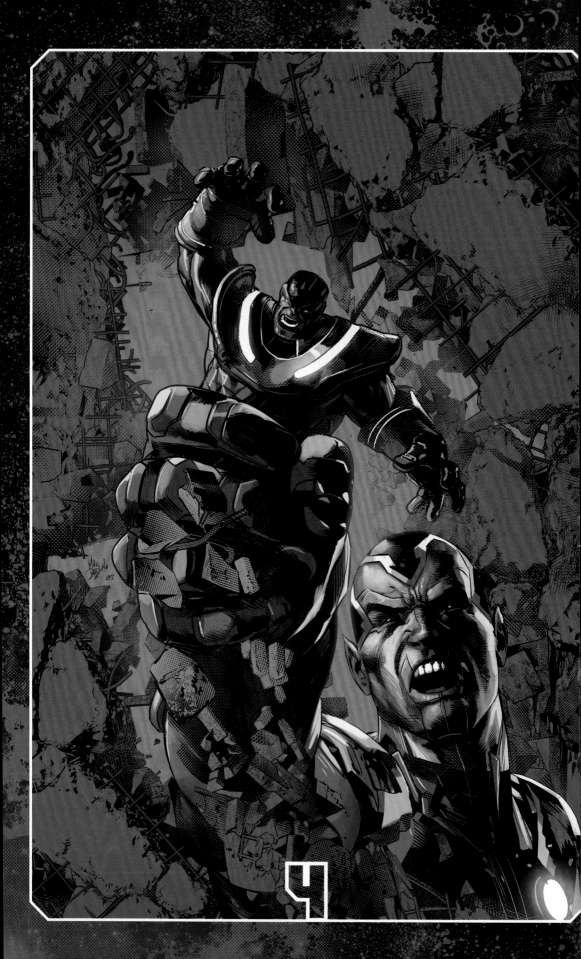

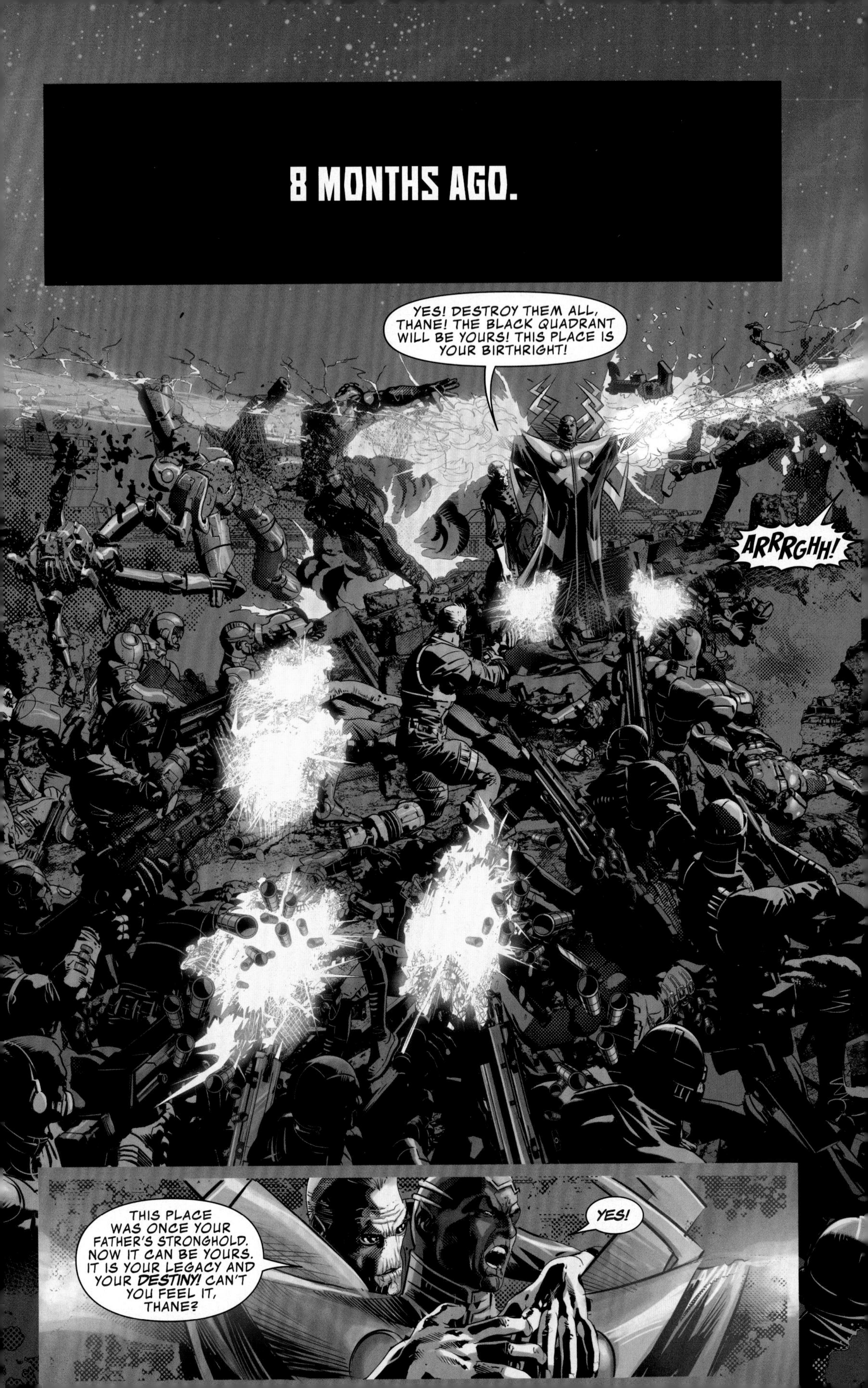
8 MONTHS AGO.
YES! DESTROY THEM ALL, THANE! THE BLACK QUADRANT WILL BE YOURS! THIS PLACE IS YOUR BIRTHRIGHT!
ARRRGHH!
THIS PLACE WAS ONCE YOUR FATHER'S STRONGHOLD. NOW IT CAN BE YOURS. IT IS YOUR LEGACY AND YOUR DESTINY! CAN'T YOU FEEL IT, THANE?
YES!

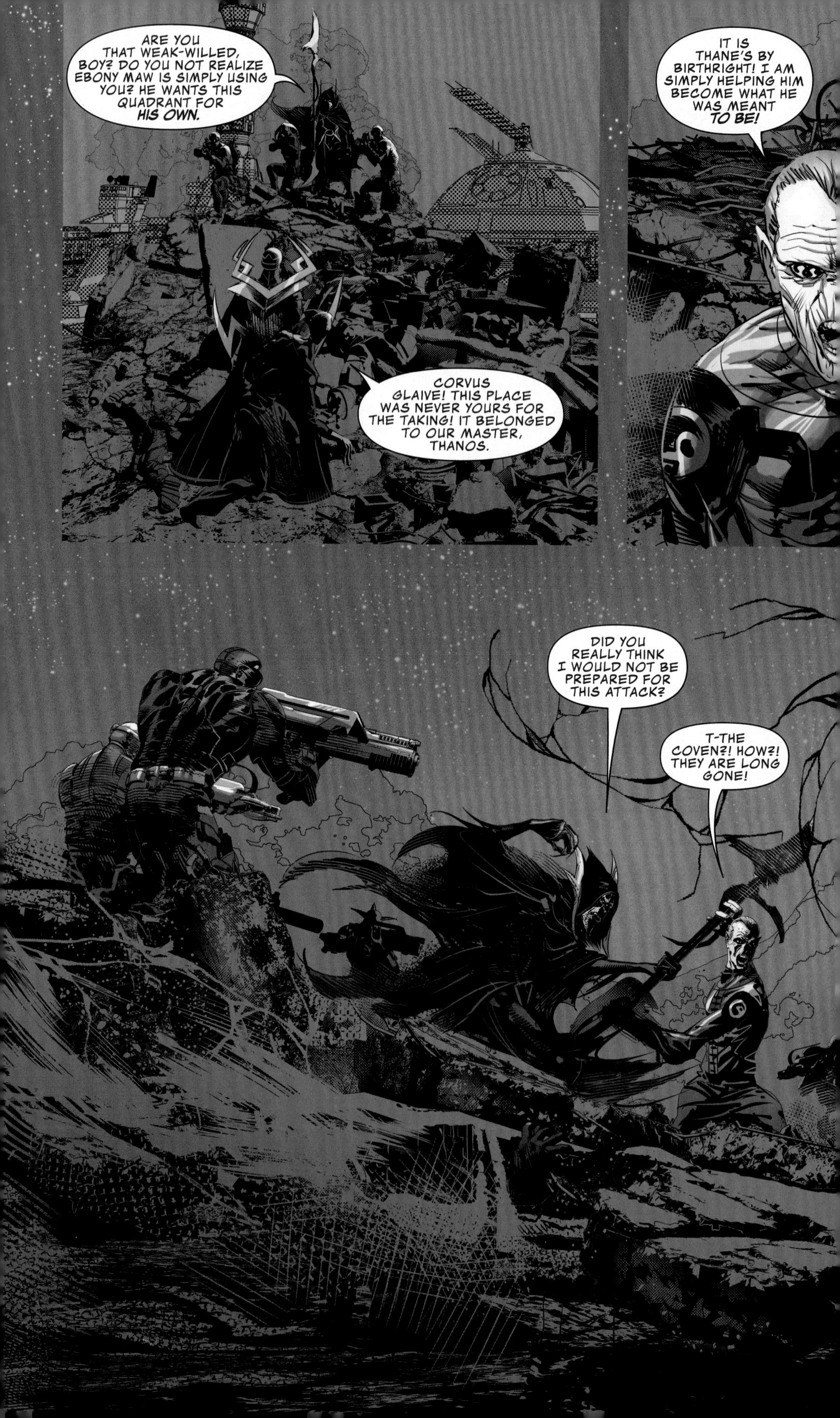
ARE YOU THAT WEAK-WILLED, BOY? DO YOU NOT REALIZE EBONY MAW IS SIMPLY USING YOU? HE WANTS THIS QUADRANT FOR **HIS OWN.**
CORVUS GLAIVE! THIS PLACE WAS NEVER YOURS FOR THE TAKING! IT BELONGED TO OUR MASTER, THANOS.
IT IS THANE'S BY BIRTHRIGHT! I AM SIMPLY HELPING HIM BECOME WHAT HE WAS MEANT **TO BE!**
DID YOU REALLY THINK I WOULD NOT BE PREPARED FOR THIS ATTACK?
T-THE COVEN?! HOW?! THEY ARE LONG GONE!

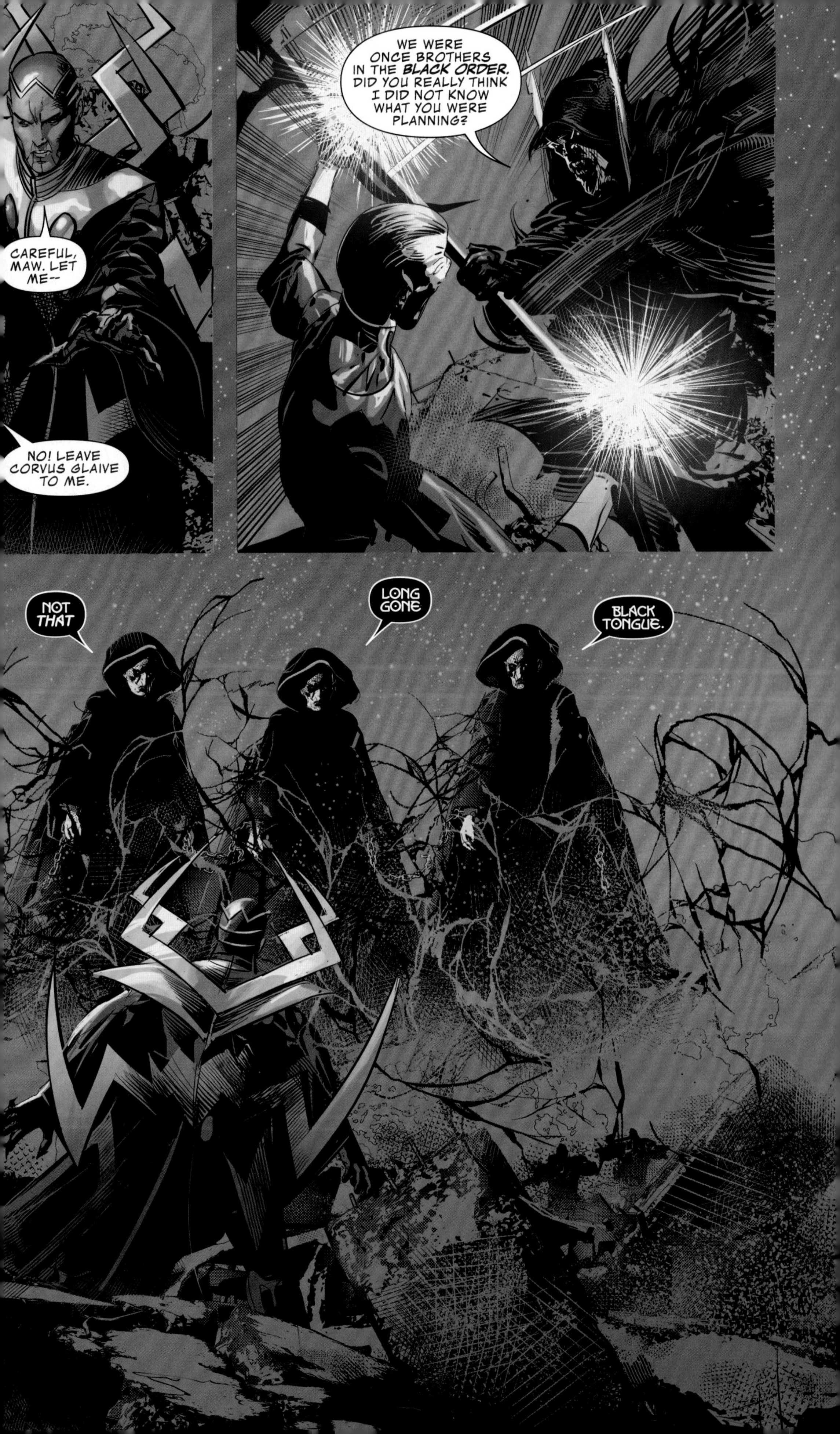
CAREFUL, MAW. LET ME--
NO! LEAVE CORVUS GLAIVE TO ME.
WE WERE ONCE BROTHERS IN THE BLACK ORDER. DID YOU REALLY THINK I DID NOT KNOW WHAT YOU WERE PLANNING?
NOT THAT
LONG GONE
BLACK TONGUE.

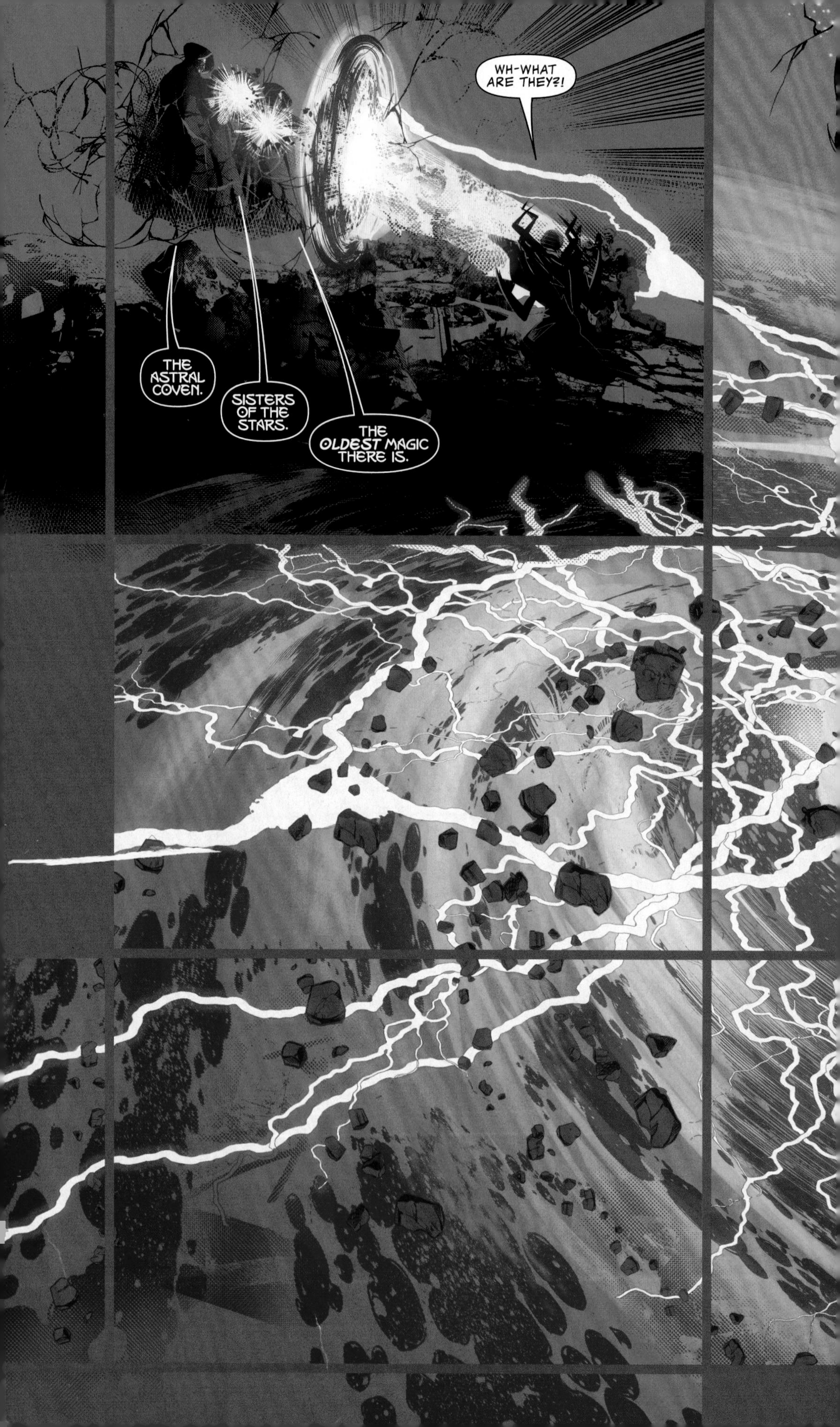

WH-WHAT ARE THEY?!
THE ASTRAL COVEN.
SISTERS OF THE STARS.
THE OLDEST MAGIC THERE IS.

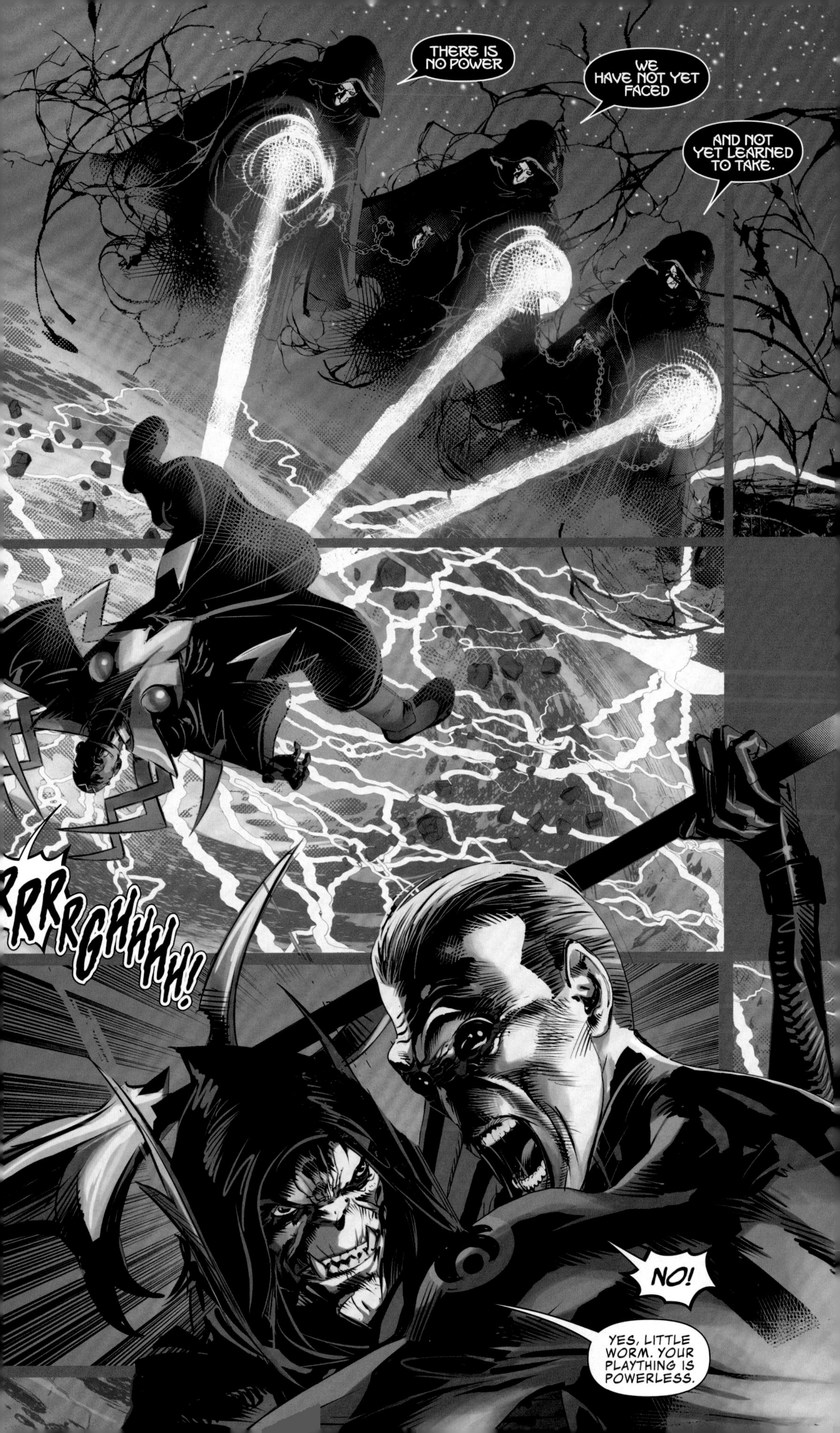
THERE IS NO POWER
WE HAVE NOT YET FACED
AND NOT YET LEARNED TO TAKE.
RRRRGHHHHH!
NO!
YES, LITTLE WORM. YOUR PLAYTHING IS POWERLESS.

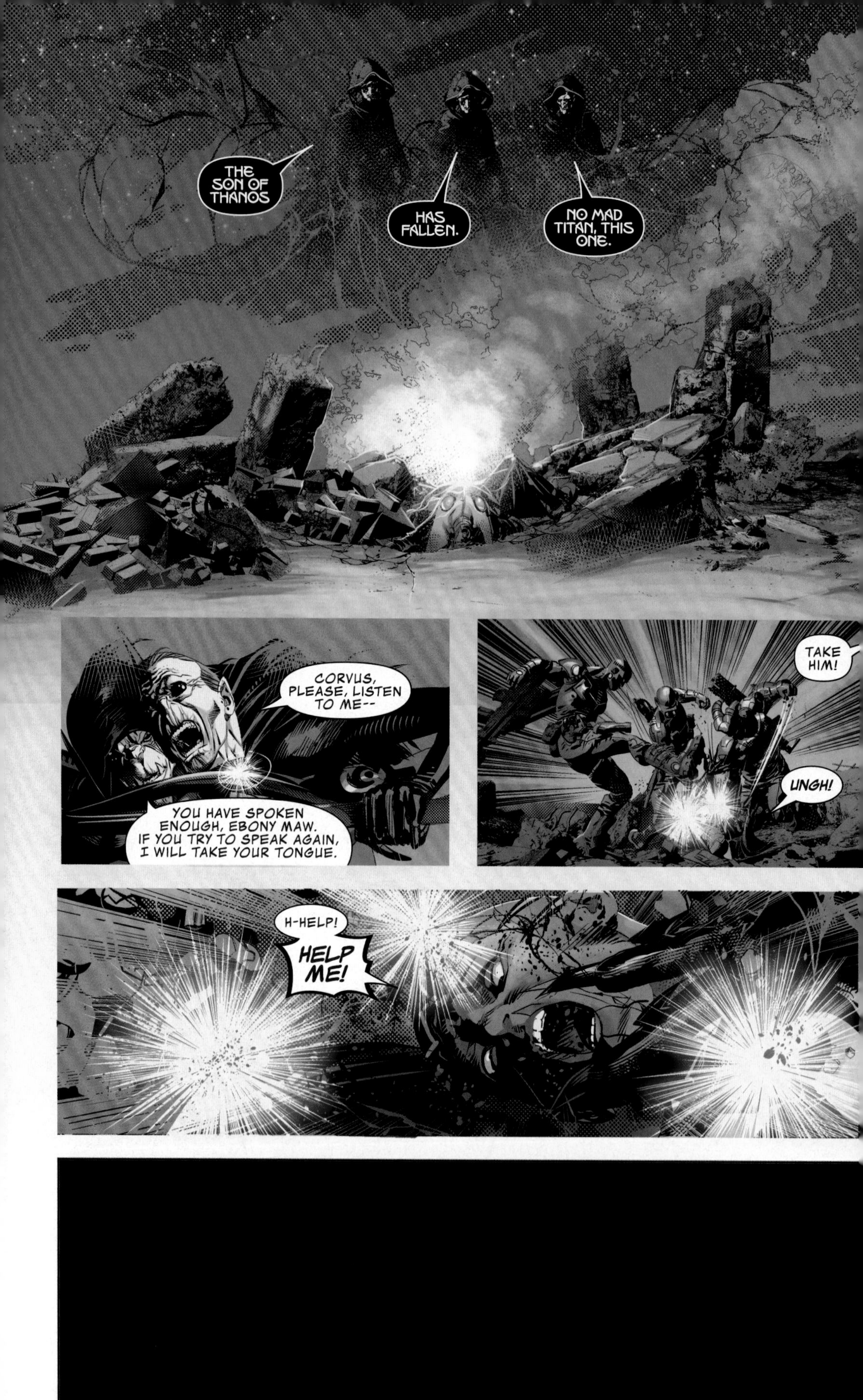
THE SON OF THANOS
HAS FALLEN.
NO MAD TITAN, THIS ONE.
CORVUS, PLEASE, LISTEN TO ME--
YOU HAVE SPOKEN ENOUGH, EBONY MAW. IF YOU TRY TO SPEAK AGAIN, I WILL TAKE YOUR TONGUE.
TAKE HIM!
UNGH!
H-HELP!
HELP ME!

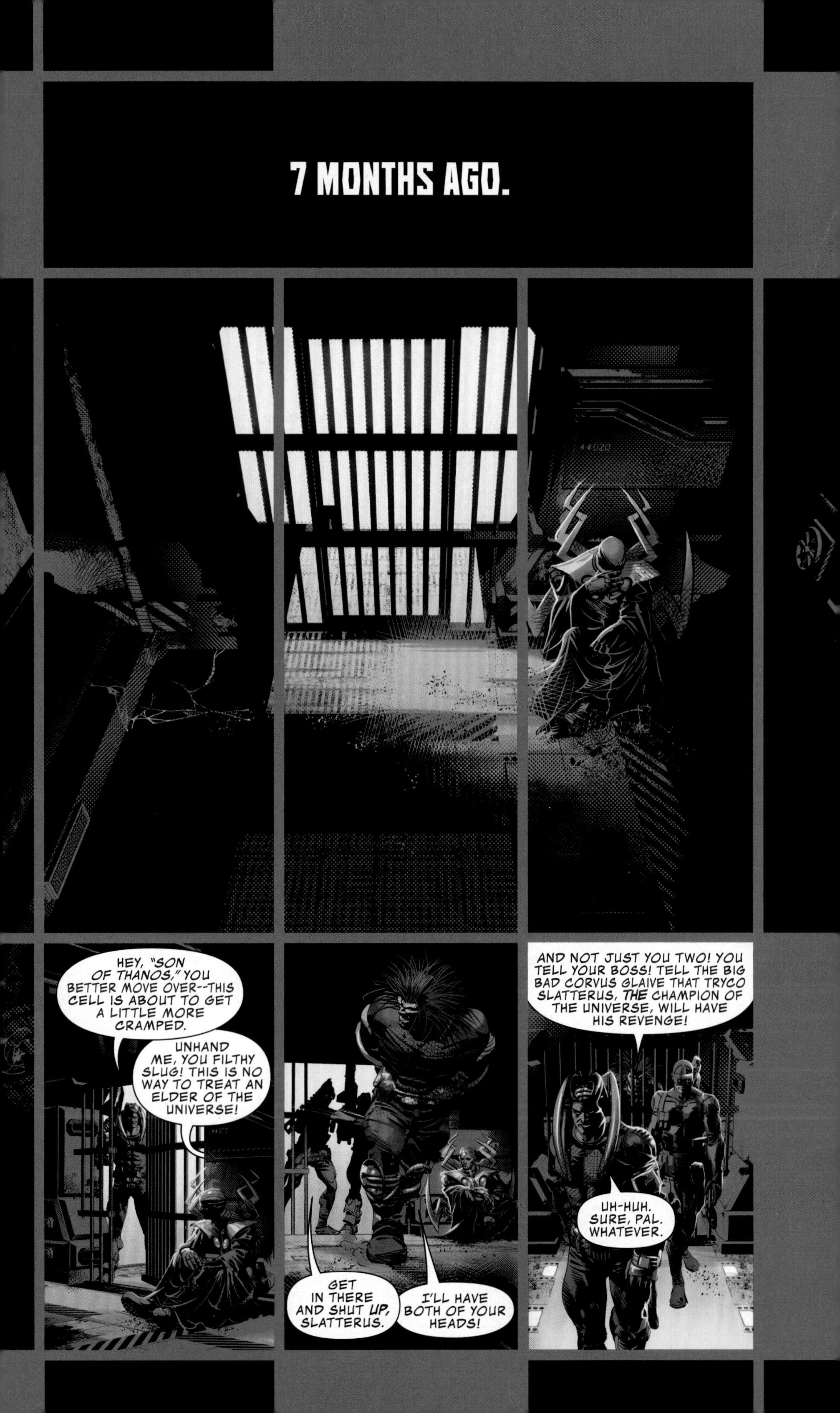
7 MONTHS AGO.
HEY, "SON OF THANOS," YOU BETTER MOVE OVER--THIS CELL IS ABOUT TO GET A LITTLE MORE CRAMPED.
UNHAND ME, YOU FILTHY SLUG! THIS IS NO WAY TO TREAT AN ELDER OF THE UNIVERSE!
GET IN THERE AND SHUT *UP*, SLATTERUS.
I'LL HAVE BOTH OF YOUR HEADS!
AND NOT JUST YOU TWO! YOU TELL YOUR BOSS! TELL THE BIG BAD CORVUS GLAIVE THAT TRYCO SLATTERUS, *THE* CHAMPION OF THE UNIVERSE, WILL HAVE HIS REVENGE!
UH-HUH. SURE, PAL. WHATEVER.

AH, HELLO THERE. DIDN'T SEE YOU COWERING IN THE SHADOWS, LITTLE MAN.
THE NAME IS SLATTERUS. TRYCO SLATTERUS. BUT MANY KNOW ME AS THE *CHAMPION OF THE UNIVERSE.*
UM, YEAH, I HEARD.
RIGHT, OF COURSE. WELL, THIS PLACE IS A REAL DUMP, ISN'T IT? SMELLS LIKE A ZOMPMUTT FART, TOO.
HOW LONG HAVE YOU BEEN STUCK IN HERE...?
THANE. MY NAME IS THANE.
AND... I DON'T KNOW HOW LONG I'VE BEEN HERE. WEEKS? IT--IT'S HARD TO TELL.
THANE? AS IN THE PUP OF THANOS HIMSELF? HA! I HEARD ABOUT YOU, BOY!
Y-YOU HAVE?
SURE! WORD OF YOUR "CONQUESTS" SPREAD AROUND PRETTY QUICK.
BUT, UH, I SEE THINGS DIDN'T GO SO WELL, EH? NOT QUITE YOUR DADDY, ARE YOU?
NO. I *AM NOT MY FATHER.* DO YOU HAVE A PROBLEM WITH THAT?
WHOA! NO PROBLEM. RELAX, LITTLE MAN. NO HARM, NO FOUL, EH?
JUST--JUST DON'T TALK TO ME, OKAY? I WAS DOING FINE BEFORE YOU SHOWED UP.
HUMPH! SUITS ME FINE!

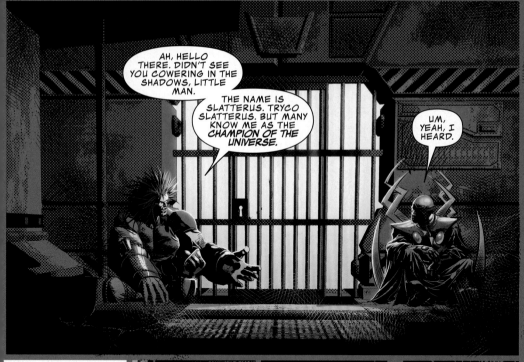

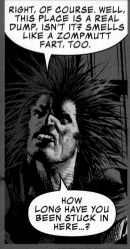

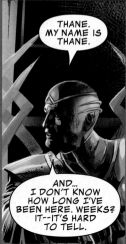

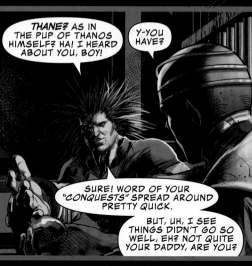

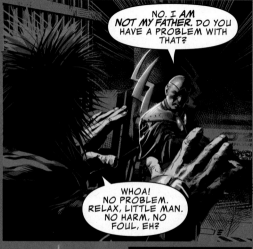

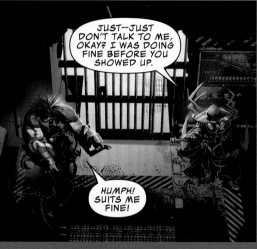

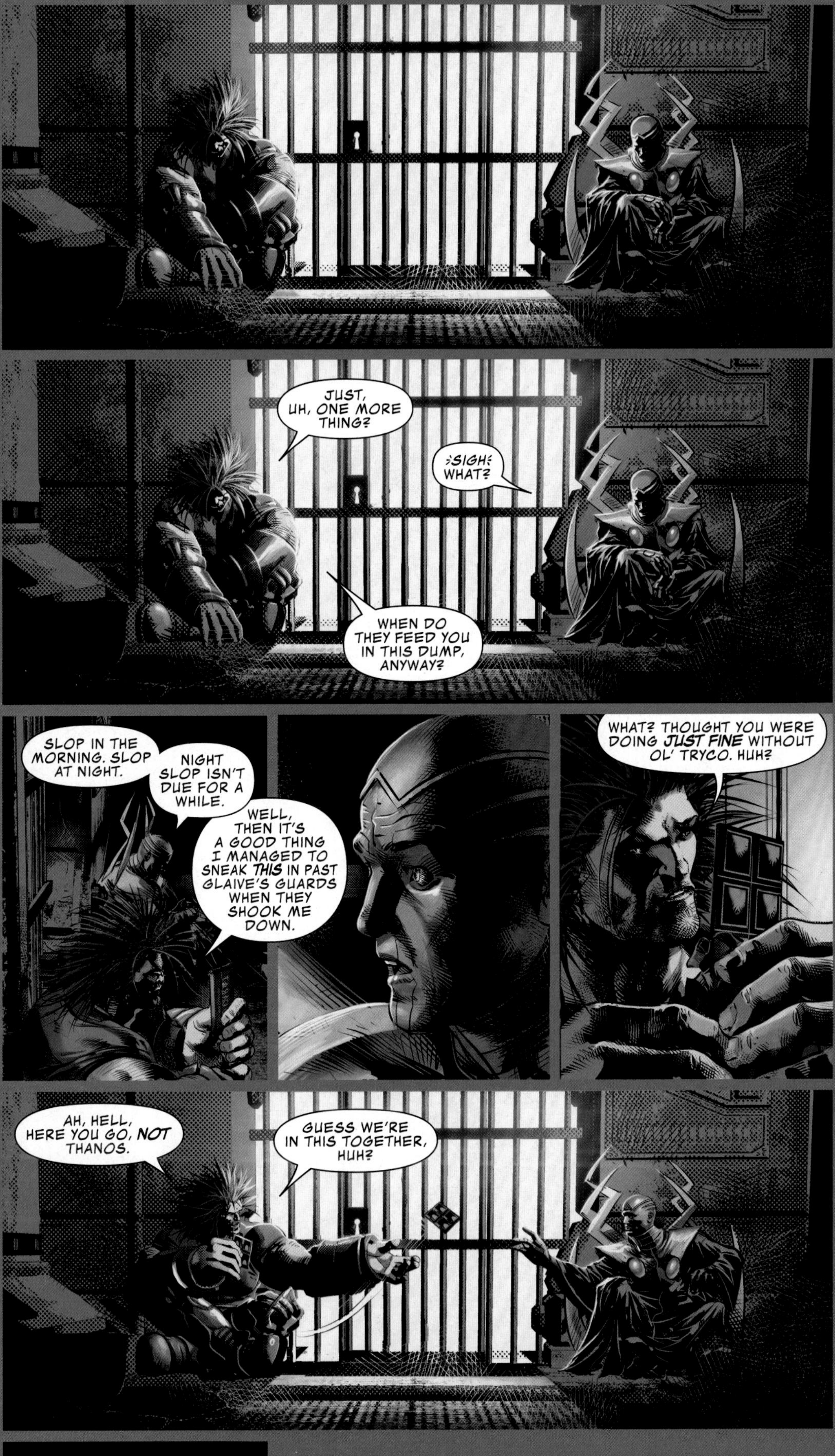
JUST, UH, ONE MORE THING?
SIGH WHAT?
WHEN DO THEY FEED YOU IN THIS DUMP, ANYWAY?
SLOP IN THE MORNING. SLOP AT NIGHT.
NIGHT SLOP ISN'T DUE FOR A WHILE.
WELL, THEN IT'S A GOOD THING I MANAGED TO SNEAK **THIS** IN PAST GLAIVE'S GUARDS WHEN THEY SHOOK ME DOWN.
WHAT? THOUGHT YOU WERE DOING **JUST FINE** WITHOUT OL' TRYCO. HUH?
AH, HELL, HERE YOU GO, **NOT** THANOS.
GUESS WE'RE IN THIS TOGETHER, HUH?

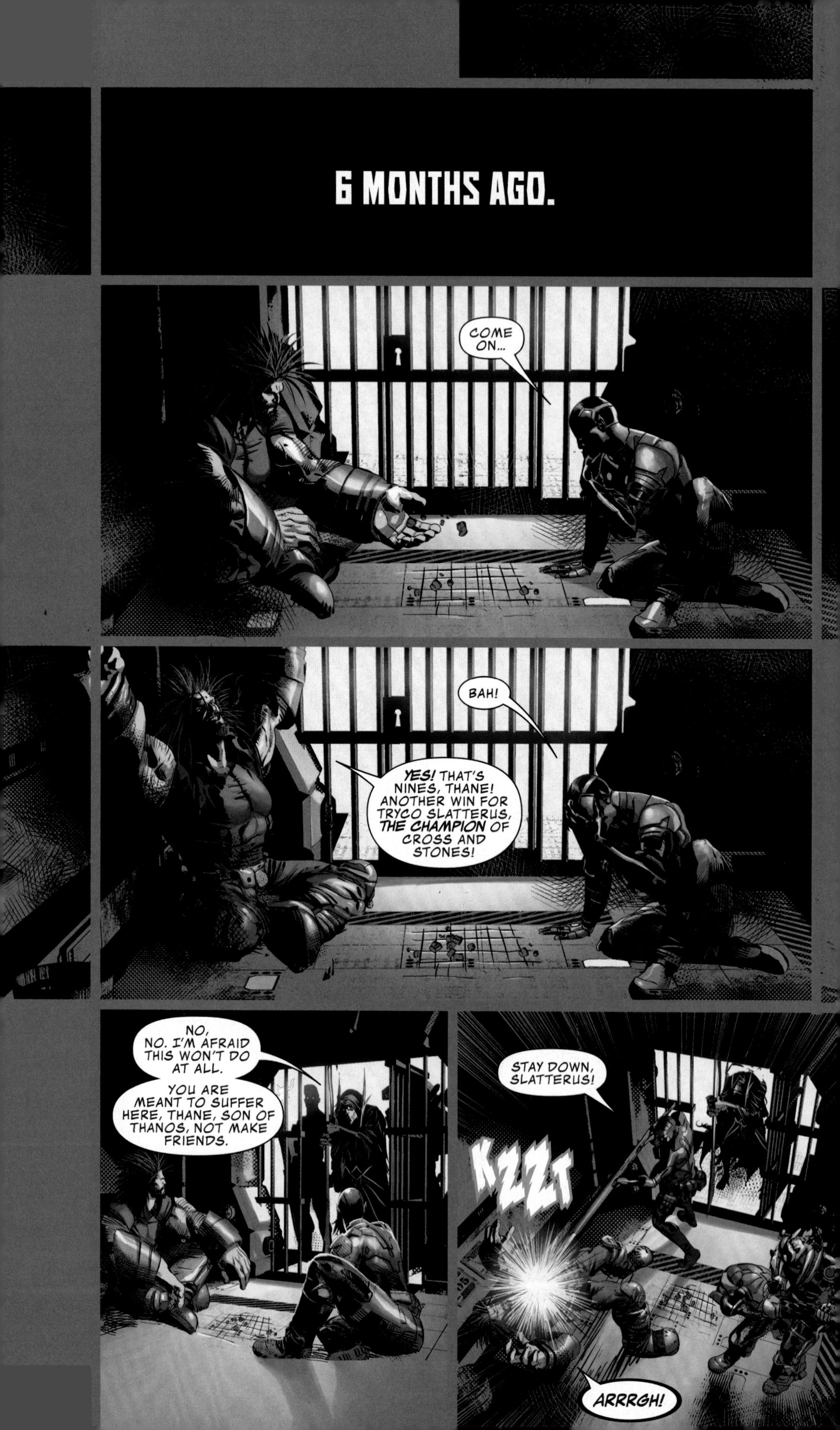
6 MONTHS AGO.
COME ON...
BAH!
YES! THAT'S NINES, THANE! ANOTHER WIN FOR TRYCO SLATTERUS, THE CHAMPION OF CROSS AND STONES!
NO, NO. I'M AFRAID THIS WON'T DO AT ALL.
YOU ARE MEANT TO SUFFER HERE, THANE, SON OF THANOS, NOT MAKE FRIENDS.
STAY DOWN, SLATTERUS!
KZZZT
ARRRGH!

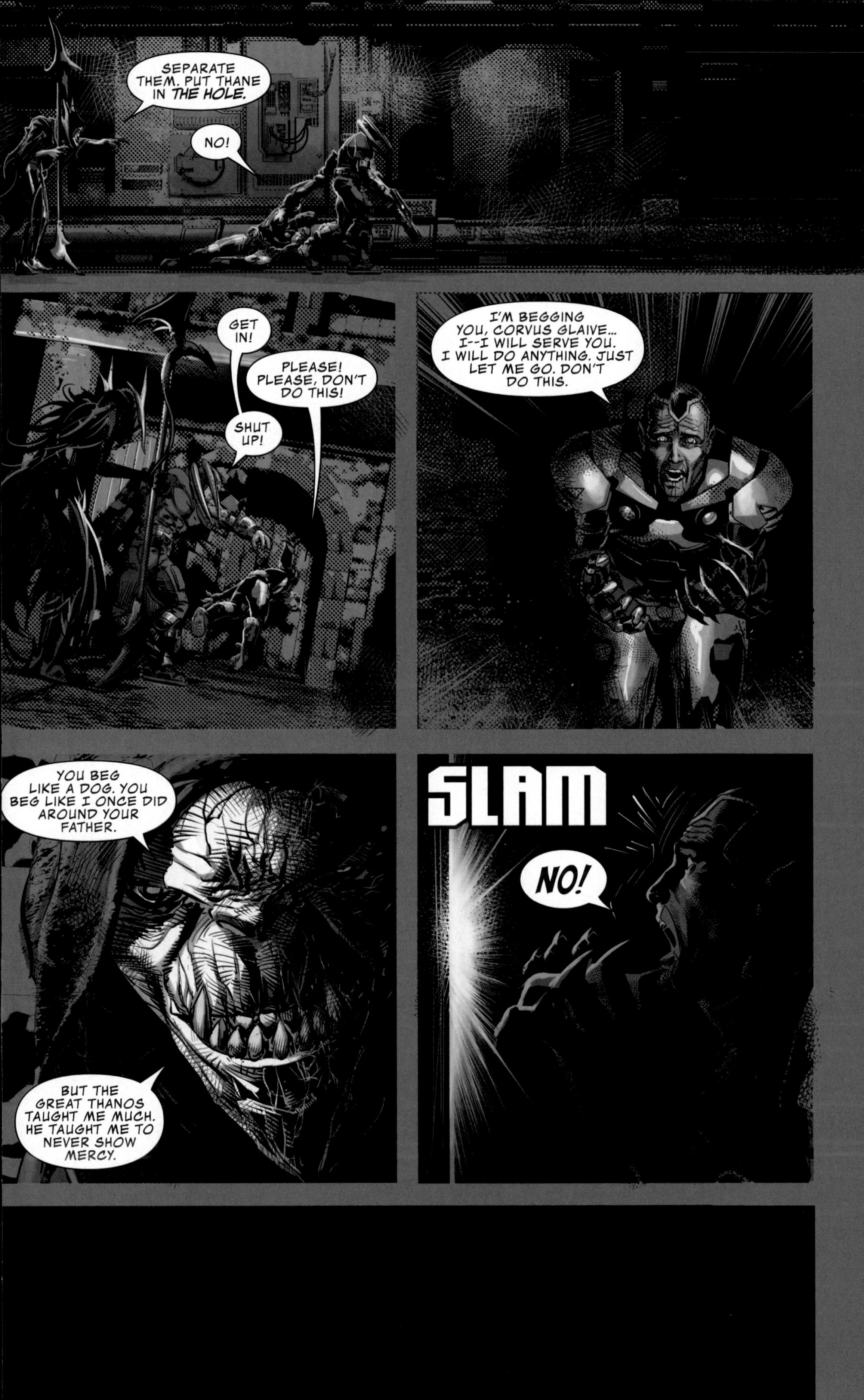
SEPARATE THEM. PUT THANE IN *THE HOLE.*
NO!
GET IN!
PLEASE! PLEASE, DON'T DO THIS!
SHUT UP!
I'M BEGGING YOU, CORVUS GLAIVE... I--I WILL SERVE YOU. I WILL DO ANYTHING. JUST LET ME GO. DON'T DO THIS.
YOU BEG LIKE A DOG. YOU BEG LIKE I ONCE DID AROUND YOUR FATHER.
BUT THE GREAT THANOS TAUGHT ME MUCH. HE TAUGHT ME TO NEVER SHOW MERCY.
SLAM
NO!

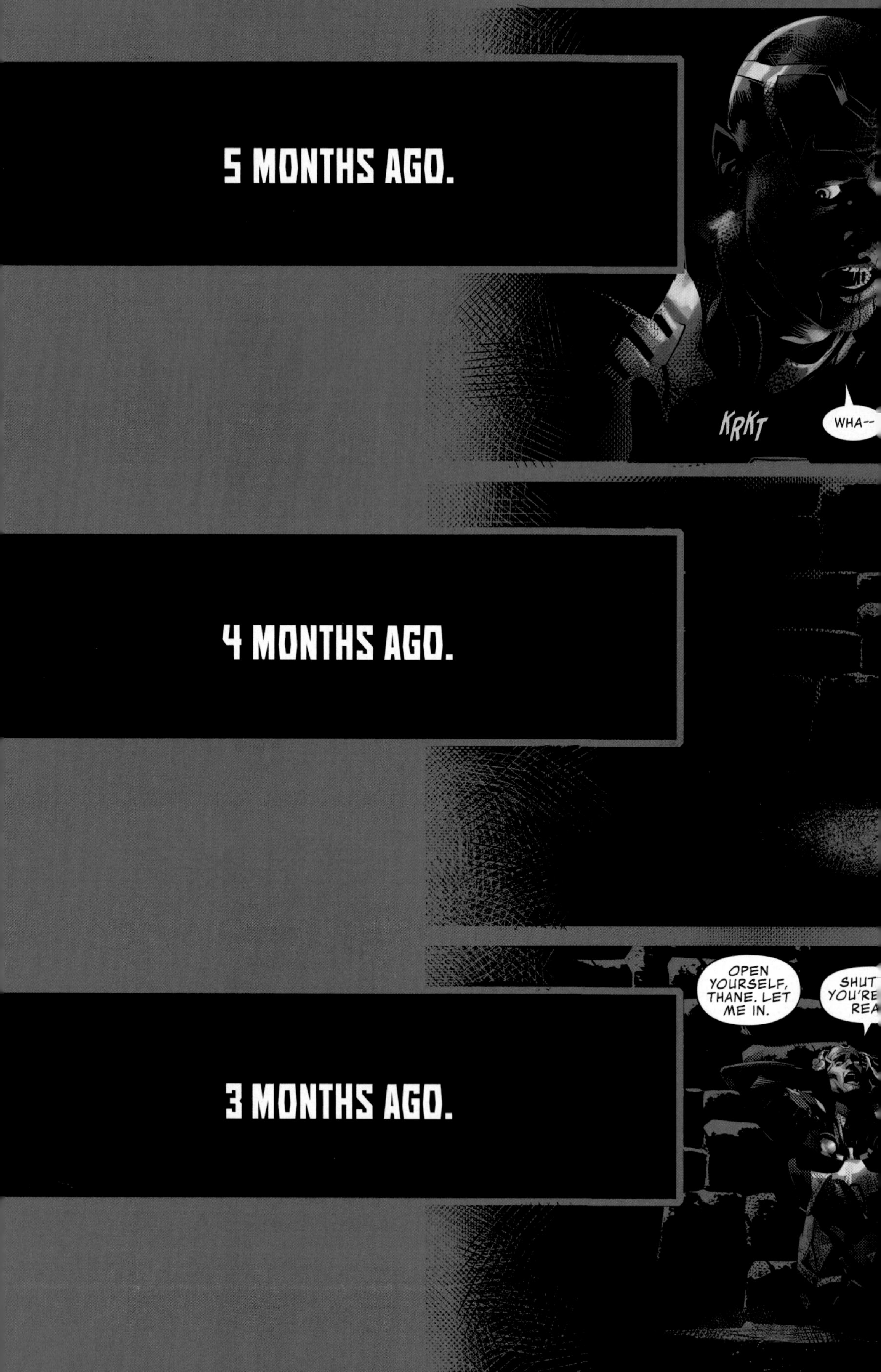
5 MONTHS AGO.
KRKT
WHA--
4 MONTHS AGO.
3 MONTHS AGO.
OPEN YOURSELF, THANE. LET ME IN.
SHUT YOU'RE

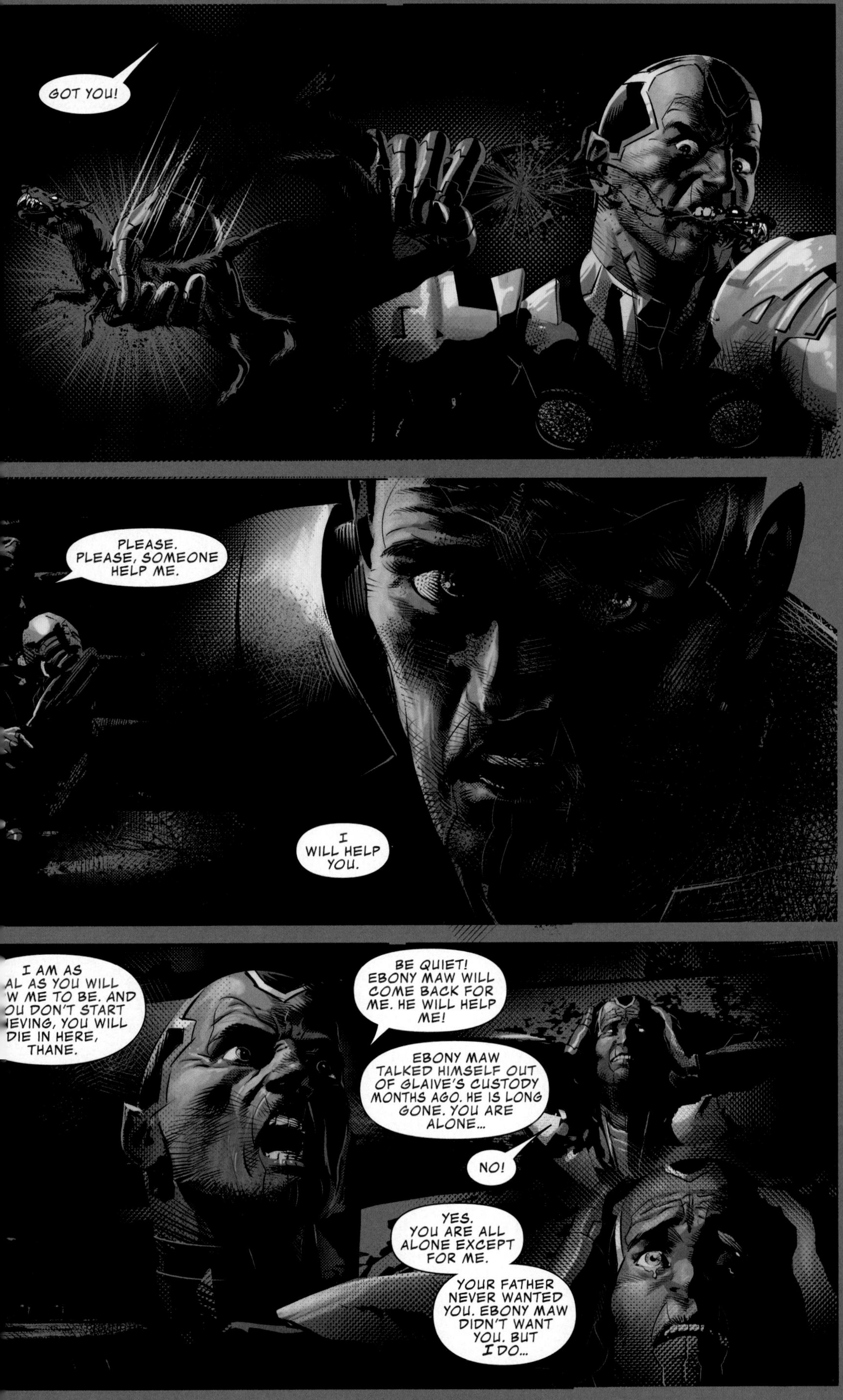
GOT YOU!
PLEASE. PLEASE, SOMEONE HELP ME.
I WILL HELP YOU.
I AM AS
AL AS YOU WILL
W ME TO BE. AND
OU DON'T START
IEVING, YOU WILL
DIE IN HERE,
THANE.
BE QUIET! EBONY MAW WILL COME BACK FOR ME. HE WILL HELP ME!
EBONY MAW TALKED HIMSELF OUT OF GLAIVE'S CUSTODY MONTHS AGO. HE IS LONG GONE. YOU ARE ALONE...
NO!
YES. YOU ARE ALL ALONE EXCEPT FOR ME.
YOUR FATHER NEVER WANTED YOU. EBONY MAW DIDN'T WANT YOU. BUT *I* DO...

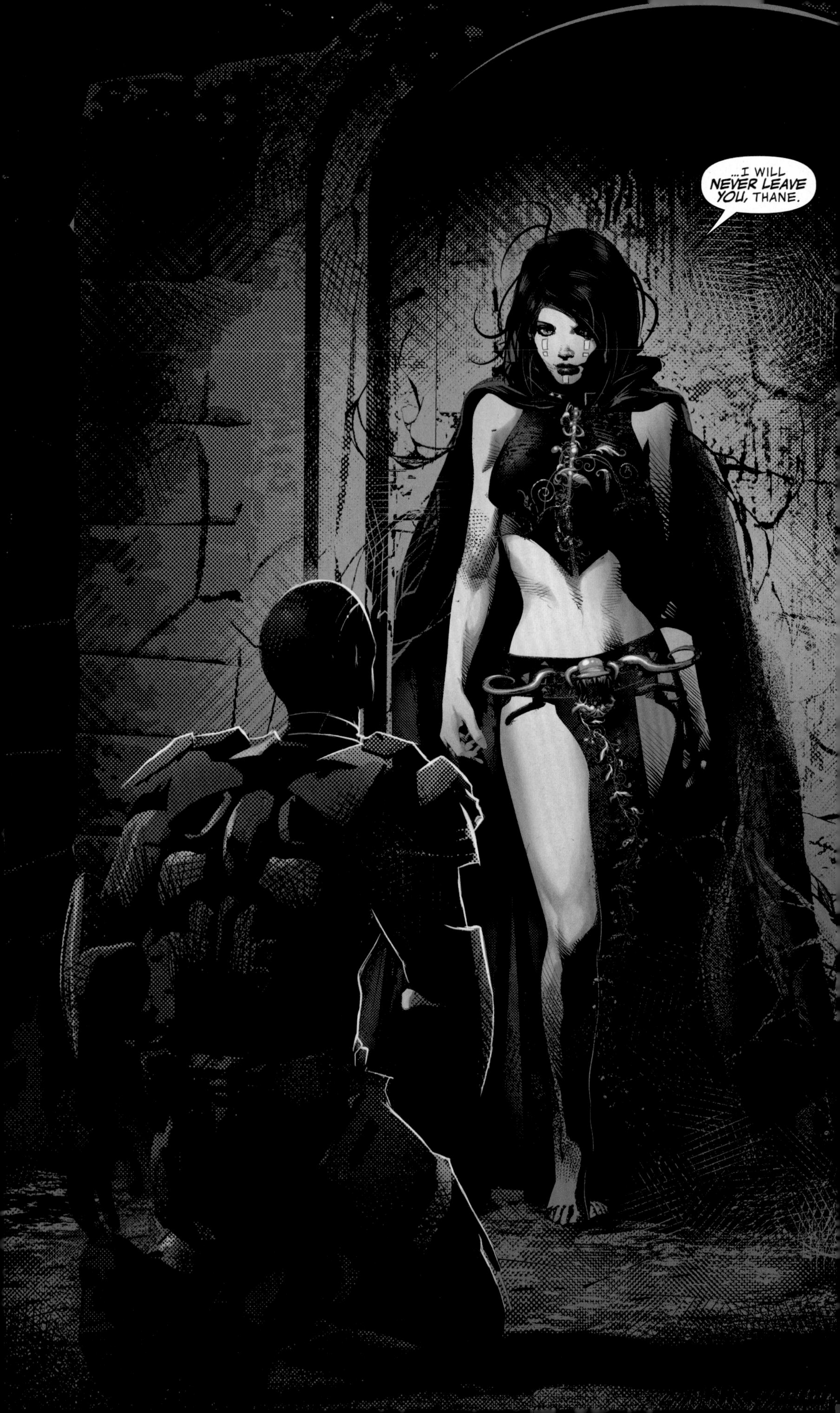
...I WILL NEVER LEAVE YOU, THANE.

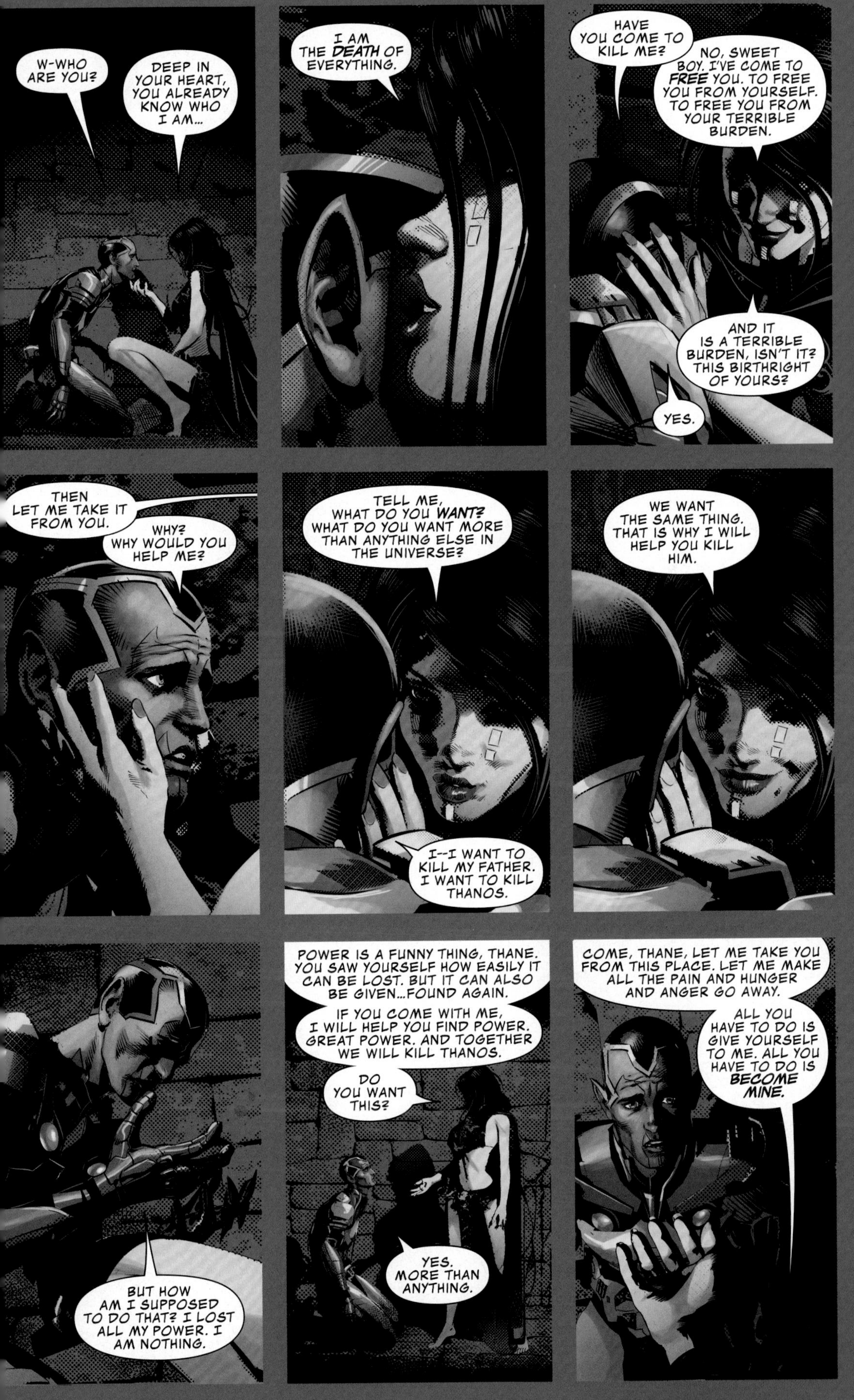
W-WHO ARE YOU?
DEEP IN YOUR HEART, YOU ALREADY KNOW WHO I AM...
I AM THE DEATH OF EVERYTHING.
HAVE YOU COME TO KILL ME?
NO, SWEET BOY. I'VE COME TO FREE YOU. TO FREE YOU FROM YOURSELF. TO FREE YOU FROM YOUR TERRIBLE BURDEN.
AND IT IS A TERRIBLE BURDEN, ISN'T IT? THIS BIRTHRIGHT OF YOURS?
YES.
THEN LET ME TAKE IT FROM YOU.
WHY? WHY WOULD YOU HELP ME?
TELL ME, WHAT DO YOU WANT? WHAT DO YOU WANT MORE THAN ANYTHING ELSE IN THE UNIVERSE?
I--I WANT TO KILL MY FATHER. I WANT TO KILL THANOS.
WE WANT THE SAME THING. THAT IS WHY I WILL HELP YOU KILL HIM.
BUT HOW AM I SUPPOSED TO DO THAT? I LOST ALL MY POWER. I AM NOTHING.
POWER IS A FUNNY THING, THANE. YOU SAW YOURSELF HOW EASILY IT CAN BE LOST. BUT IT CAN ALSO BE GIVEN...FOUND AGAIN.
IF YOU COME WITH ME, I WILL HELP YOU FIND POWER. GREAT POWER. AND TOGETHER WE WILL KILL THANOS.
DO YOU WANT THIS?
YES. MORE THAN ANYTHING.
COME, THANE, LET ME TAKE YOU FROM THIS PLACE. LET ME MAKE ALL THE PAIN AND HUNGER AND ANGER GO AWAY.
ALL YOU HAVE TO DO IS GIVE YOURSELF TO ME. ALL YOU HAVE TO DO IS BECOME MINE.

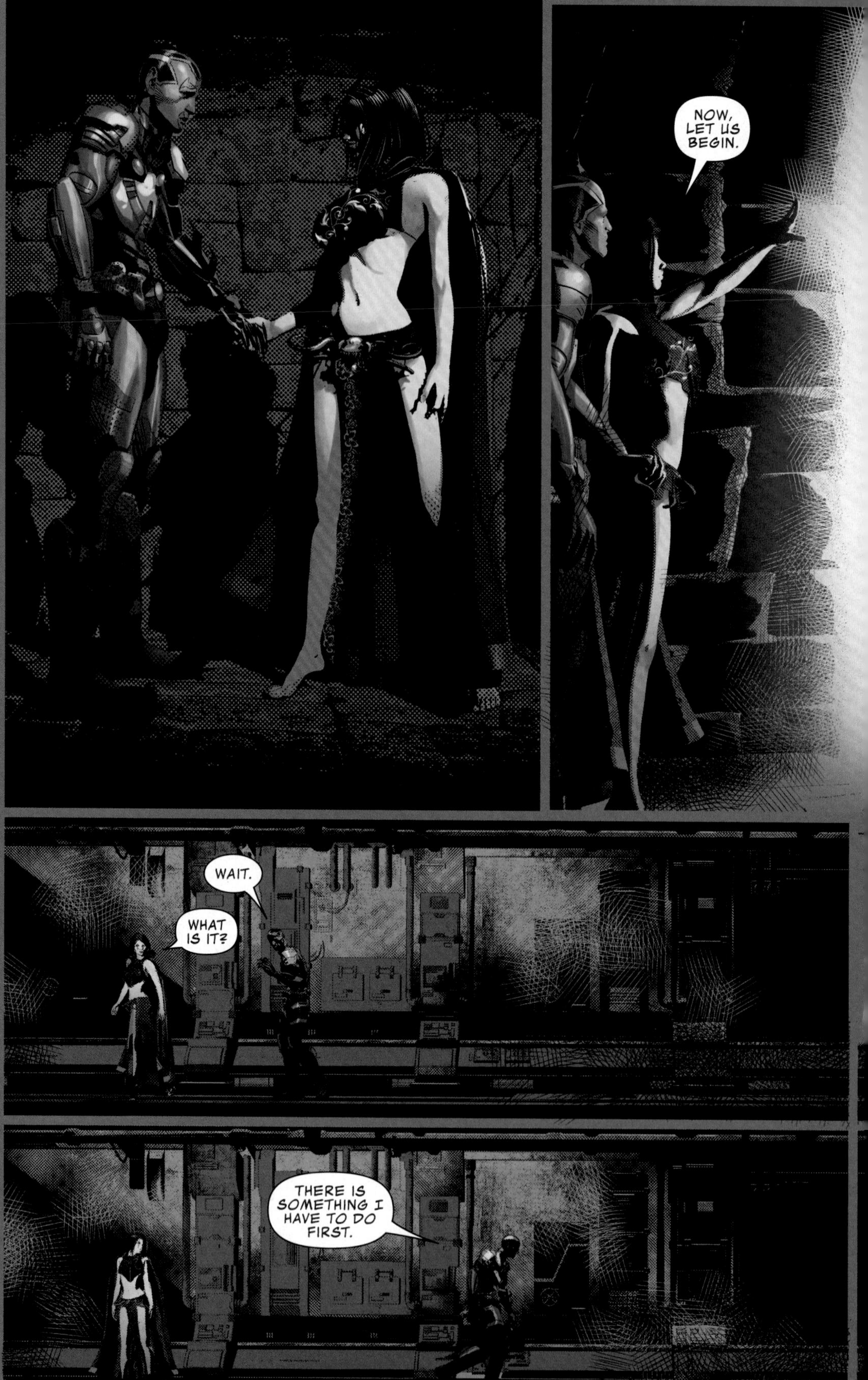
NOW, LET US BEGIN.
WAIT.
WHAT IS IT?
THERE IS SOMETHING I HAVE TO DO FIRST.

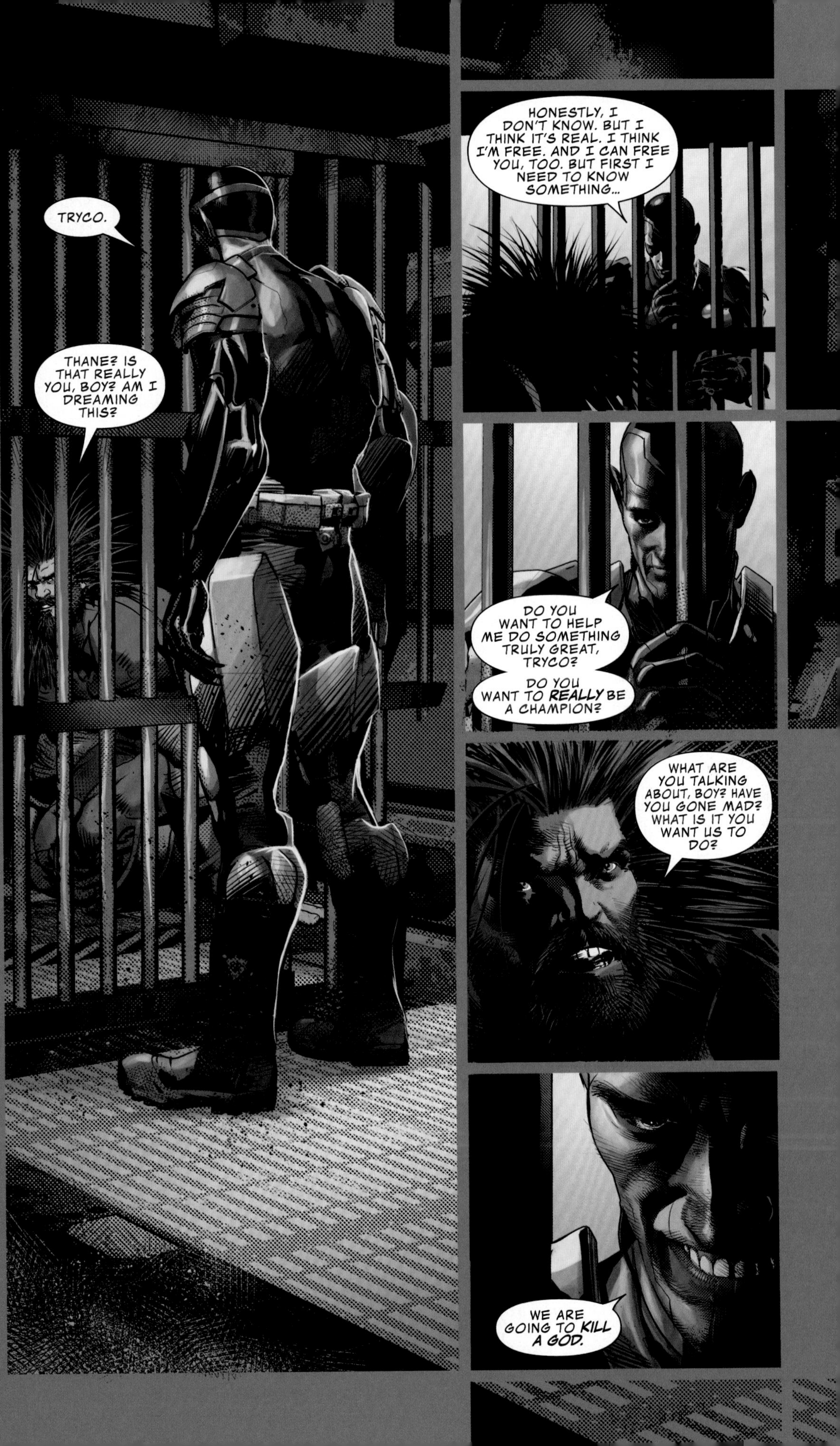
TRYCO.
THANE? IS THAT REALLY YOU, BOY? AM I DREAMING THIS?
HONESTLY, I DON'T KNOW. BUT I THINK IT'S REAL. I THINK I'M FREE. AND I CAN FREE YOU, TOO. BUT FIRST I NEED TO KNOW SOMETHING...
DO YOU WANT TO HELP ME DO SOMETHING TRULY GREAT, TRYCO?
DO YOU WANT TO *REALLY* BE A CHAMPION?
WHAT ARE YOU TALKING ABOUT, BOY? HAVE YOU GONE MAD? WHAT IS IT YOU WANT US TO DO?
WE ARE GOING TO *KILL A GOD.*

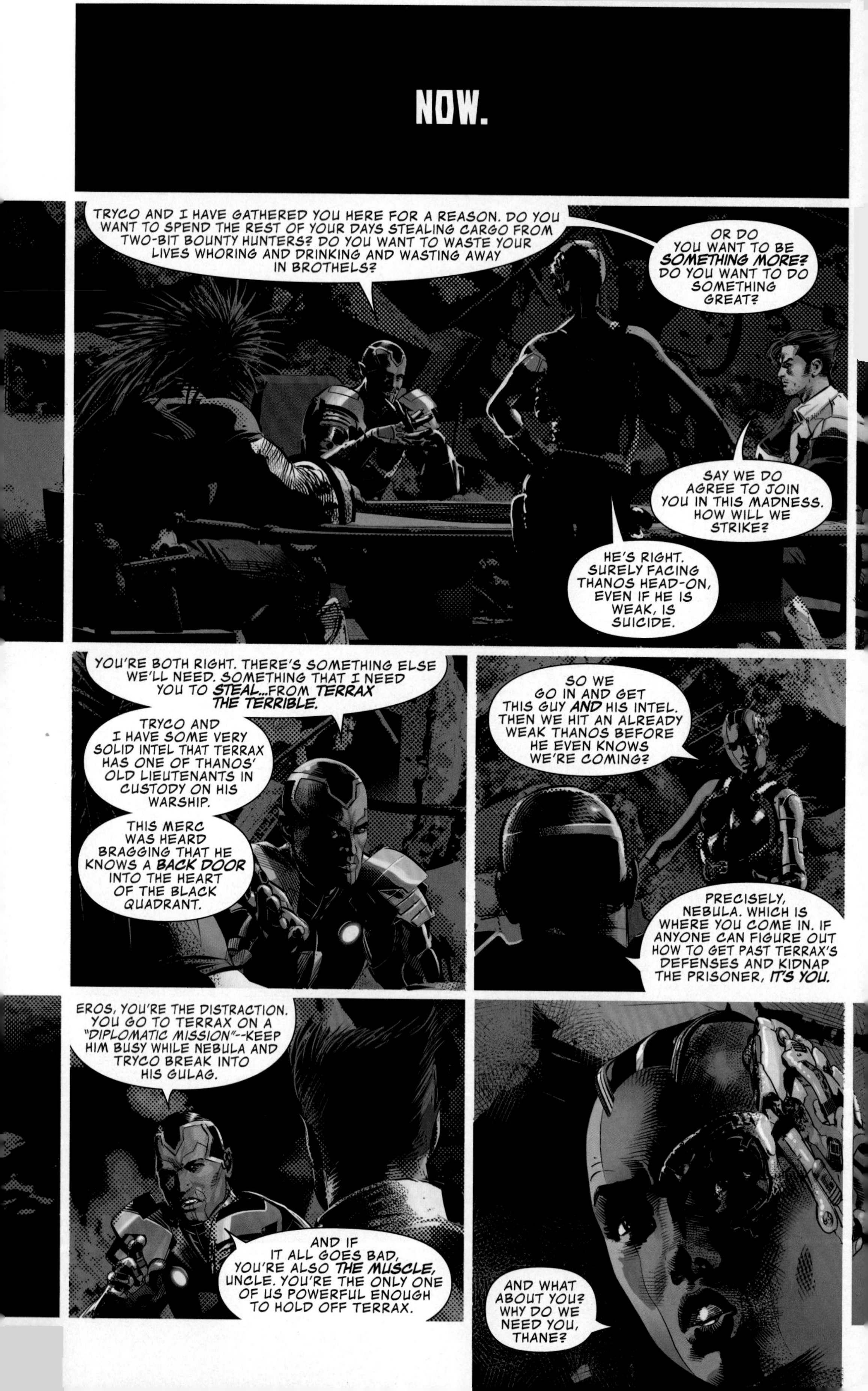
NOW.
TRYCO AND I HAVE GATHERED YOU HERE FOR A REASON. DO YOU WANT TO SPEND THE REST OF YOUR DAYS STEALING CARGO FROM TWO-BIT BOUNTY HUNTERS? DO YOU WANT TO WASTE YOUR LIVES WHORING AND DRINKING AND WASTING AWAY IN BROTHELS?
OR DO YOU WANT TO BE SOMETHING MORE? DO YOU WANT TO DO SOMETHING GREAT?
SAY WE DO AGREE TO JOIN YOU IN THIS MADNESS. HOW WILL WE STRIKE?
HE'S RIGHT. SURELY FACING THANOS HEAD-ON, EVEN IF HE IS WEAK, IS SUICIDE.
YOU'RE BOTH RIGHT. THERE'S SOMETHING ELSE WE'LL NEED. SOMETHING THAT I NEED YOU TO STEAL...FROM TERRAX THE TERRIBLE.
TRYCO AND I HAVE SOME VERY SOLID INTEL THAT TERRAX HAS ONE OF THANOS' OLD LIEUTENANTS IN CUSTODY ON HIS WARSHIP.
THIS MERC WAS HEARD BRAGGING THAT HE KNOWS A BACK DOOR INTO THE HEART OF THE BLACK QUADRANT.
SO WE GO IN AND GET THIS GUY AND HIS INTEL. THEN WE HIT AN ALREADY WEAK THANOS BEFORE HE EVEN KNOWS WE'RE COMING?
PRECISELY, NEBULA. WHICH IS WHERE YOU COME IN. IF ANYONE CAN FIGURE OUT HOW TO GET PAST TERRAX'S DEFENSES AND KIDNAP THE PRISONER, IT'S YOU.
EROS, YOU'RE THE DISTRACTION. YOU GO TO TERRAX ON A "DIPLOMATIC MISSION"--KEEP HIM BUSY WHILE NEBULA AND TRYCO BREAK INTO HIS GULAG.
AND IF IT ALL GOES BAD, YOU'RE ALSO THE MUSCLE, UNCLE. YOU'RE THE ONLY ONE OF US POWERFUL ENOUGH TO HOLD OFF TERRAX.
AND WHAT ABOUT YOU? WHY DO WE NEED YOU, THANE?

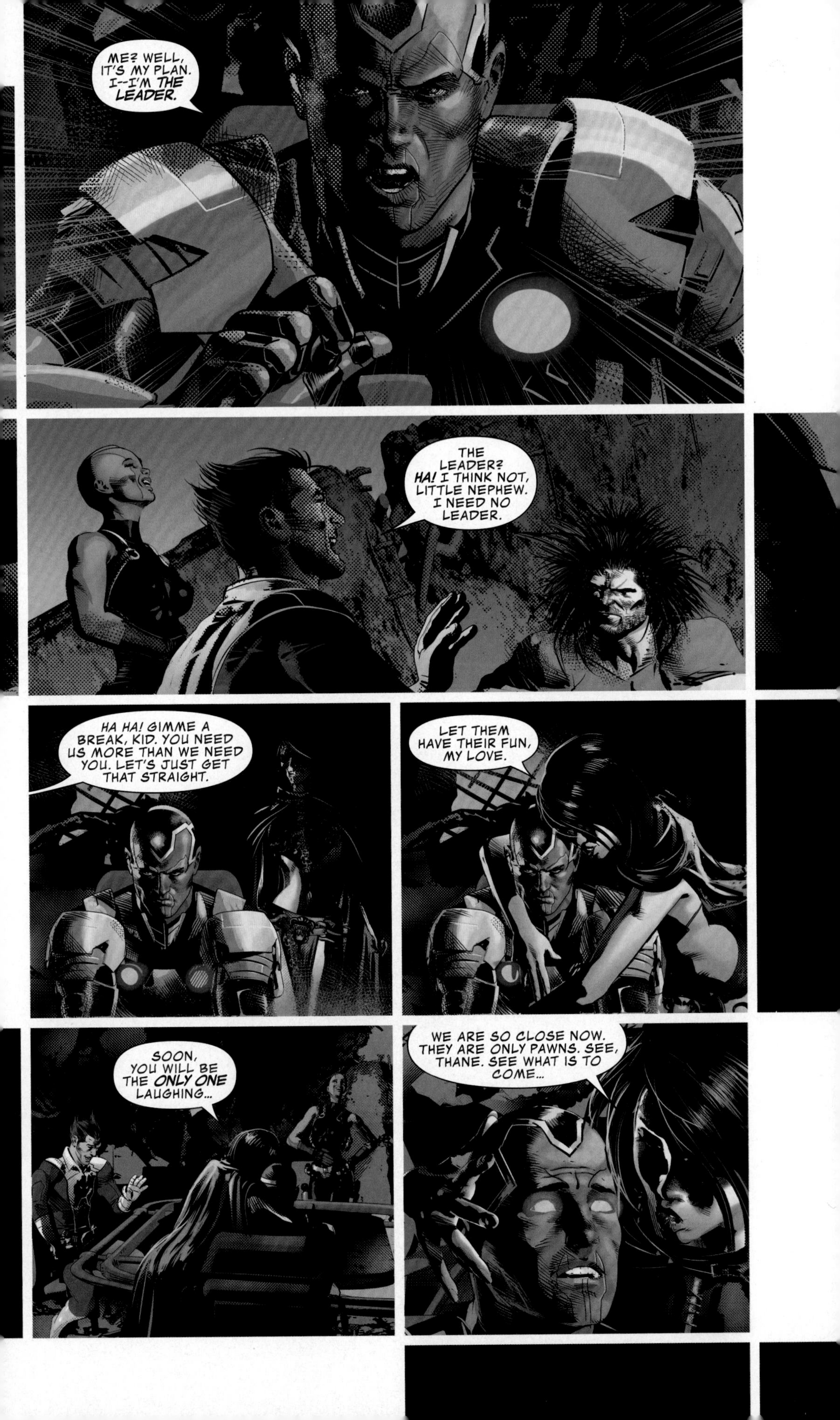
ME? WELL, IT'S MY PLAN. I--I'M THE LEADER.
THE LEADER? HA! I THINK NOT, LITTLE NEPHEW. I NEED NO LEADER.
HA HA! GIMME A BREAK, KID. YOU NEED US MORE THAN WE NEED YOU. LET'S JUST GET THAT STRAIGHT.
LET THEM HAVE THEIR FUN, MY LOVE.
SOON, YOU WILL BE THE ONLY ONE LAUGHING...
WE ARE SO CLOSE NOW. THEY ARE ONLY PAWNS. SEE, THANE. SEE WHAT IS TO COME...

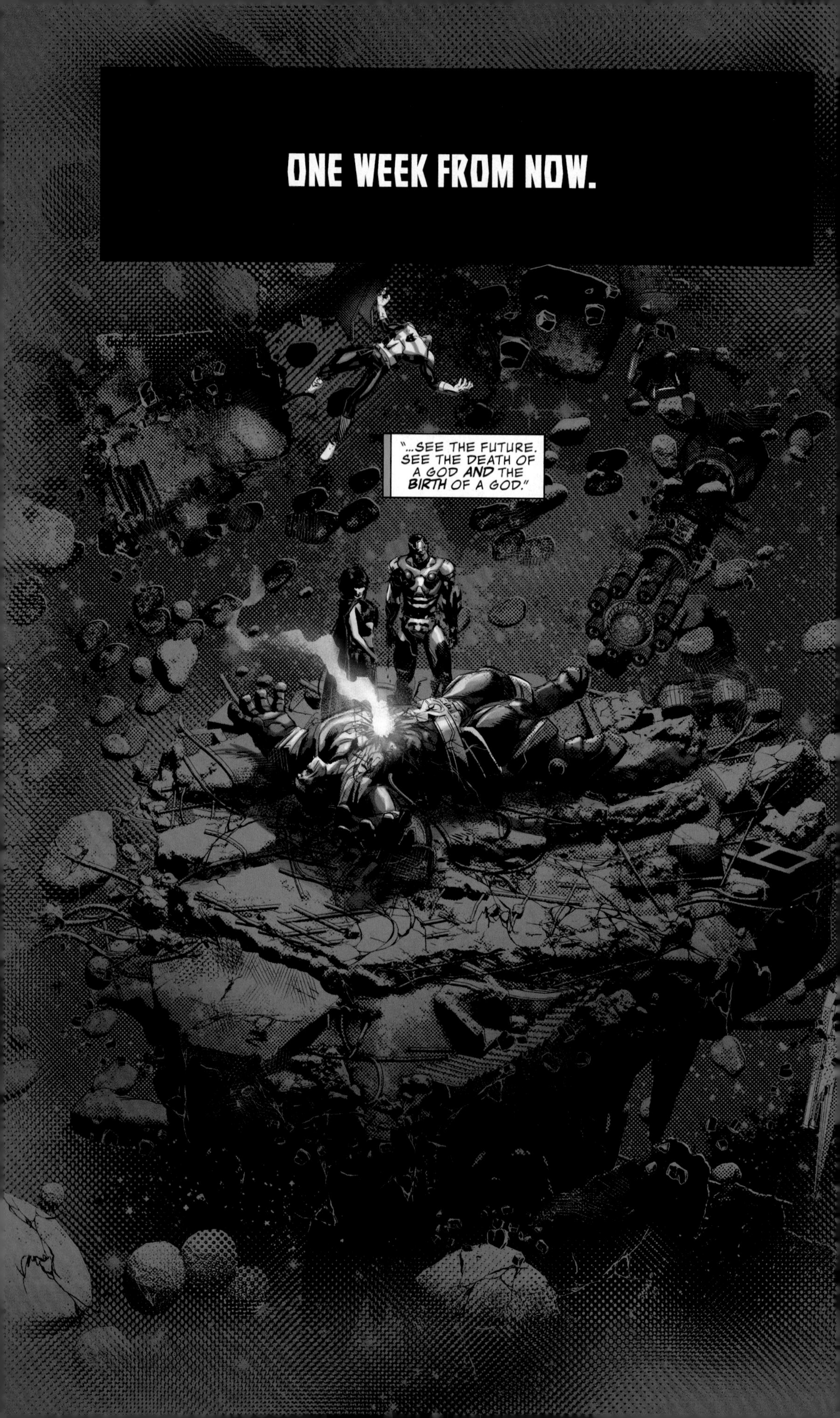
ONE WEEK FROM NOW.
"...SEE THE FUTURE. SEE THE DEATH OF A GOD AND THE BIRTH OF A GOD."

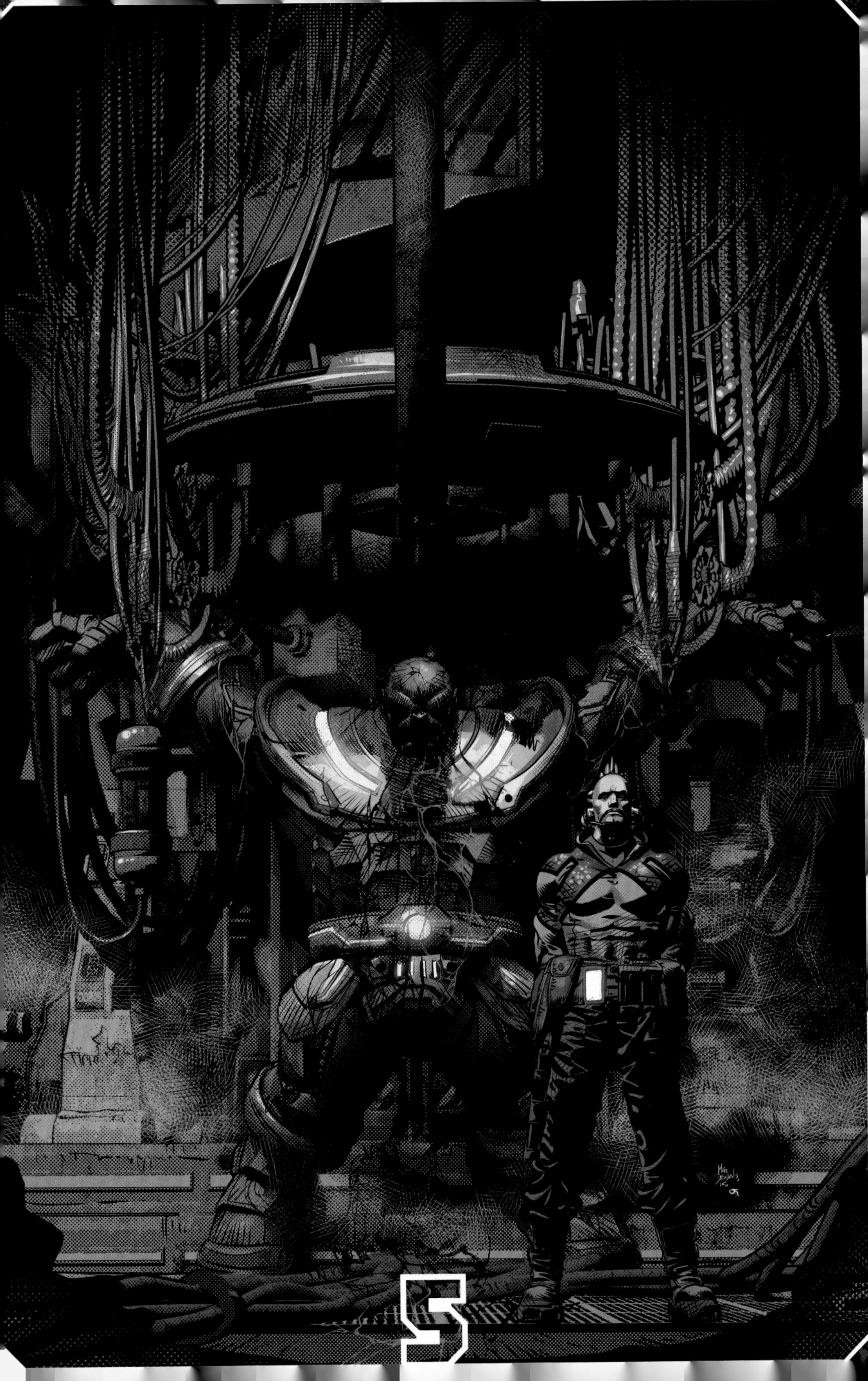
5

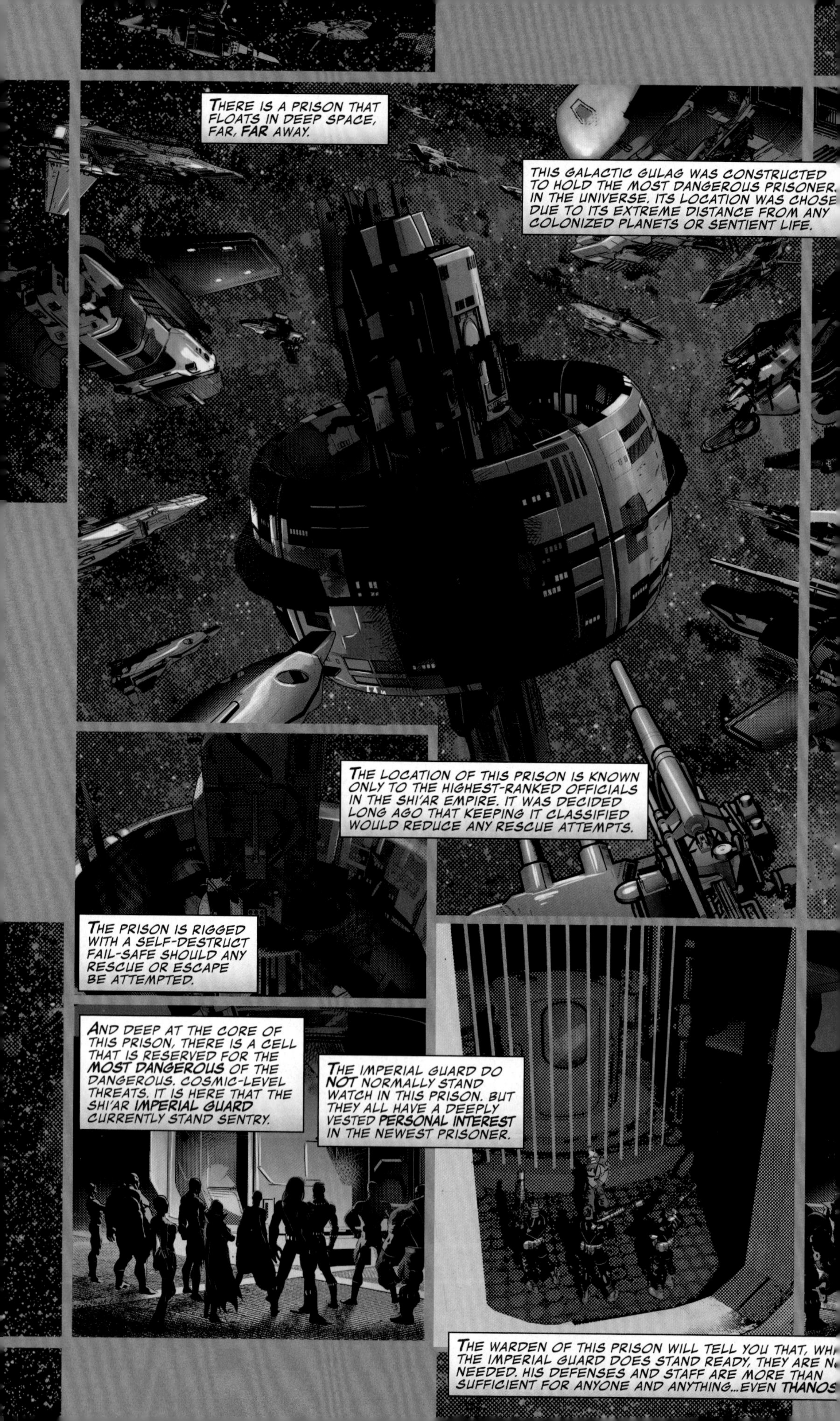
THERE IS A PRISON THAT FLOATS IN DEEP SPACE, FAR, FAR AWAY.
THIS GALACTIC GULAG WAS CONSTRUCTED TO HOLD THE MOST DANGEROUS PRISONER IN THE UNIVERSE. ITS LOCATION WAS CHOSE DUE TO ITS EXTREME DISTANCE FROM ANY COLONIZED PLANETS OR SENTIENT LIFE.
THE LOCATION OF THIS PRISON IS KNOWN ONLY TO THE HIGHEST-RANKED OFFICIALS IN THE SHI'AR EMPIRE. IT WAS DECIDED LONG AGO THAT KEEPING IT CLASSIFIED WOULD REDUCE ANY RESCUE ATTEMPTS.
THE PRISON IS RIGGED WITH A SELF-DESTRUCT FAIL-SAFE SHOULD ANY RESCUE OR ESCAPE BE ATTEMPTED.
AND DEEP AT THE CORE OF THIS PRISON, THERE IS A CELL THAT IS RESERVED FOR THE MOST DANGEROUS OF THE DANGEROUS. COSMIC-LEVEL THREATS. IT IS HERE THAT THE SHI'AR IMPERIAL GUARD CURRENTLY STAND SENTRY.
THE IMPERIAL GUARD DO NOT NORMALLY STAND WATCH IN THIS PRISON. BUT THEY ALL HAVE A DEEPLY VESTED PERSONAL INTEREST IN THE NEWEST PRISONER.
THE WARDEN OF THIS PRISON WILL TELL YOU THAT, WH THE IMPERIAL GUARD DOES STAND READY, THEY ARE N NEEDED. HIS DEFENSES AND STAFF ARE MORE THAN SUFFICIENT FOR ANYONE AND ANYTHING...EVEN THANOS

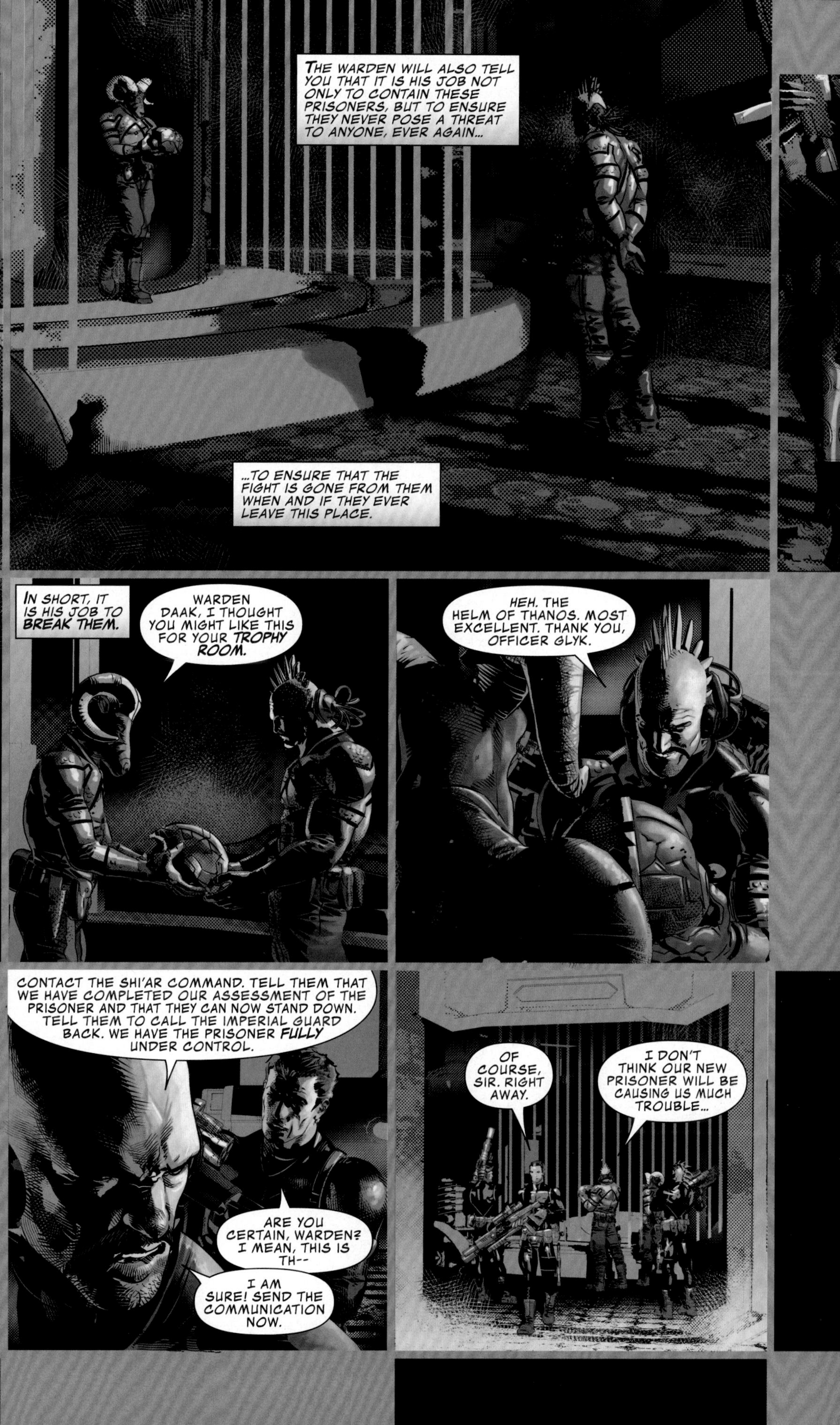
THE WARDEN WILL ALSO TELL YOU THAT IT IS HIS JOB NOT ONLY TO CONTAIN THESE PRISONERS, BUT TO ENSURE THEY NEVER POSE A THREAT TO ANYONE, EVER AGAIN...
...TO ENSURE THAT THE FIGHT IS GONE FROM THEM WHEN AND IF THEY EVER LEAVE THIS PLACE.
IN SHORT, IT IS HIS JOB TO BREAK THEM.
WARDEN DAAK, I THOUGHT YOU MIGHT LIKE THIS FOR YOUR TROPHY ROOM.
HEH. THE HELM OF THANOS. MOST EXCELLENT. THANK YOU, OFFICER GLYK.
CONTACT THE SHI'AR COMMAND. TELL THEM THAT WE HAVE COMPLETED OUR ASSESSMENT OF THE PRISONER AND THAT THEY CAN NOW STAND DOWN. TELL THEM TO CALL THE IMPERIAL GUARD BACK. WE HAVE THE PRISONER FULLY UNDER CONTROL.
ARE YOU CERTAIN, WARDEN? I MEAN, THIS IS TH--
I AM SURE! SEND THE COMMUNICATION NOW.
OF COURSE, SIR. RIGHT AWAY.
I DON'T THINK OUR NEW PRISONER WILL BE CAUSING US MUCH TROUBLE...

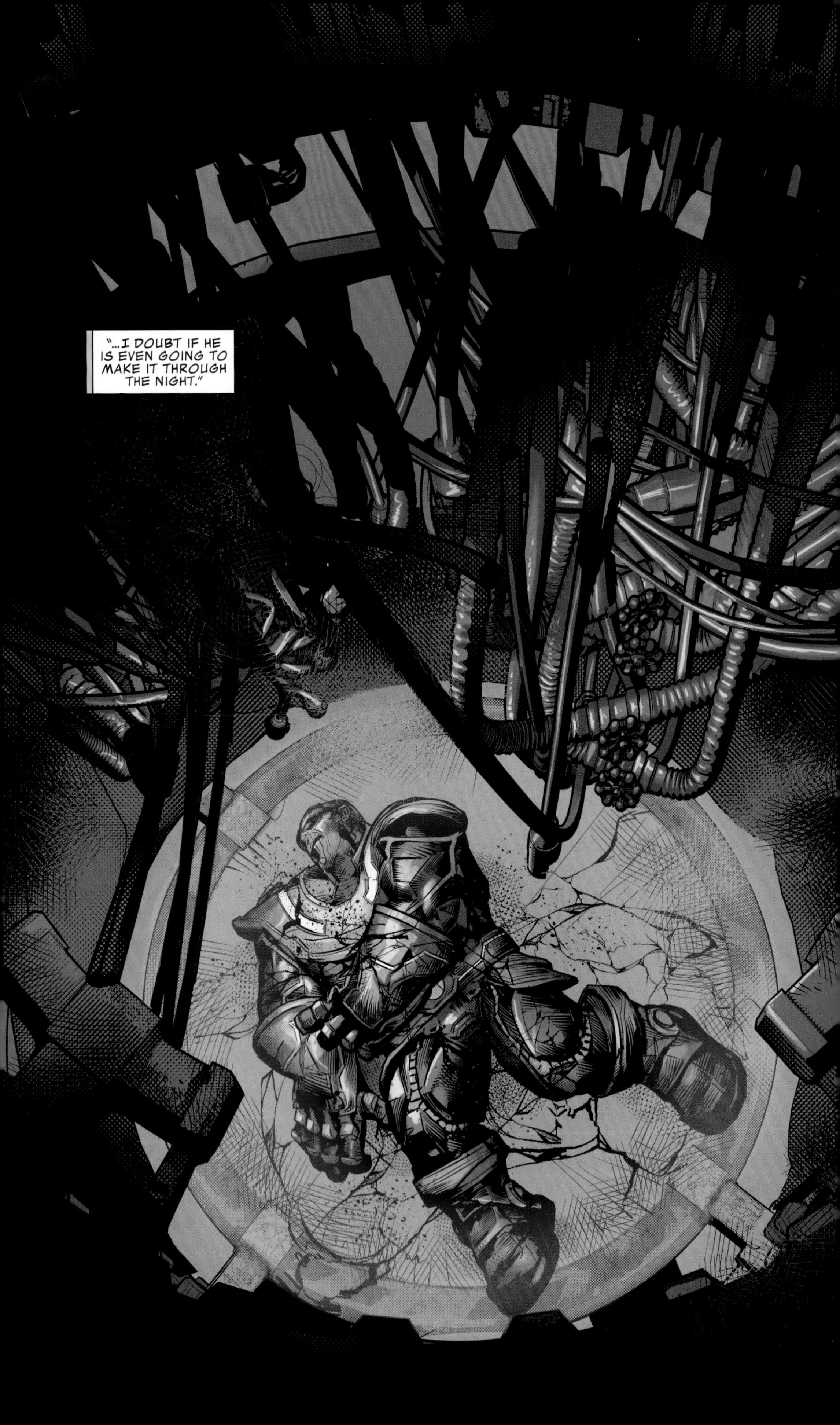
"...I DOUBT IF HE IS EVEN GOING TO MAKE IT THROUGH THE NIGHT."

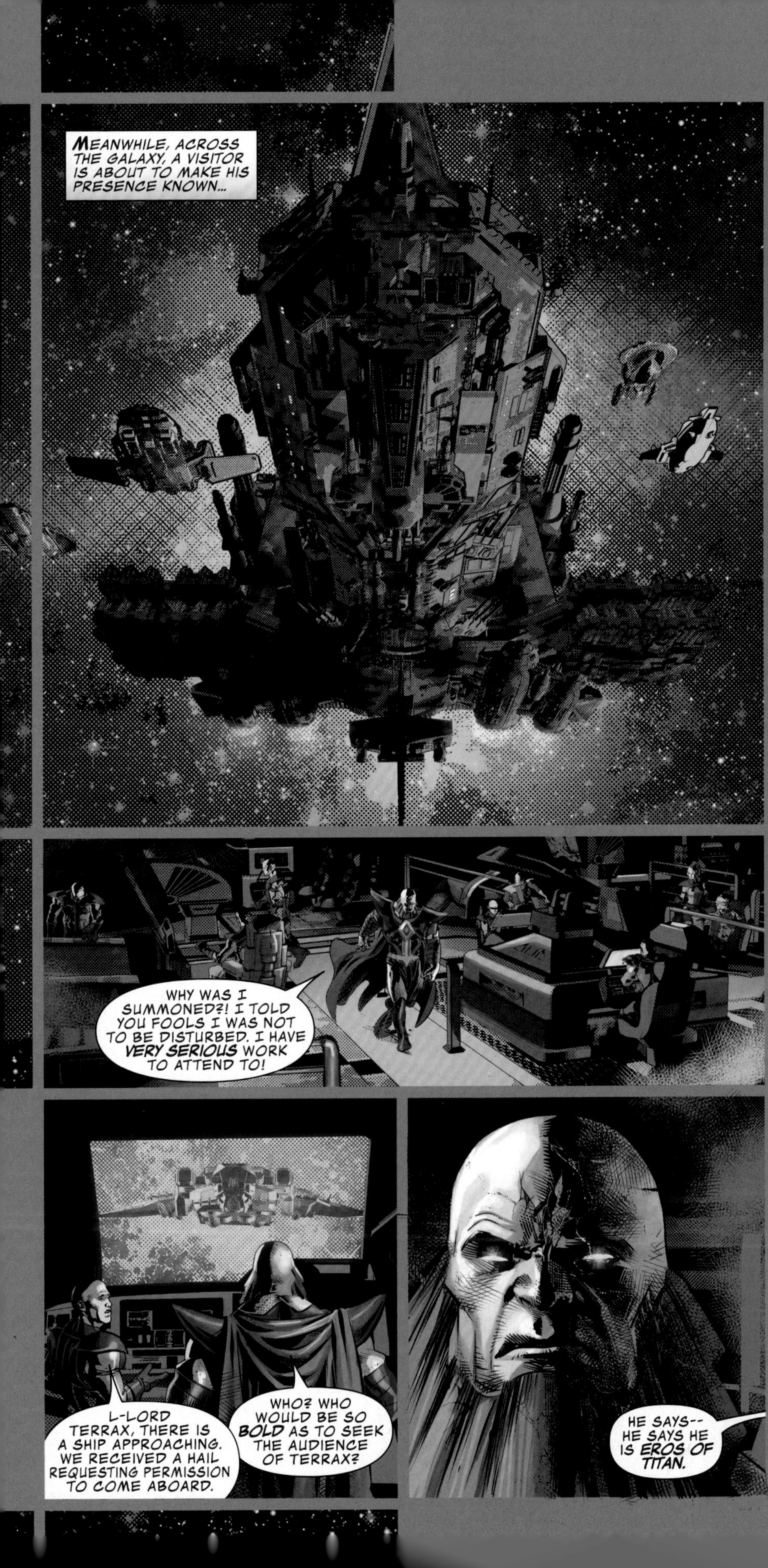
MEANWHILE, ACROSS THE GALAXY, A VISITOR IS ABOUT TO MAKE HIS PRESENCE KNOWN...
WHY WAS I SUMMONED?! I TOLD YOU FOOLS I WAS NOT TO BE DISTURBED. I HAVE VERY SERIOUS WORK TO ATTEND TO!
L-LORD TERRAX, THERE IS A SHIP APPROACHING. WE RECEIVED A HAIL REQUESTING PERMISSION TO COME ABOARD.
WHO? WHO WOULD BE SO BOLD AS TO SEEK THE AUDIENCE OF TERRAX?
HE SAYS-- HE SAYS HE IS EROS OF TITAN.

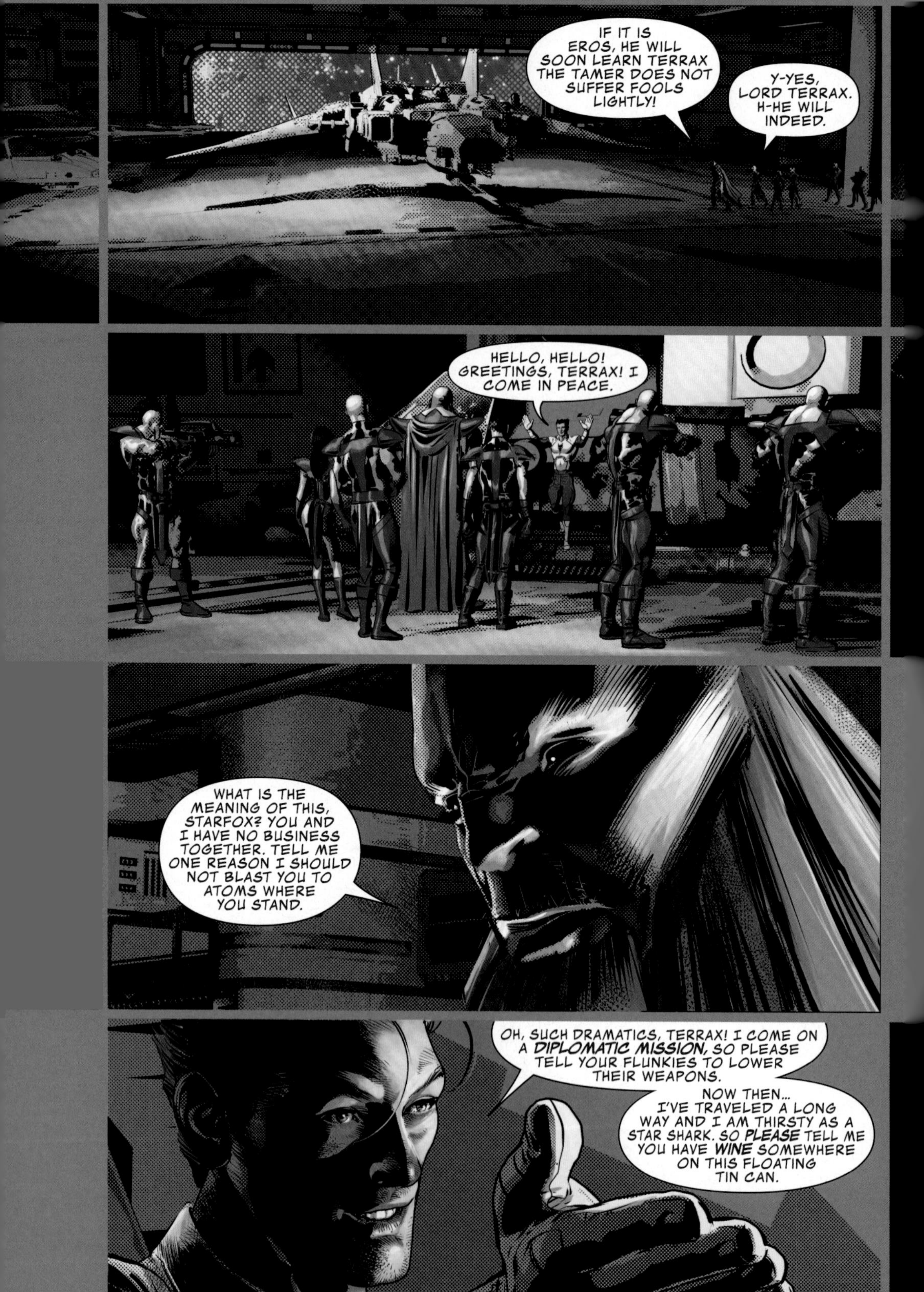
IF IT IS EROS, HE WILL SOON LEARN TERRAX THE TAMER DOES NOT SUFFER FOOLS LIGHTLY!
Y-YES, LORD TERRAX. H-HE WILL INDEED.
HELLO, HELLO! GREETINGS, TERRAX! I COME IN PEACE.
WHAT IS THE MEANING OF THIS, STARFOX? YOU AND I HAVE NO BUSINESS TOGETHER. TELL ME ONE REASON I SHOULD NOT BLAST YOU TO ATOMS WHERE YOU STAND.
OH, SUCH DRAMATICS, TERRAX! I COME ON A DIPLOMATIC MISSION, SO PLEASE TELL YOUR FLUNKIES TO LOWER THEIR WEAPONS.
NOW THEN... I'VE TRAVELED A LONG WAY AND I AM THIRSTY AS A STAR SHARK. SO PLEASE TELL ME YOU HAVE WINE SOMEWHERE ON THIS FLOATING TIN CAN.

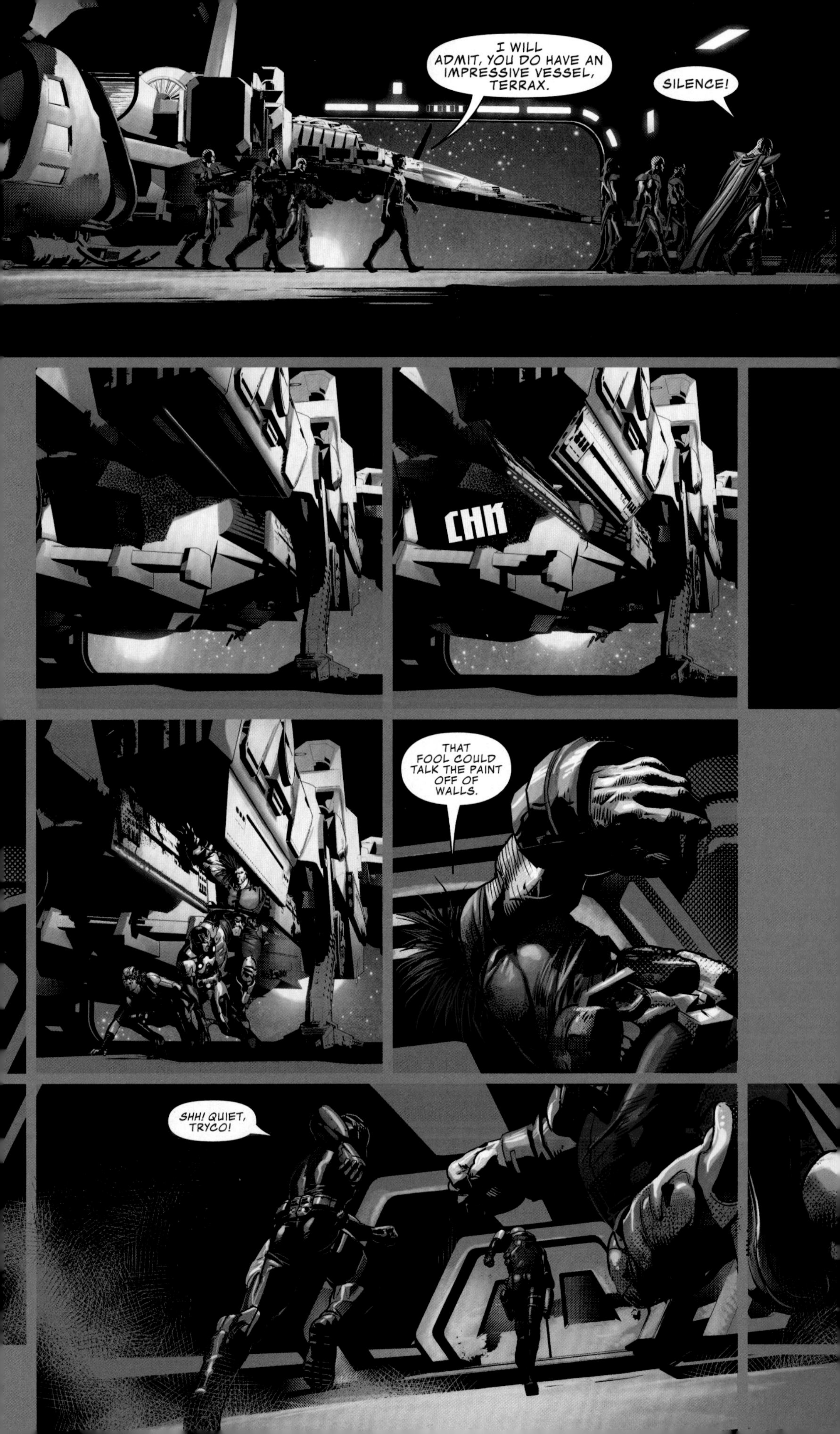
I WILL ADMIT, YOU DO HAVE AN IMPRESSIVE VESSEL, TERRAX.
SILENCE!
CHK
THAT FOOL COULD TALK THE PAINT OFF OF WALLS.
SHH! QUIET, TRYCO!

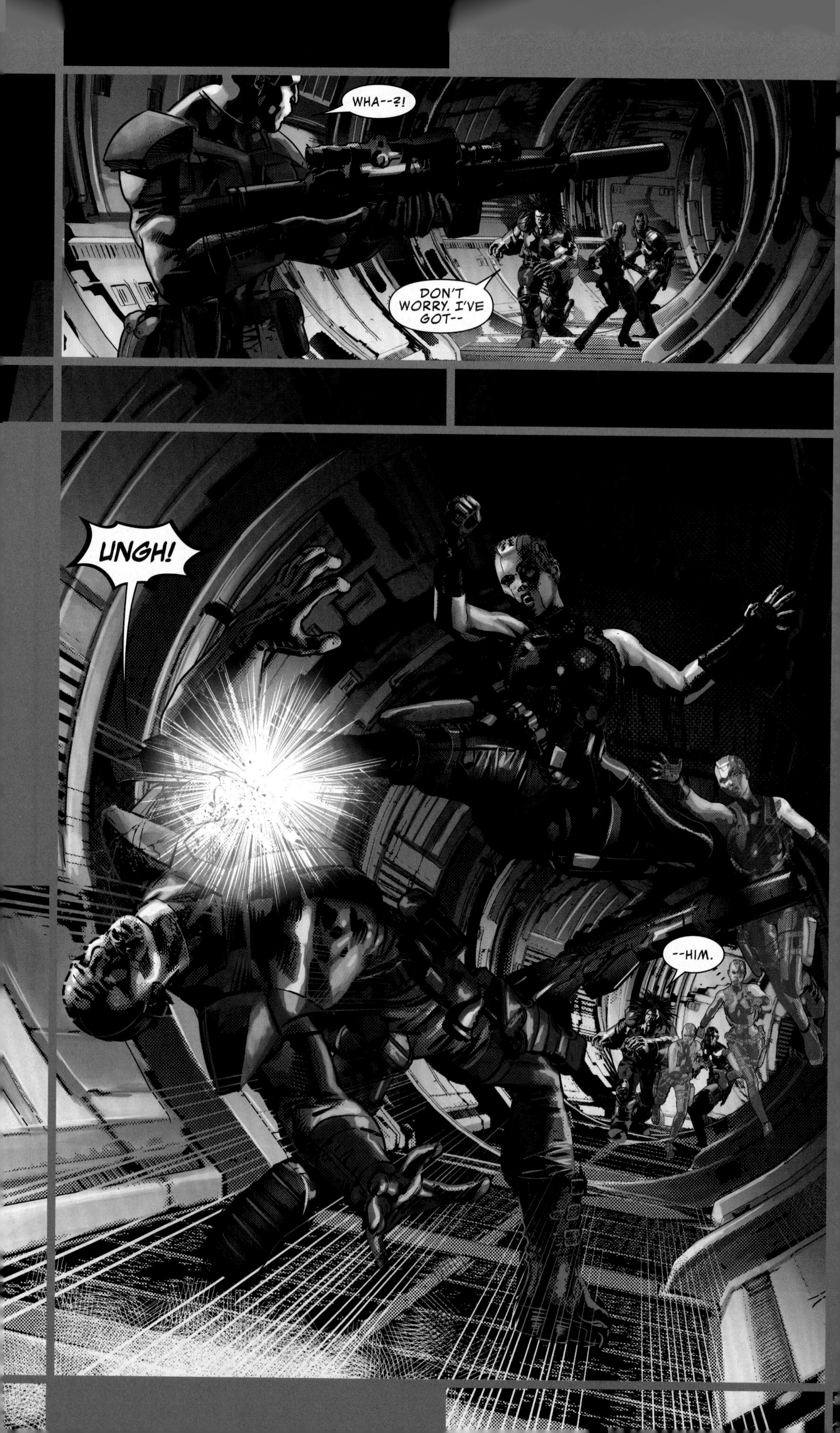
WHA--?!
DON'T WORRY. I'VE GOT--
UNGH!
--HIM.

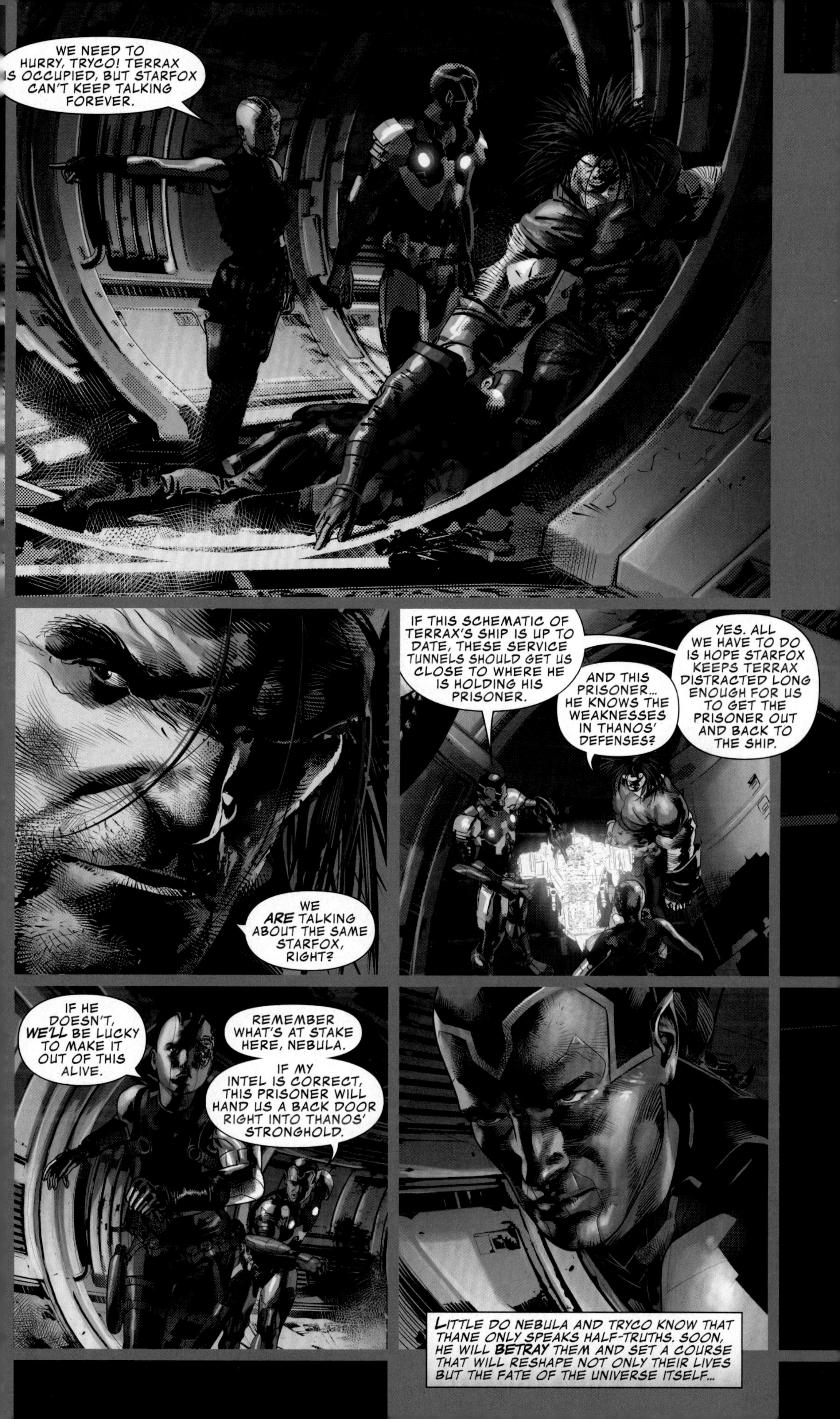
WE NEED TO HURRY, TRYCO! TERRAX IS OCCUPIED, BUT STARFOX CAN'T KEEP TALKING FOREVER.
WE ARE TALKING ABOUT THE SAME STARFOX, RIGHT?
IF THIS SCHEMATIC OF TERRAX'S SHIP IS UP TO DATE, THESE SERVICE TUNNELS SHOULD GET US CLOSE TO WHERE HE IS HOLDING HIS PRISONER.
AND THIS PRISONER... HE KNOWS THE WEAKNESSES IN THANOS' DEFENSES?
YES. ALL WE HAVE TO DO IS HOPE STARFOX KEEPS TERRAX DISTRACTED LONG ENOUGH FOR US TO GET THE PRISONER OUT AND BACK TO THE SHIP.
IF HE DOESN'T, WE'LL BE LUCKY TO MAKE IT OUT OF THIS ALIVE.
REMEMBER WHAT'S AT STAKE HERE, NEBULA.
IF MY INTEL IS CORRECT, THIS PRISONER WILL HAND US A BACK DOOR RIGHT INTO THANOS' STRONGHOLD.
LITTLE DO NEBULA AND TRYCO KNOW THAT THANE ONLY SPEAKS HALF-TRUTHS. SOON, HE WILL BETRAY THEM AND SET A COURSE THAT WILL RESHAPE NOT ONLY THEIR LIVES BUT THE FATE OF THE UNIVERSE ITSELF...

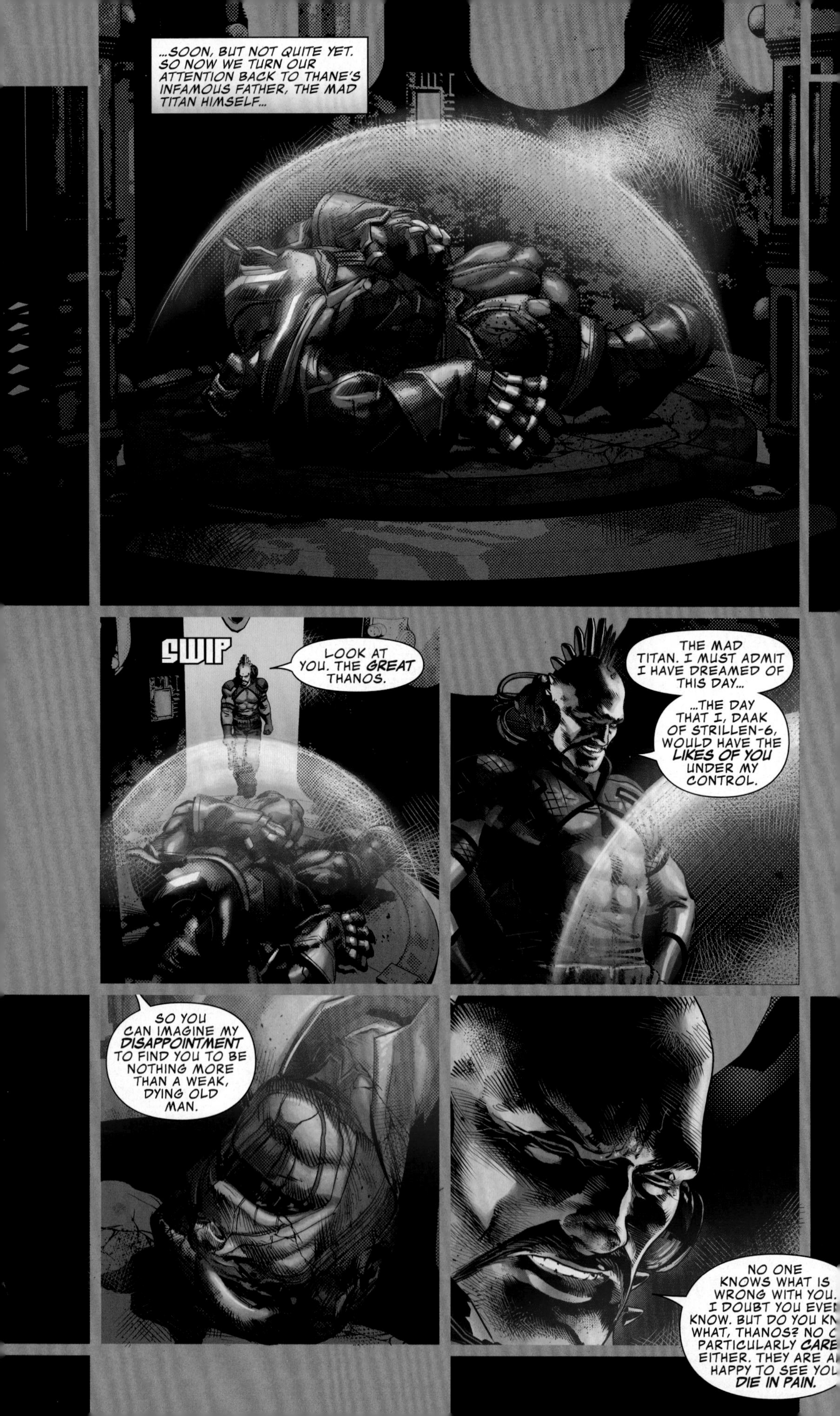

...SOON, BUT NOT QUITE YET. SO NOW WE TURN OUR ATTENTION BACK TO THANE'S INFAMOUS FATHER, THE MAD TITAN HIMSELF...
SWIP
LOOK AT YOU. THE GREAT THANOS.
THE MAD TITAN. I MUST ADMIT I HAVE DREAMED OF THIS DAY...
...THE DAY THAT I, DAAK OF STRILLEN-6, WOULD HAVE THE LIKES OF YOU UNDER MY CONTROL.
SO YOU CAN IMAGINE MY DISAPPOINTMENT TO FIND YOU TO BE NOTHING MORE THAN A WEAK, DYING OLD MAN.
NO ONE KNOWS WHAT IS WRONG WITH YOU. I DOUBT YOU EVE KNOW. BUT DO YOU K WHAT, THANOS? NO PARTICULARLY CARE EITHER. THEY ARE A HAPPY TO SEE YOU DIE IN PAIN.

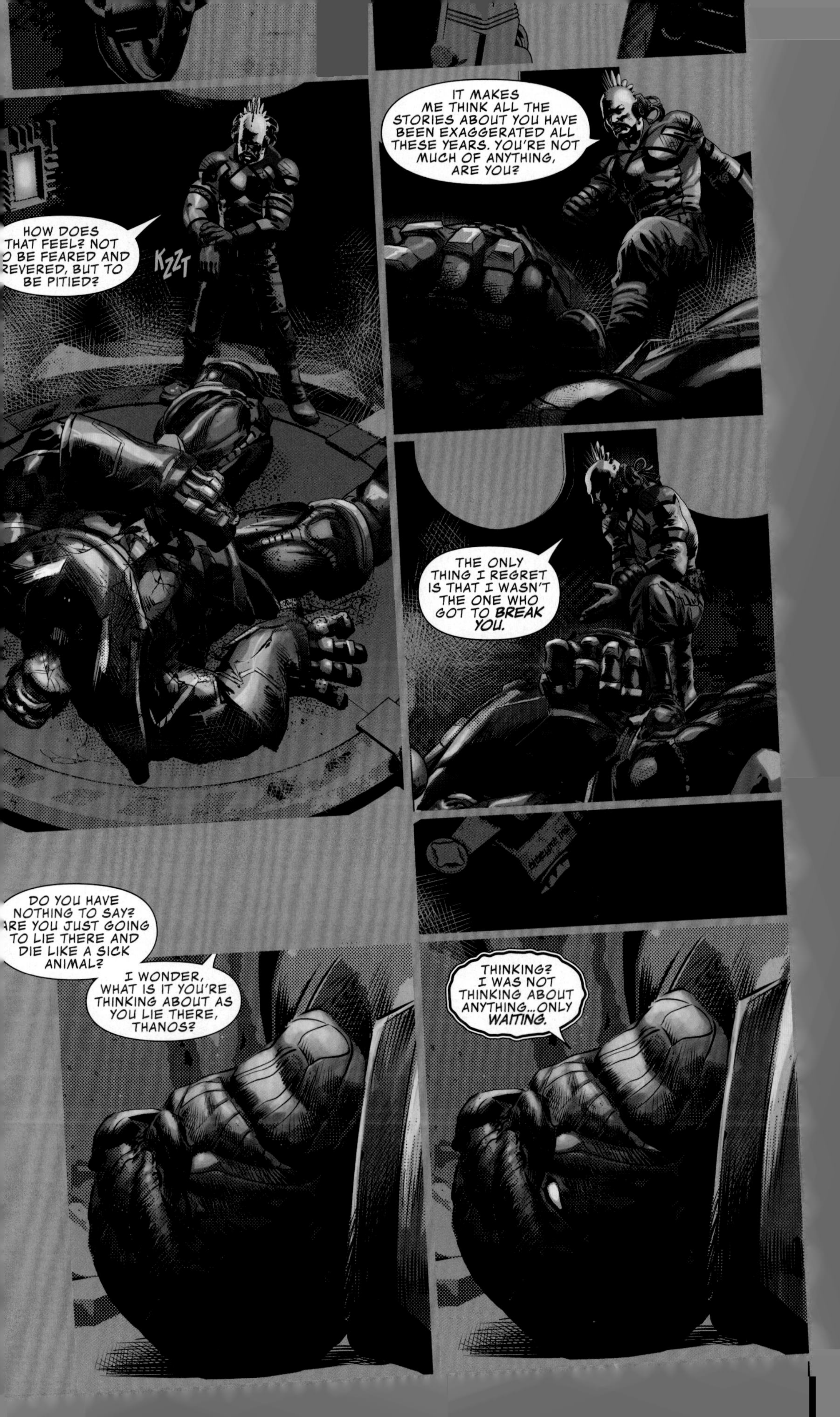
HOW DOES THAT FEEL? NOT TO BE FEARED AND REVERED, BUT TO BE PITIED?
KZZT
IT MAKES ME THINK ALL THE STORIES ABOUT YOU HAVE BEEN EXAGGERATED ALL THESE YEARS. YOU'RE NOT MUCH OF ANYTHING, ARE YOU?
THE ONLY THING I REGRET IS THAT I WASN'T THE ONE WHO GOT TO **BREAK YOU.**
DO YOU HAVE NOTHING TO SAY? ARE YOU JUST GOING TO LIE THERE AND DIE LIKE A SICK ANIMAL?
I WONDER, WHAT IS IT YOU'RE THINKING ABOUT AS YOU LIE THERE, THANOS?
THINKING? I WAS NOT THINKING ABOUT ANYTHING...ONLY ***WAITING.***

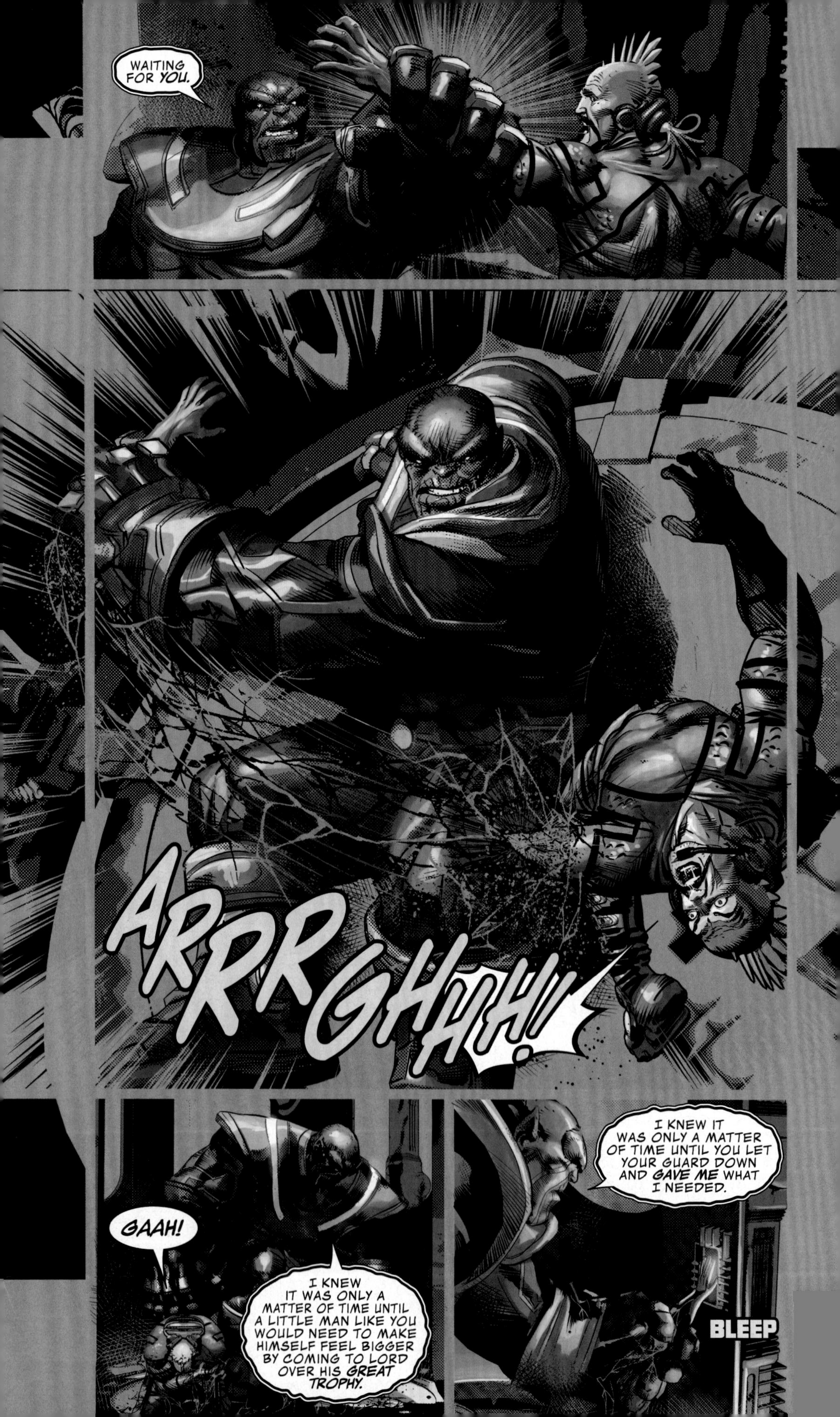

WAITING FOR YOU.
ARRRGHHH!
GAAH!
I KNEW IT WAS ONLY A MATTER OF TIME UNTIL A LITTLE MAN LIKE YOU WOULD NEED TO MAKE HIMSELF FEEL BIGGER BY COMING TO LORD OVER HIS GREAT TROPHY.
I KNEW IT WAS ONLY A MATTER OF TIME UNTIL YOU LET YOUR GUARD DOWN AND GAVE ME WHAT I NEEDED.
BLEEP

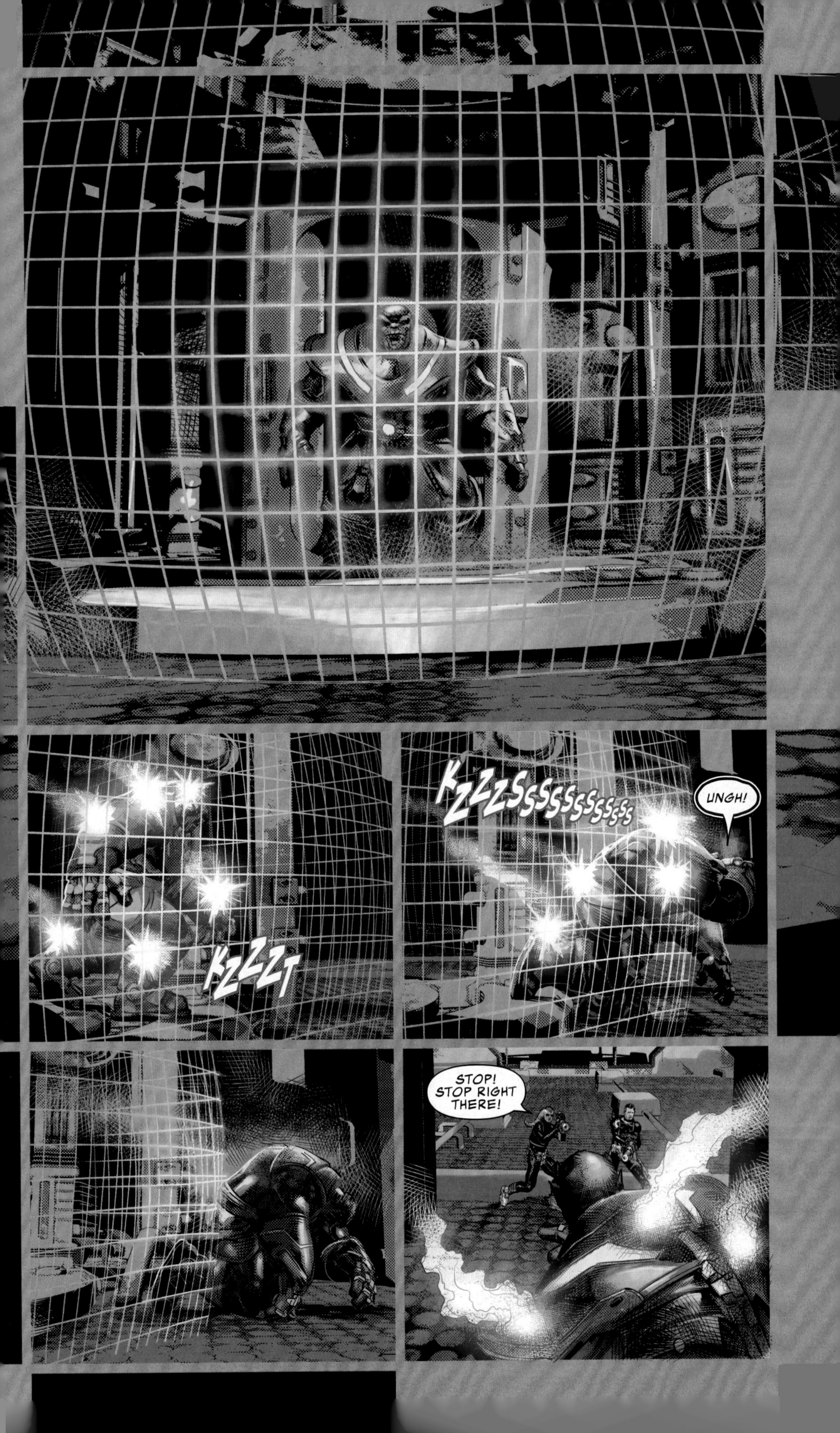
KZZZT
KZZZSSSSSSSSSSSSS
UNGH!
STOP! STOP RIGHT THERE!

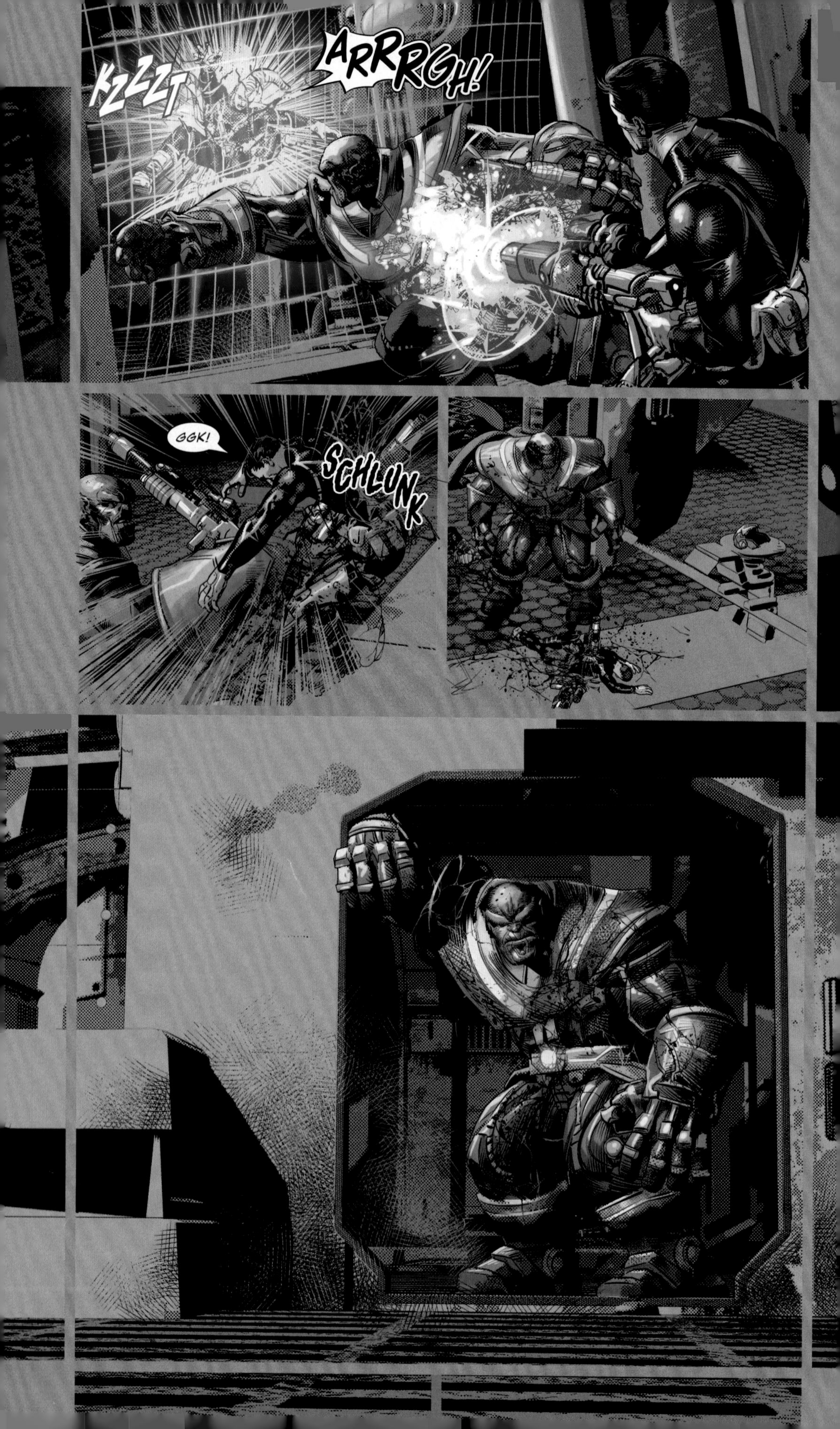
KZZZT
ARRRGH!
GGK!
SCHLUNK

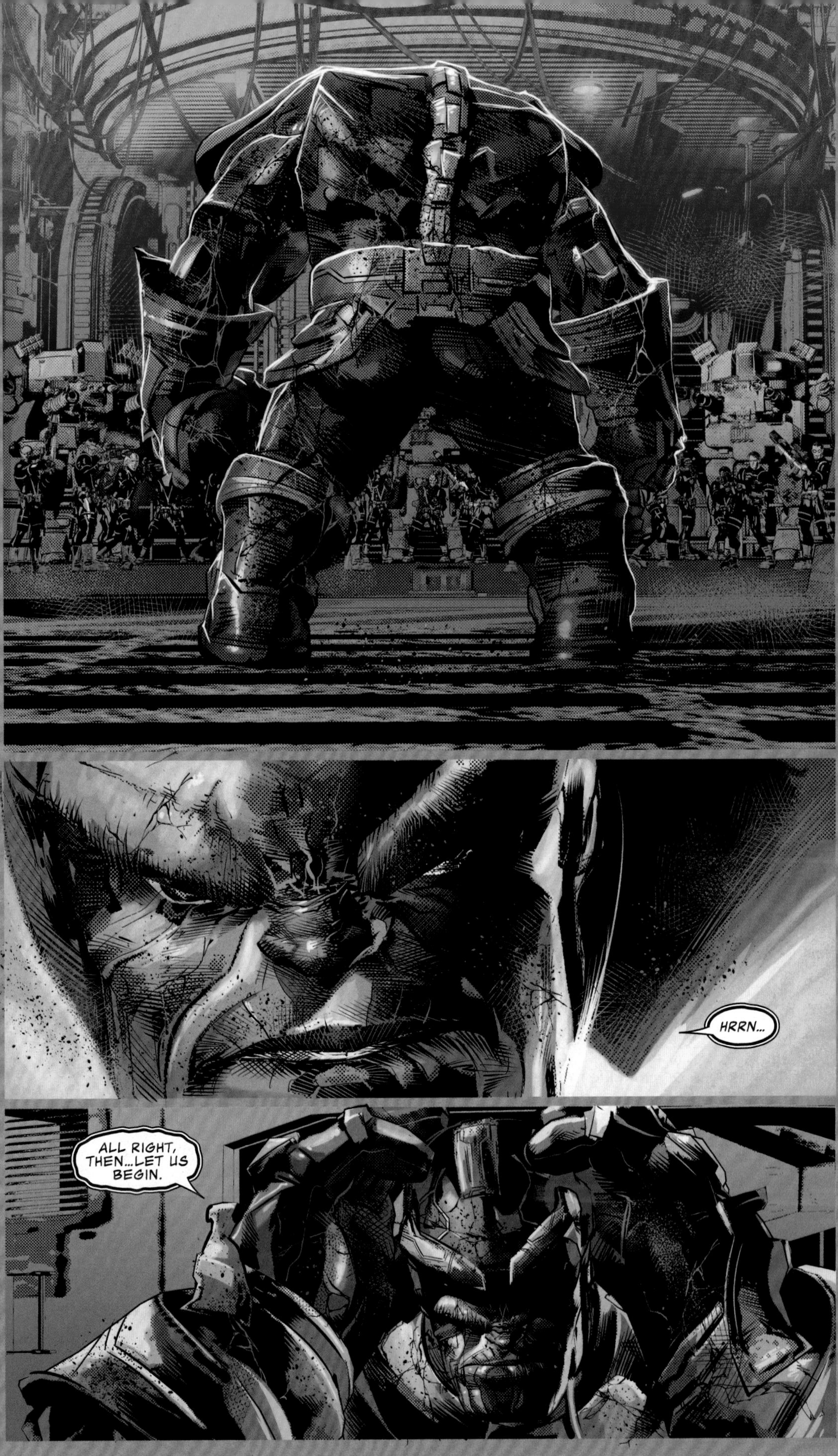
HRRN...
ALL RIGHT, THEN...LET US BEGIN.

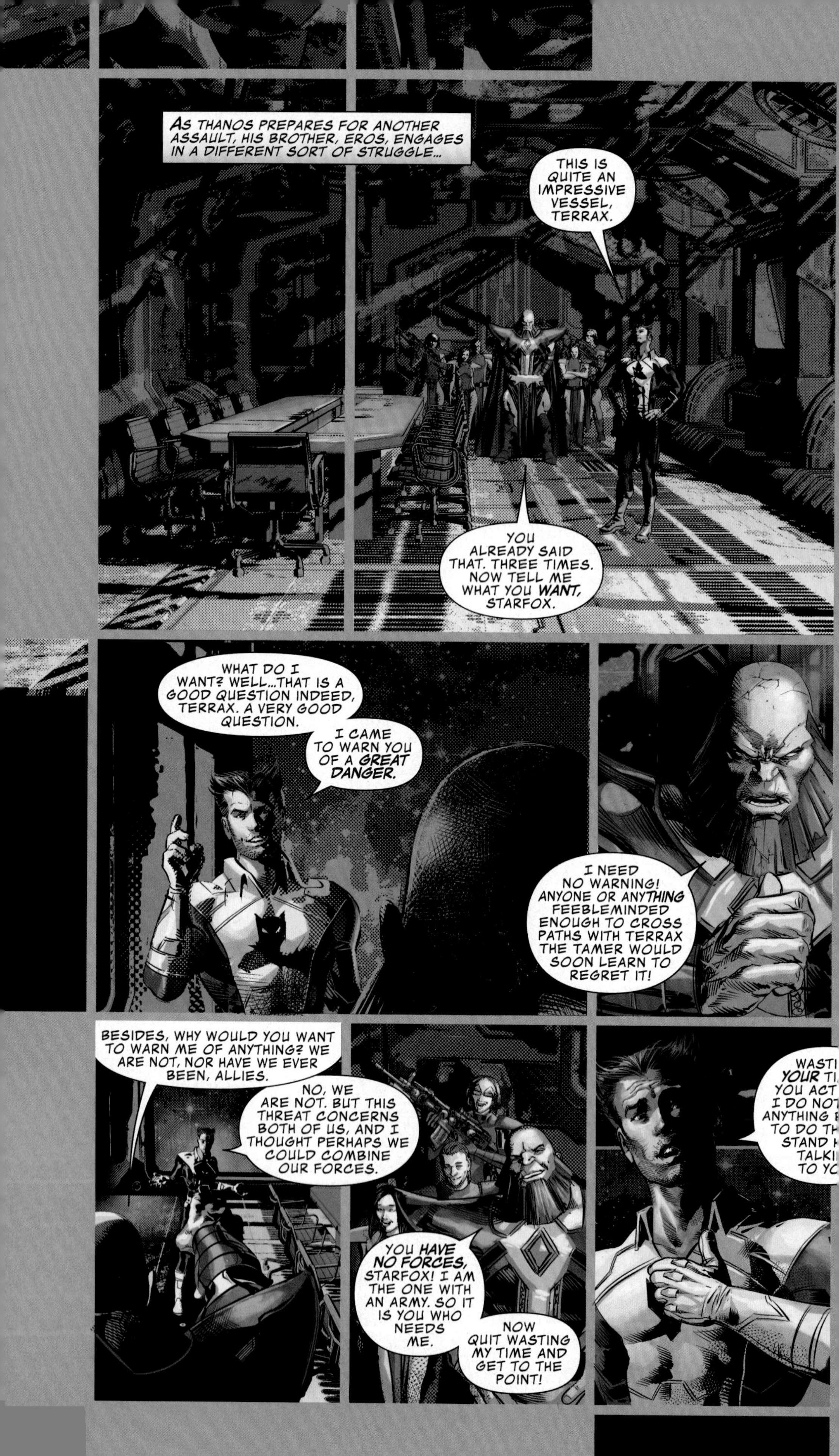

AS THANOS PREPARES FOR ANOTHER ASSAULT, HIS BROTHER, EROS, ENGAGES IN A DIFFERENT SORT OF STRUGGLE...
THIS IS QUITE AN IMPRESSIVE VESSEL, TERRAX.
YOU ALREADY SAID THAT. THREE TIMES. NOW TELL ME WHAT YOU WANT, STARFOX.
WHAT DO I WANT? WELL...THAT IS A GOOD QUESTION INDEED, TERRAX. A VERY GOOD QUESTION.
I CAME TO WARN YOU OF A GREAT DANGER.
I NEED NO WARNING! ANYONE OR ANYTHING FEEBLEMINDED ENOUGH TO CROSS PATHS WITH TERRAX THE TAMER WOULD SOON LEARN TO REGRET IT!
BESIDES, WHY WOULD YOU WANT TO WARN ME OF ANYTHING? WE ARE NOT, NOR HAVE WE EVER BEEN, ALLIES.
NO, WE ARE NOT. BUT THIS THREAT CONCERNS BOTH OF US, AND I THOUGHT PERHAPS WE COULD COMBINE OUR FORCES.
YOU HAVE NO FORCES, STARFOX! I AM THE ONE WITH AN ARMY. SO IT IS YOU WHO NEEDS ME.
NOW QUIT WASTING MY TIME AND GET TO THE POINT!
WASTI YOUR TI YOU ACT I DO NOT ANYTHING TO DO TH STAND TALKI TO YO

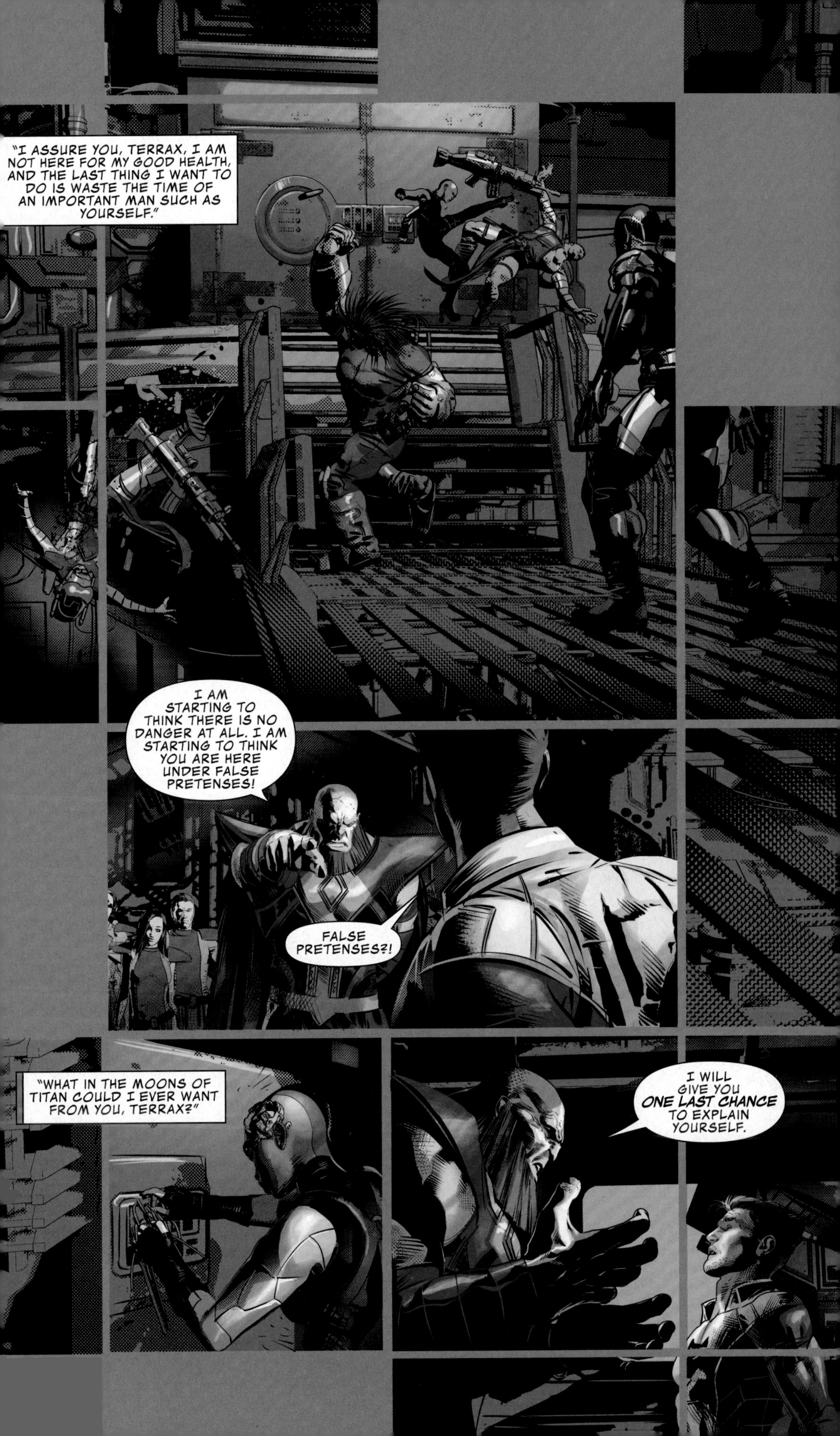
"I ASSURE YOU, TERRAX, I AM NOT HERE FOR MY GOOD HEALTH, AND THE LAST THING I WANT TO DO IS WASTE THE TIME OF AN IMPORTANT MAN SUCH AS YOURSELF."
I AM STARTING TO THINK THERE IS NO DANGER AT ALL. I AM STARTING TO THINK YOU ARE HERE UNDER FALSE PRETENSES!
FALSE PRETENSES?!
"WHAT IN THE MOONS OF TITAN COULD I EVER WANT FROM YOU, TERRAX?"
I WILL GIVE YOU ONE LAST CHANCE TO EXPLAIN YOURSELF.

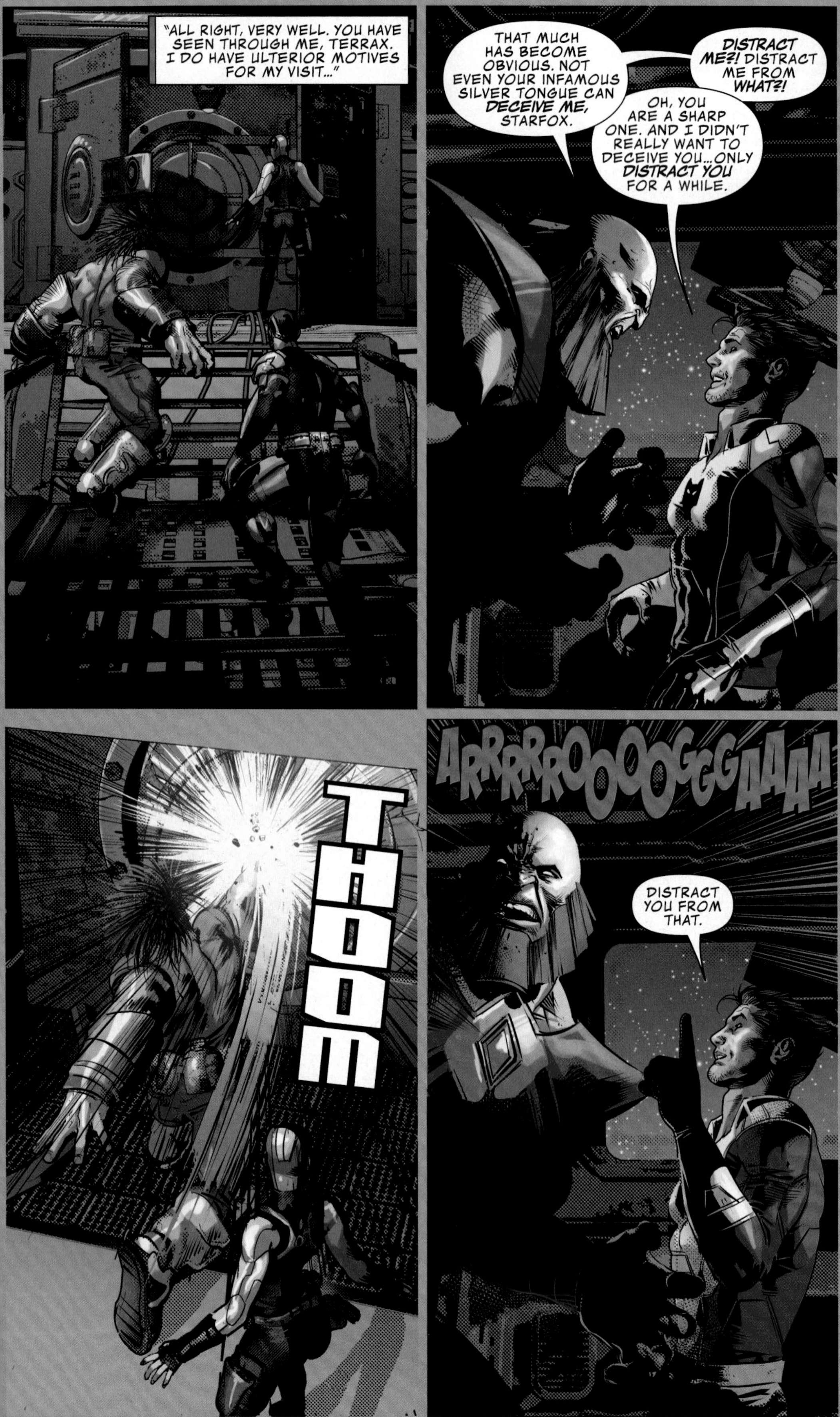
"ALL RIGHT, VERY WELL. YOU HAVE SEEN THROUGH ME, TERRAX. I DO HAVE ULTERIOR MOTIVES FOR MY VISIT..."
THAT MUCH HAS BECOME OBVIOUS. NOT EVEN YOUR INFAMOUS SILVER TONGUE CAN DECEIVE ME, STARFOX.
OH, YOU ARE A SHARP ONE. AND I DIDN'T REALLY WANT TO DECEIVE YOU...ONLY DISTRACT YOU FOR A WHILE.
DISTRACT ME?! DISTRACT ME FROM WHAT?!
THOOM
ARRRRROOOOGGAAAA
DISTRACT YOU FROM THAT.

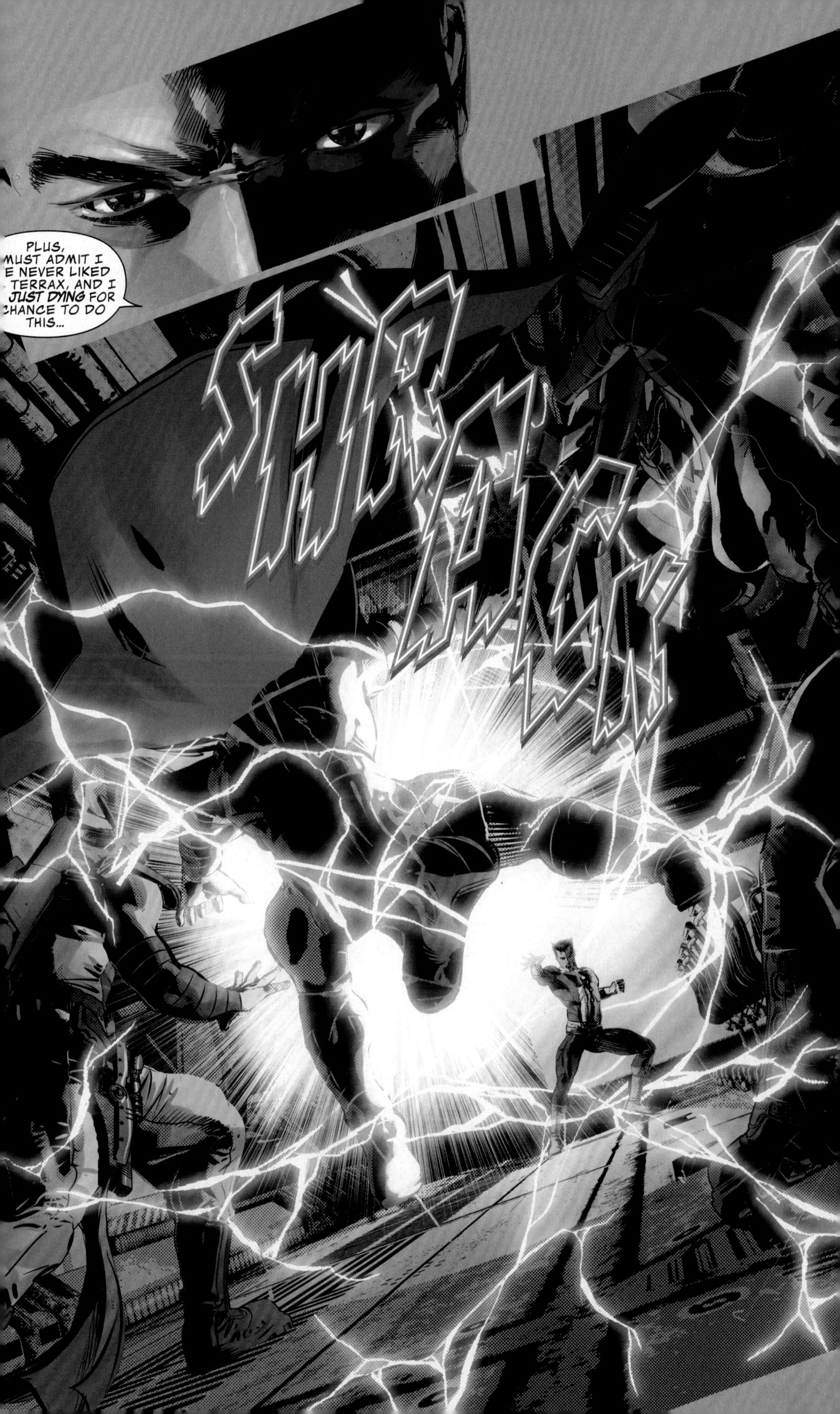
PLUS, MUST ADMIT I E NEVER LIKED TERRAX, AND I JUST DYING FOR CHANCE TO DO THIS...

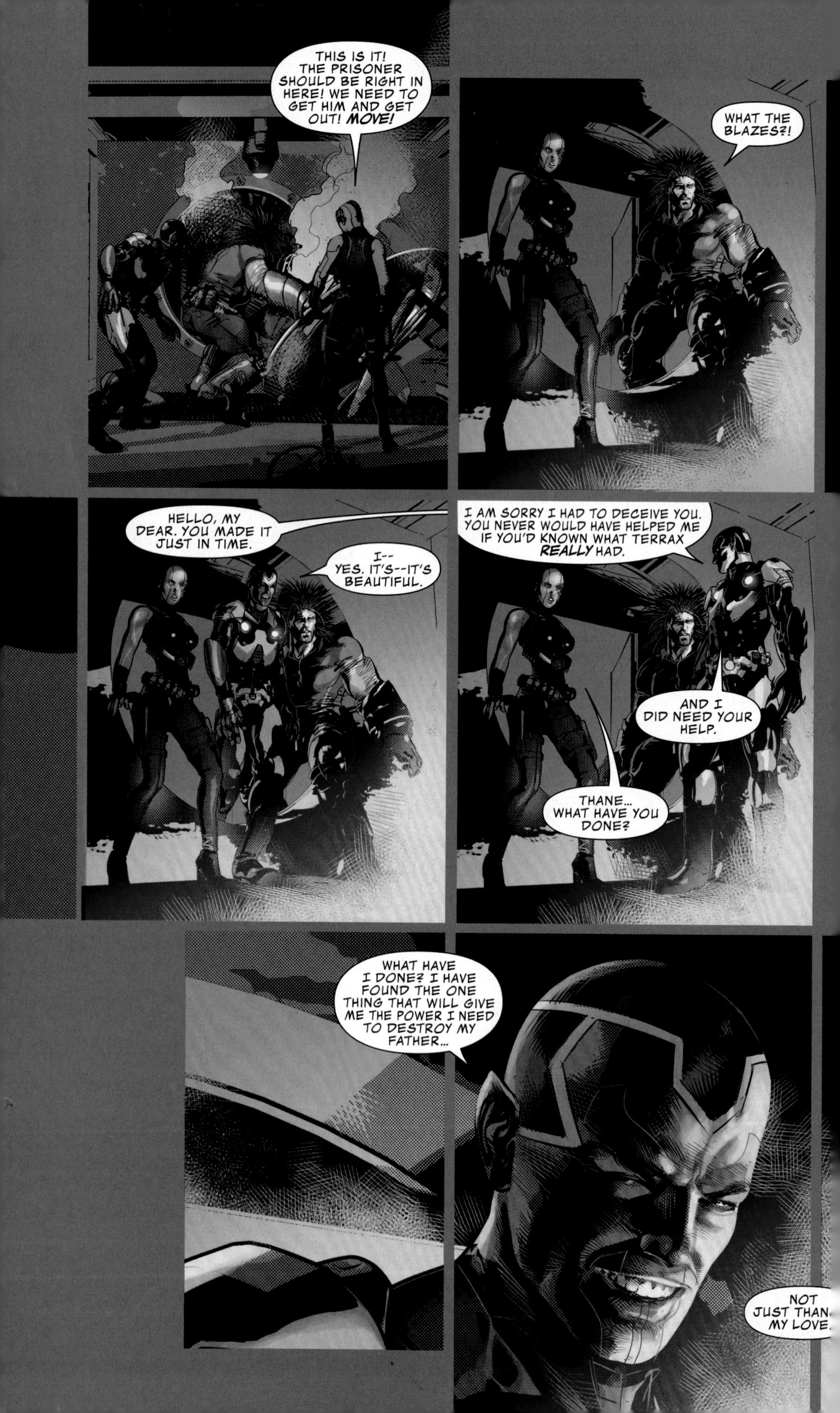

THIS IS IT! THE PRISONER SHOULD BE RIGHT IN HERE! WE NEED TO GET HIM AND GET OUT! MOVE!
WHAT THE BLAZES?!
HELLO, MY DEAR. YOU MADE IT JUST IN TIME.
I-- YES. IT'S--IT'S BEAUTIFUL.
I AM SORRY I HAD TO DECEIVE YOU. YOU NEVER WOULD HAVE HELPED ME IF YOU'D KNOWN WHAT TERRAX REALLY HAD.
AND I DID NEED YOUR HELP.
THANE... WHAT HAVE YOU DONE?
WHAT HAVE I DONE? I HAVE FOUND THE ONE THING THAT WILL GIVE ME THE POWER I NEED TO DESTROY MY FATHER...

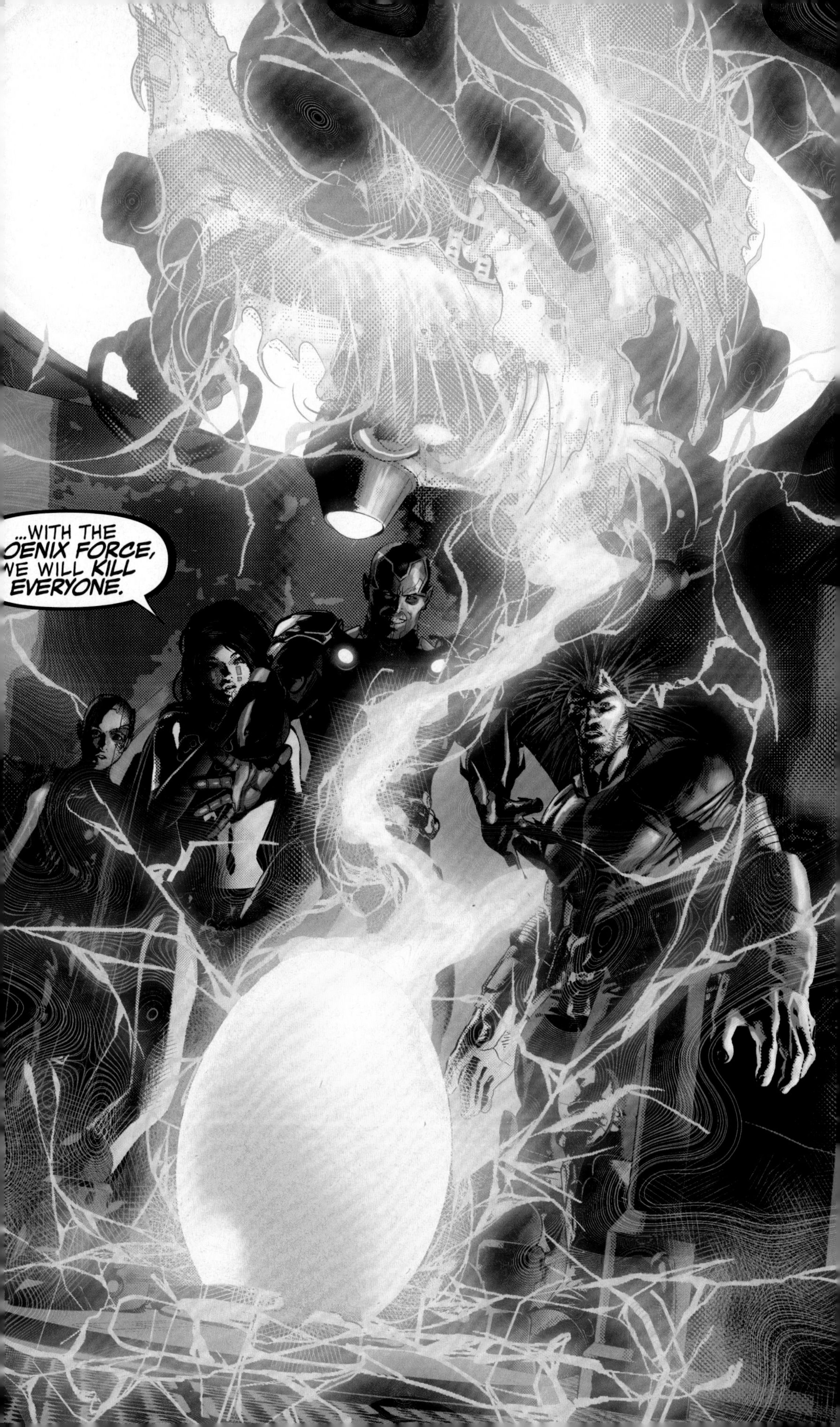
...WITH THE OENIX FORCE, WE WILL KILL EVERYONE.

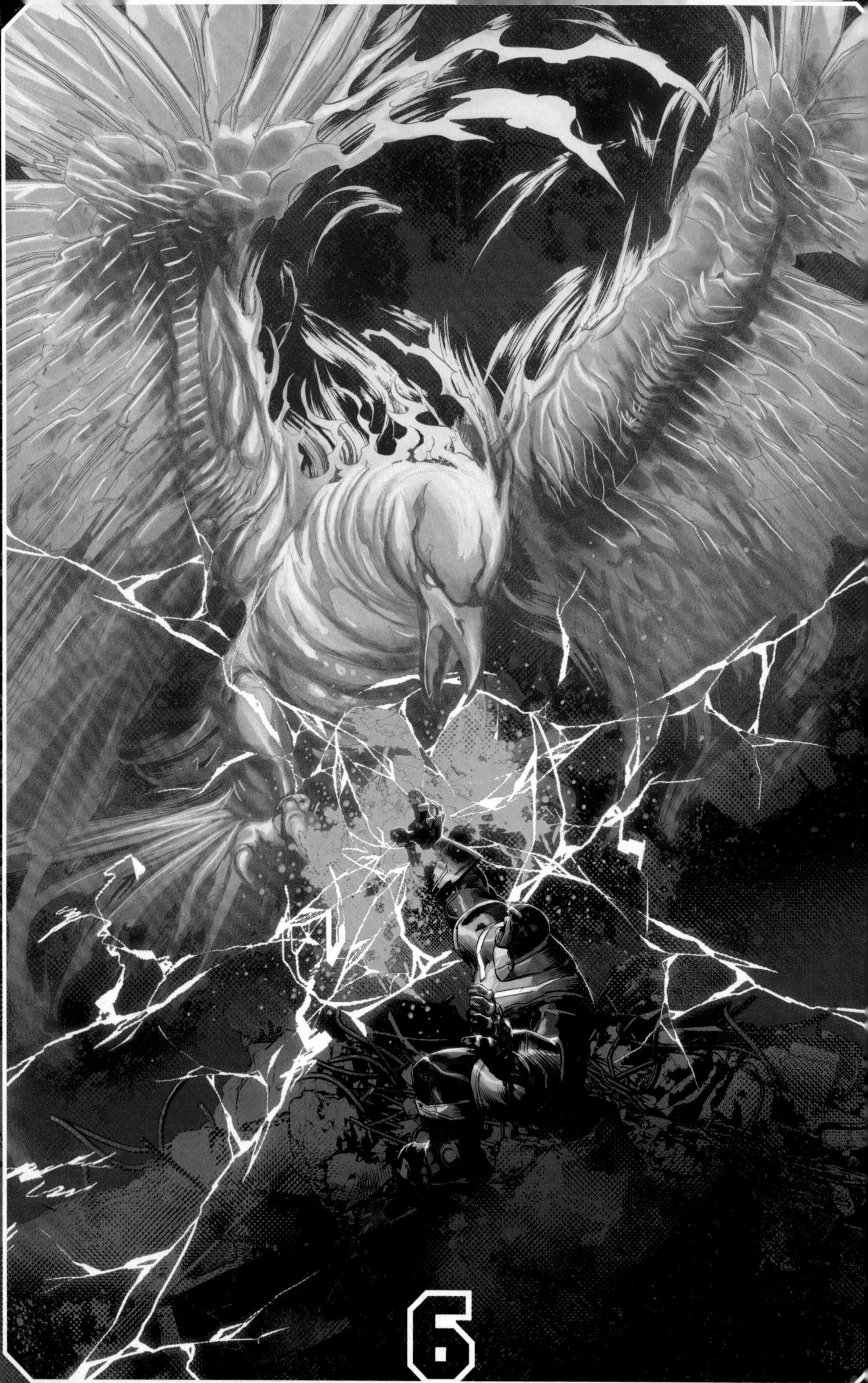
6

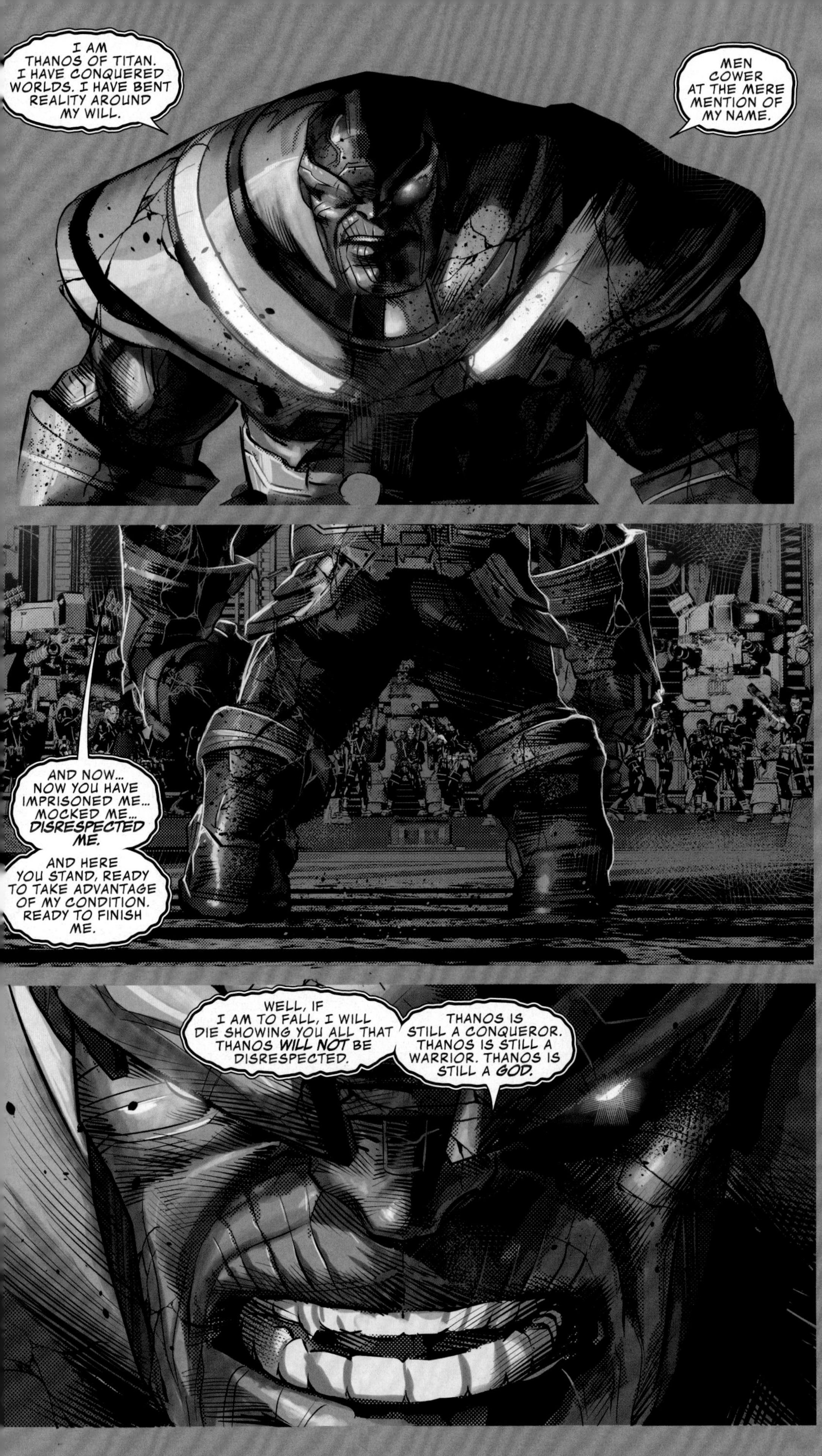
I AM THANOS OF TITAN. I HAVE CONQUERED WORLDS. I HAVE BENT REALITY AROUND MY WILL.
MEN COWER AT THE MERE MENTION OF MY NAME.
AND NOW... NOW YOU HAVE IMPRISONED ME... MOCKED ME... DISRESPECTED ME.
AND HERE YOU STAND, READY TO TAKE ADVANTAGE OF MY CONDITION. READY TO FINISH ME.
WELL, IF I AM TO FALL, I WILL DIE SHOWING YOU ALL THAT THANOS WILL NOT BE DISRESPECTED.
THANOS IS STILL A CONQUEROR. THANOS IS STILL A WARRIOR. THANOS IS STILL A GOD.

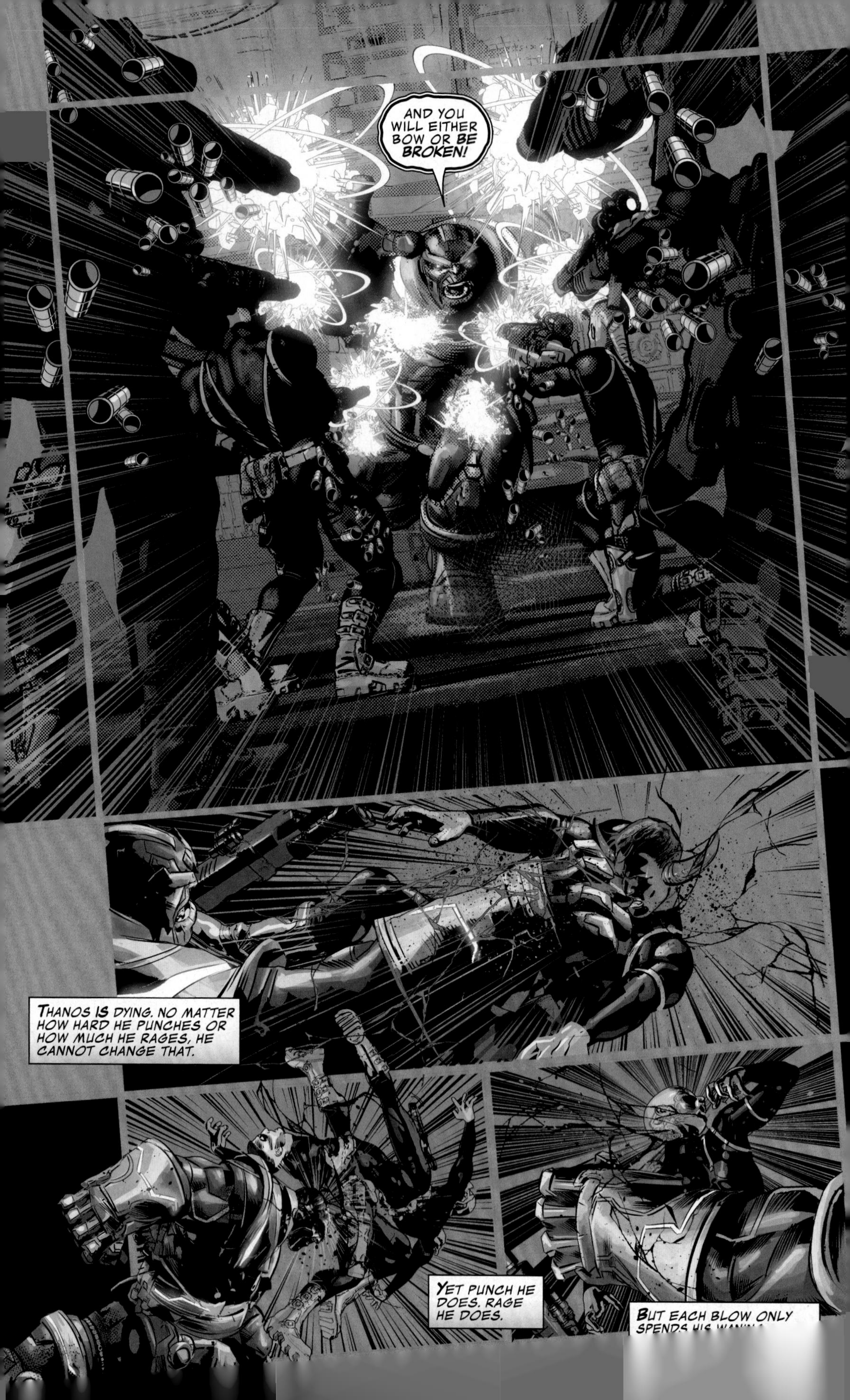
AND YOU WILL EITHER BOW OR BE BROKEN!
THANOS IS DYING. NO MATTER HOW HARD HE PUNCHES OR HOW MUCH HE RAGES, HE CANNOT CHANGE THAT.
YET PUNCH HE DOES. RAGE HE DOES.
BUT EACH BLOW ONLY SPENDS HIS

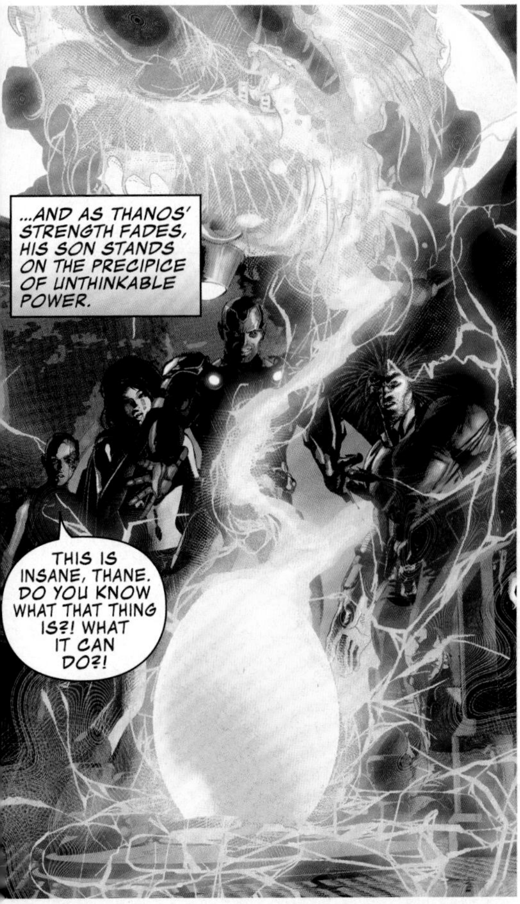
...AND AS THANOS' STRENGTH FADES, HIS SON STANDS ON THE PRECIPICE OF UNTHINKABLE POWER.
THIS IS INSANE, THANE. DO YOU KNOW WHAT THAT THING IS?! WHAT IT CAN DO?!

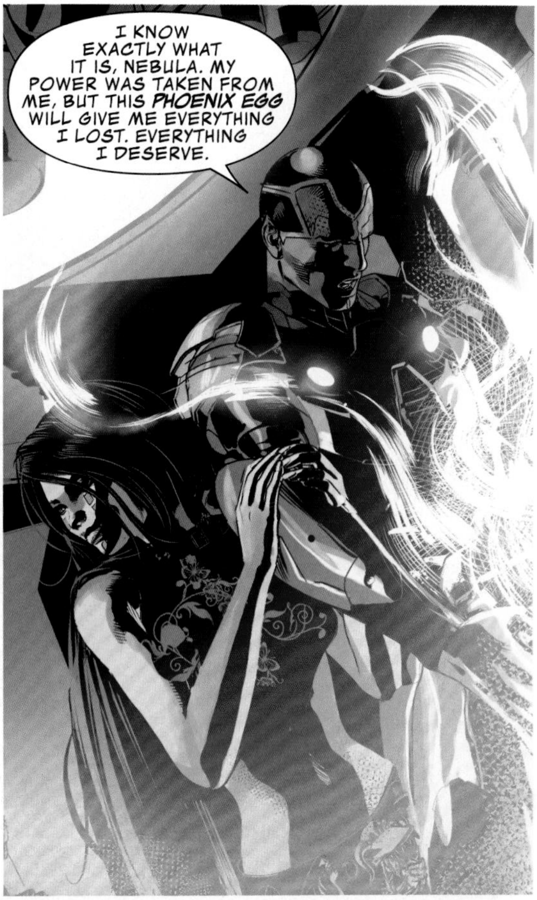
I KNOW EXACTLY WHAT IT IS, NEBULA. MY POWER WAS TAKEN FROM ME, BUT THIS PHOENIX EGG WILL GIVE ME EVERYTHING I LOST. EVERYTHING I DESERVE.

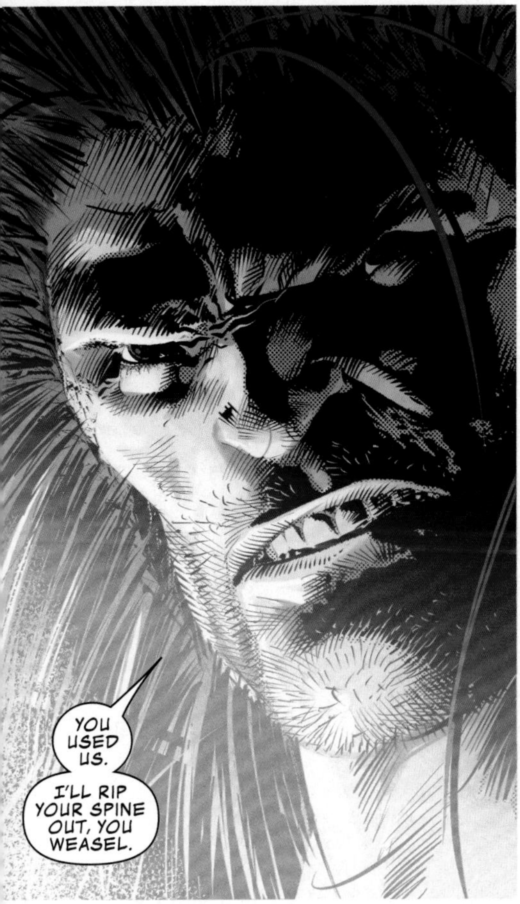
YOU USED US.
I'LL RIP YOUR SPINE OUT, YOU WEASEL.

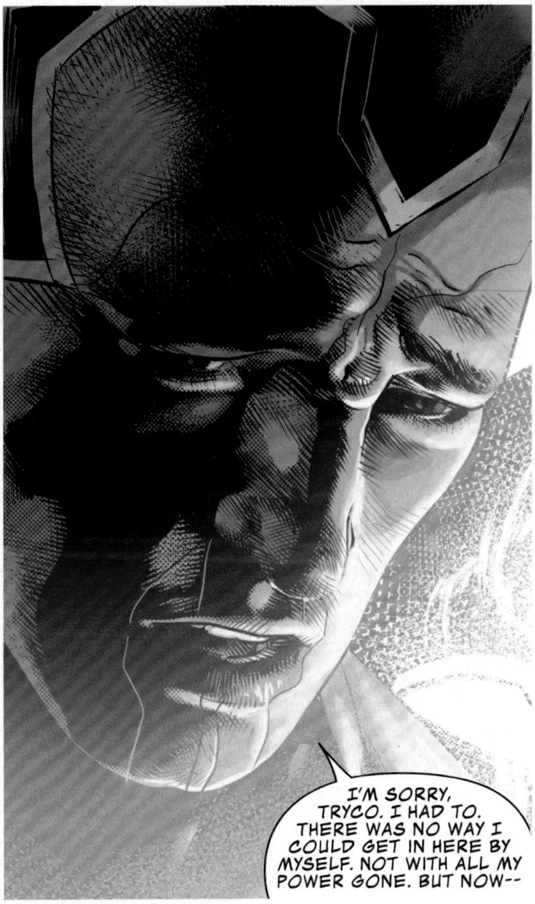
I'M SORRY, TRYCO. I HAD TO. THERE WAS NO WAY I COULD GET IN HERE BY MYSELF. NOT WITH ALL MY POWER GONE. BUT NOW--

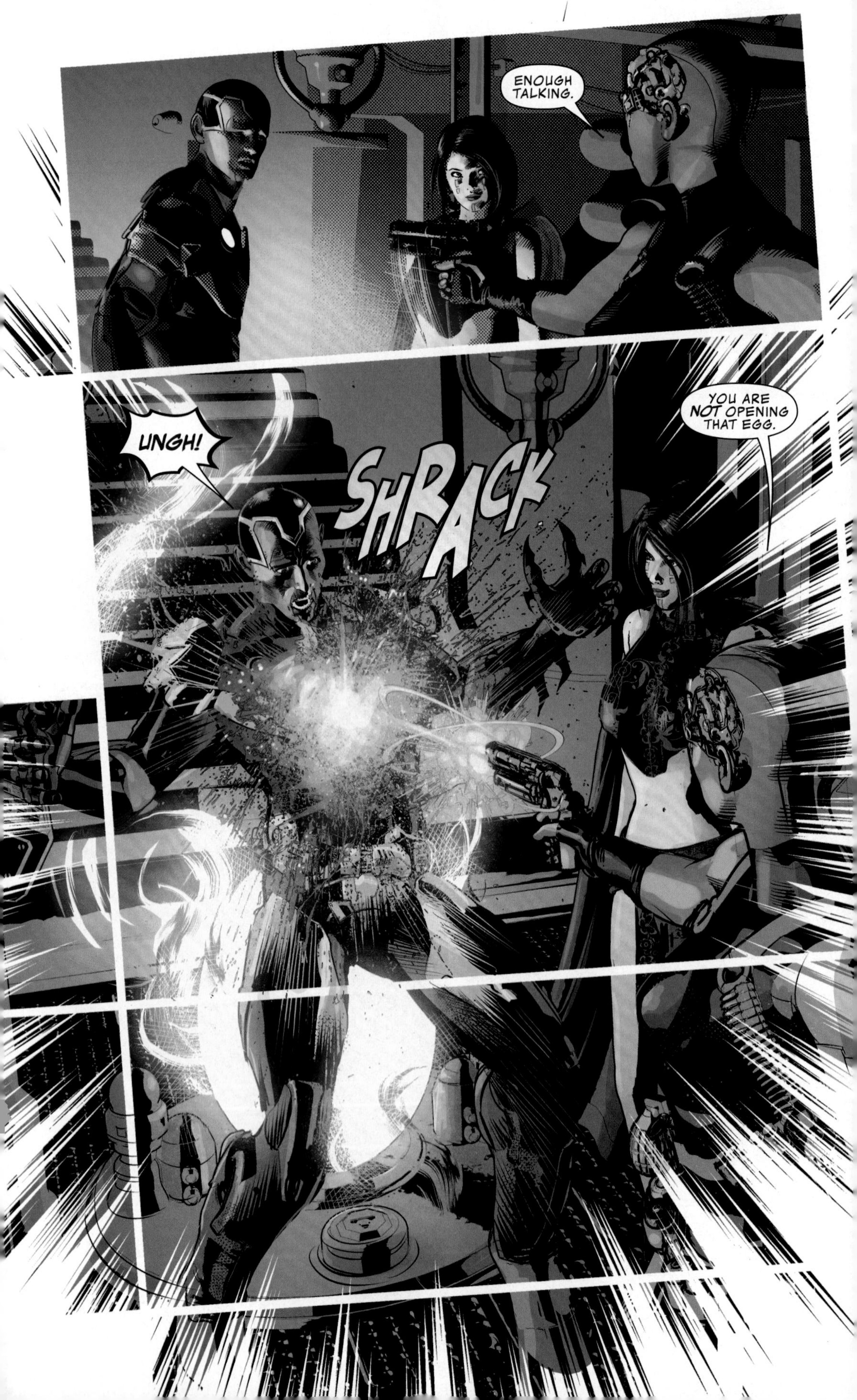
ENOUGH TALKING.
UNGH!
SHRACK
YOU ARE NOT OPENING THAT EGG.

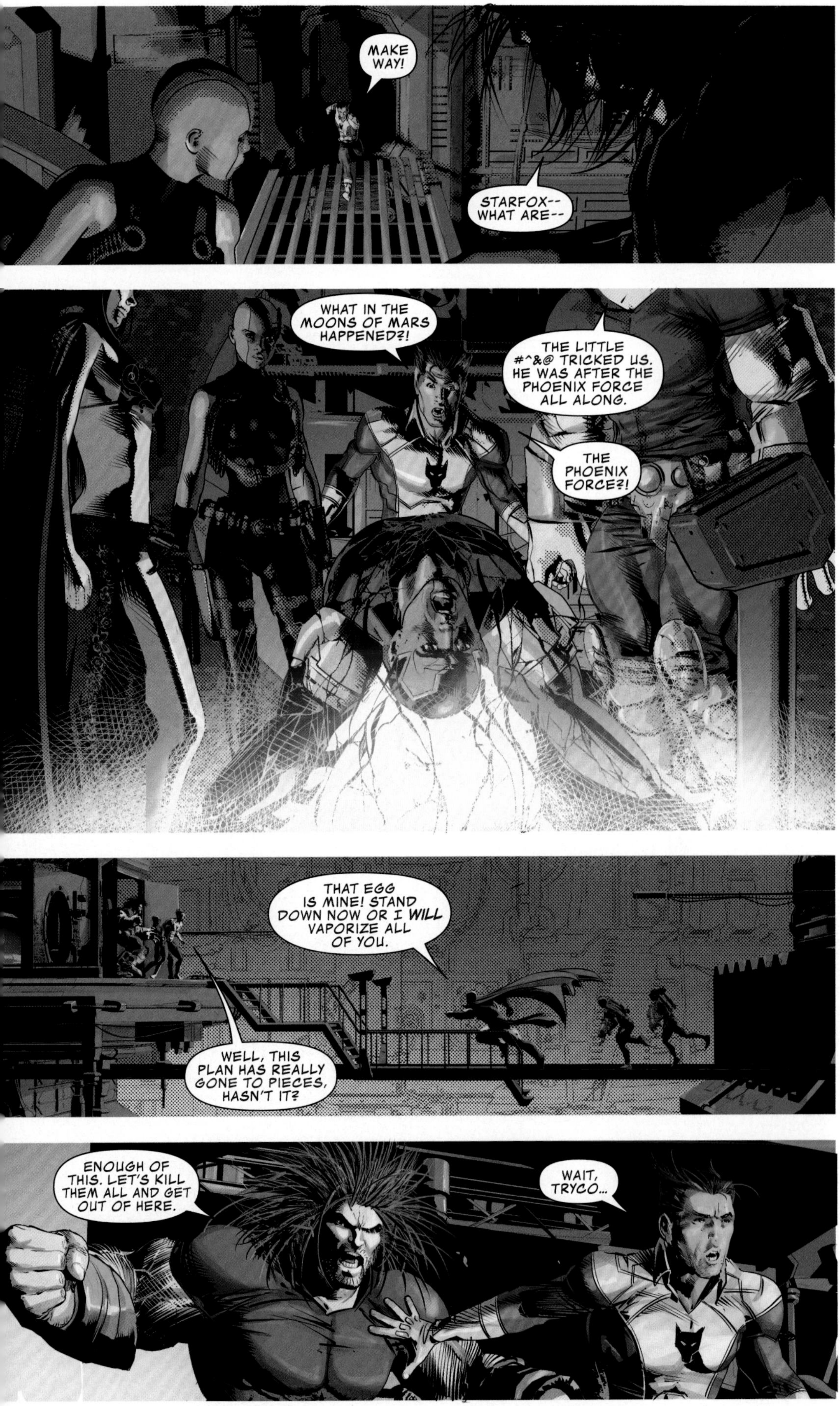
MAKE WAY!
STARFOX-- WHAT ARE--
WHAT IN THE MOONS OF MARS HAPPENED?!
THE LITTLE #^&@ TRICKED US. HE WAS AFTER THE PHOENIX FORCE ALL ALONG.
THE PHOENIX FORCE?!
THAT EGG IS MINE! STAND DOWN NOW OR I WILL VAPORIZE ALL OF YOU.
WELL, THIS PLAN HAS REALLY GONE TO PIECES, HASN'T IT?
ENOUGH OF THIS. LET'S KILL THEM ALL AND GET OUT OF HERE.
WAIT, TRYCO...

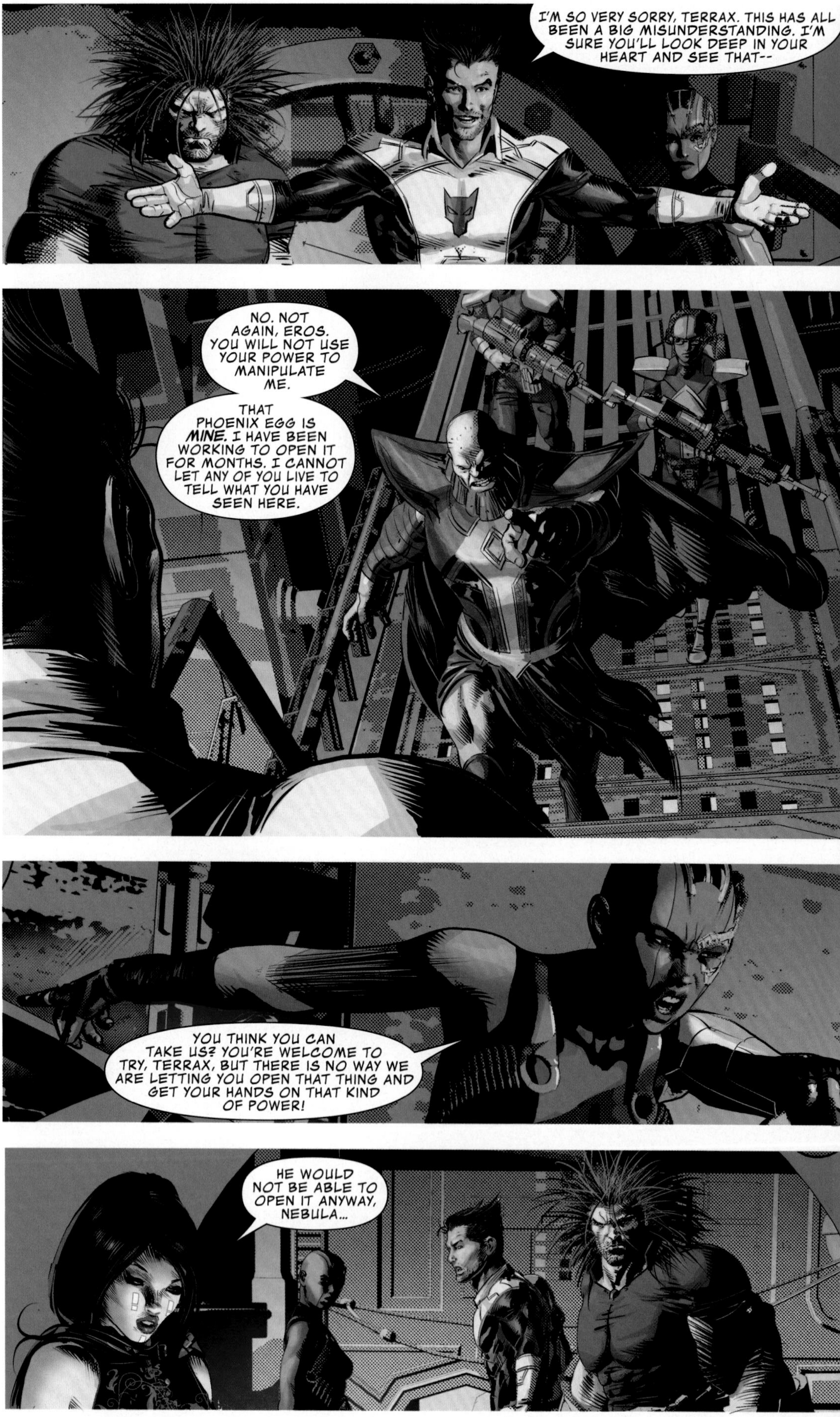
I'M SO VERY SORRY, TERRAX. THIS HAS ALL BEEN A BIG MISUNDERSTANDING. I'M SURE YOU'LL LOOK DEEP IN YOUR HEART AND SEE THAT--
NO. NOT AGAIN, EROS. YOU WILL NOT USE YOUR POWER TO MANIPULATE ME.
THAT PHOENIX EGG IS *MINE.* I HAVE BEEN WORKING TO OPEN IT FOR MONTHS. I CANNOT LET ANY OF YOU LIVE TO TELL WHAT YOU HAVE SEEN HERE.
YOU THINK YOU CAN TAKE US? YOU'RE WELCOME TO TRY, TERRAX, BUT THERE IS NO WAY WE ARE LETTING YOU OPEN THAT THING AND GET YOUR HANDS ON THAT KIND OF POWER!
HE WOULD NOT BE ABLE TO OPEN IT ANYWAY, NEBULA...

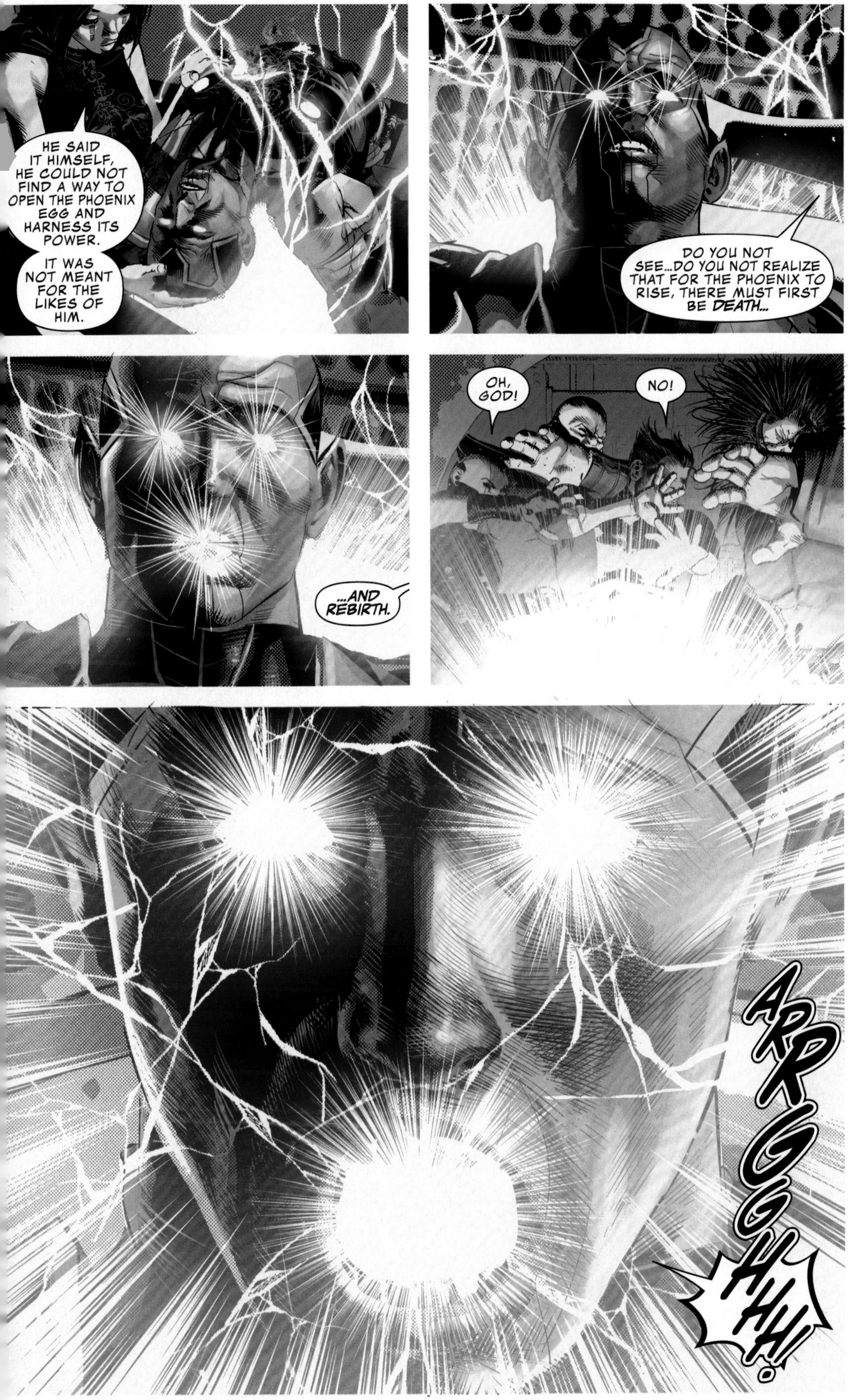
HE SAID IT HIMSELF, HE COULD NOT FIND A WAY TO OPEN THE PHOENIX EGG AND HARNESS ITS POWER.
IT WAS NOT MEANT FOR THE LIKES OF HIM.
DO YOU NOT SEE...DO YOU NOT REALIZE THAT FOR THE PHOENIX TO RISE, THERE MUST FIRST BE *DEATH*...
...AND REBIRTH.
OH, GOD!
NO!
ARRGGHHH!

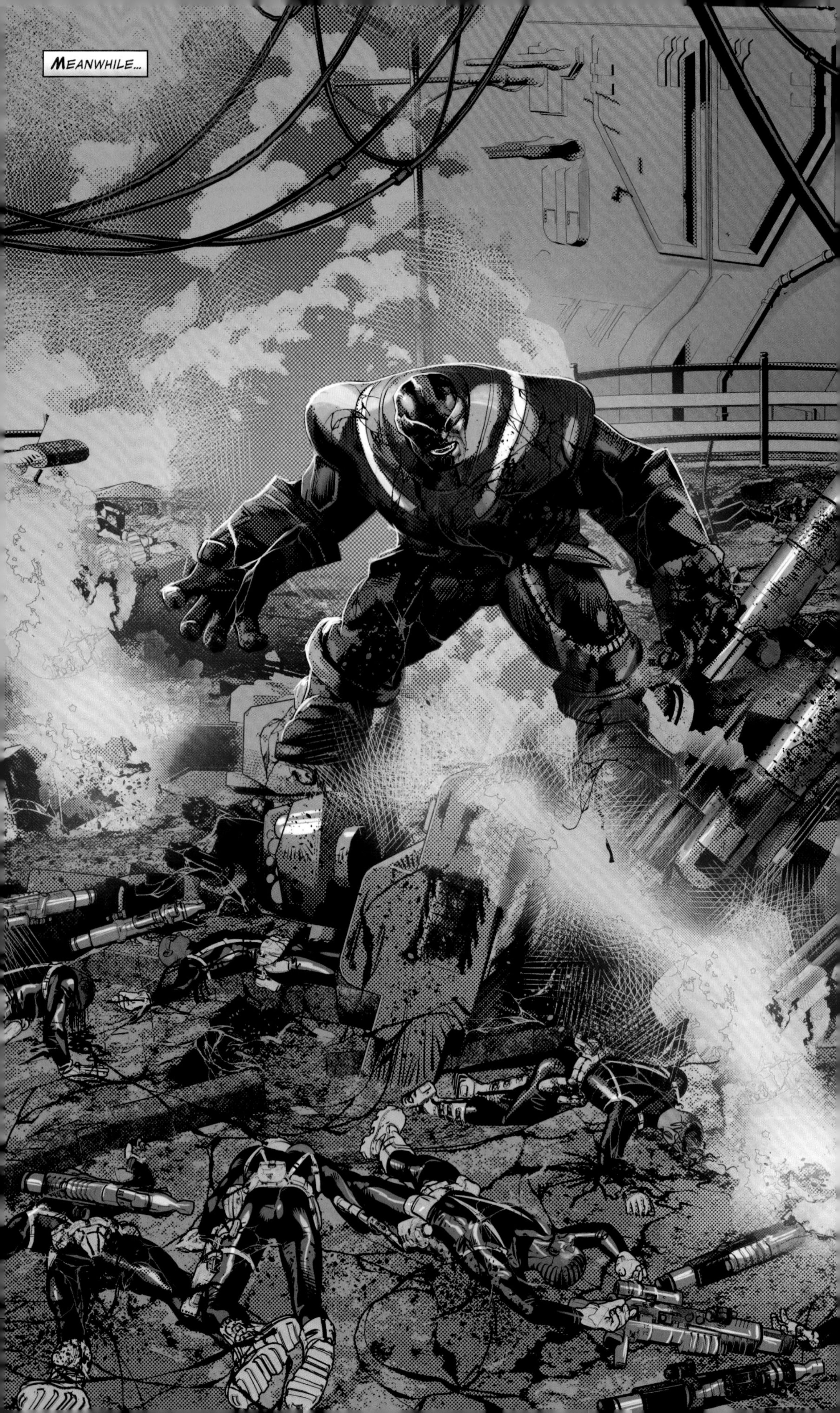
MEANWHILE...

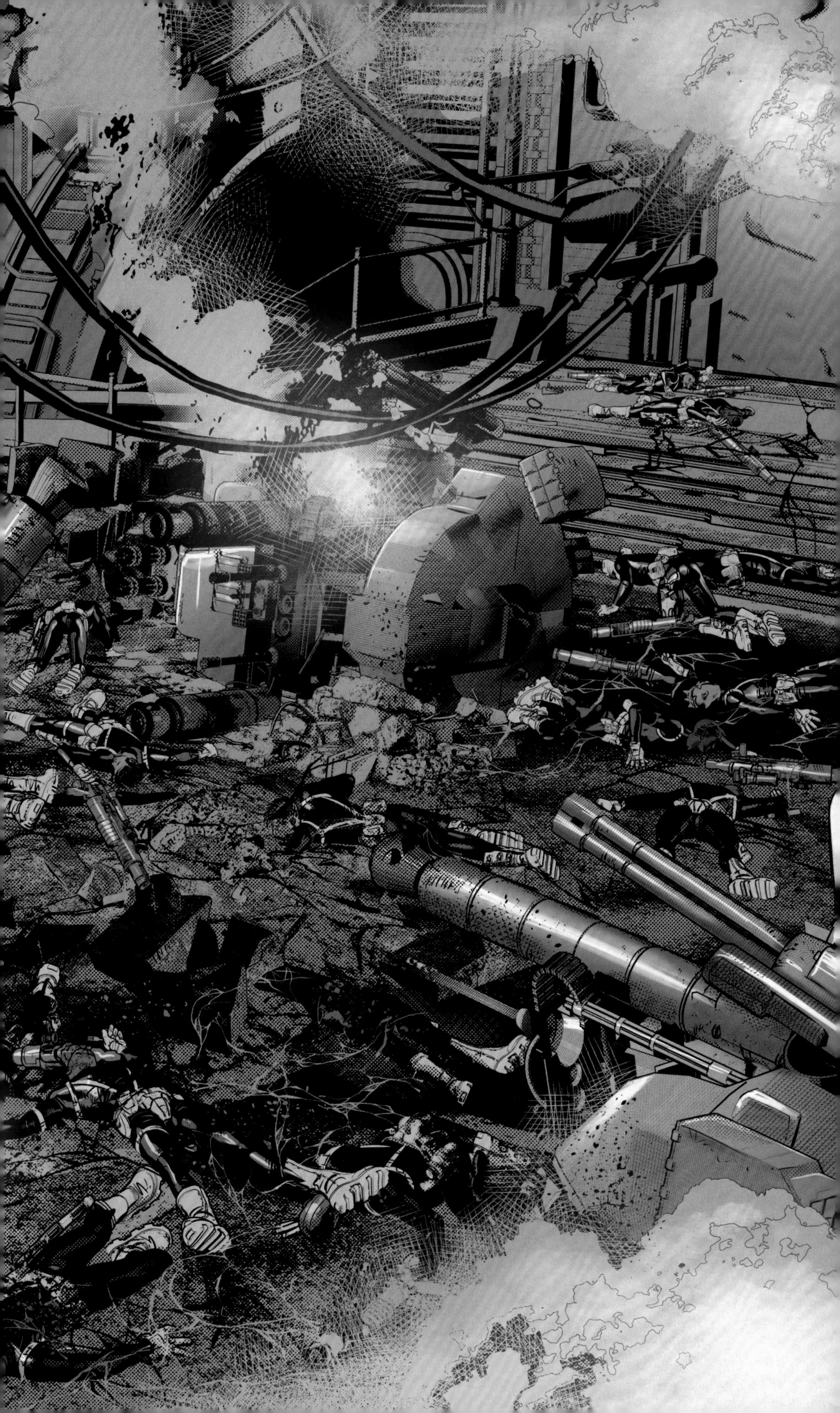

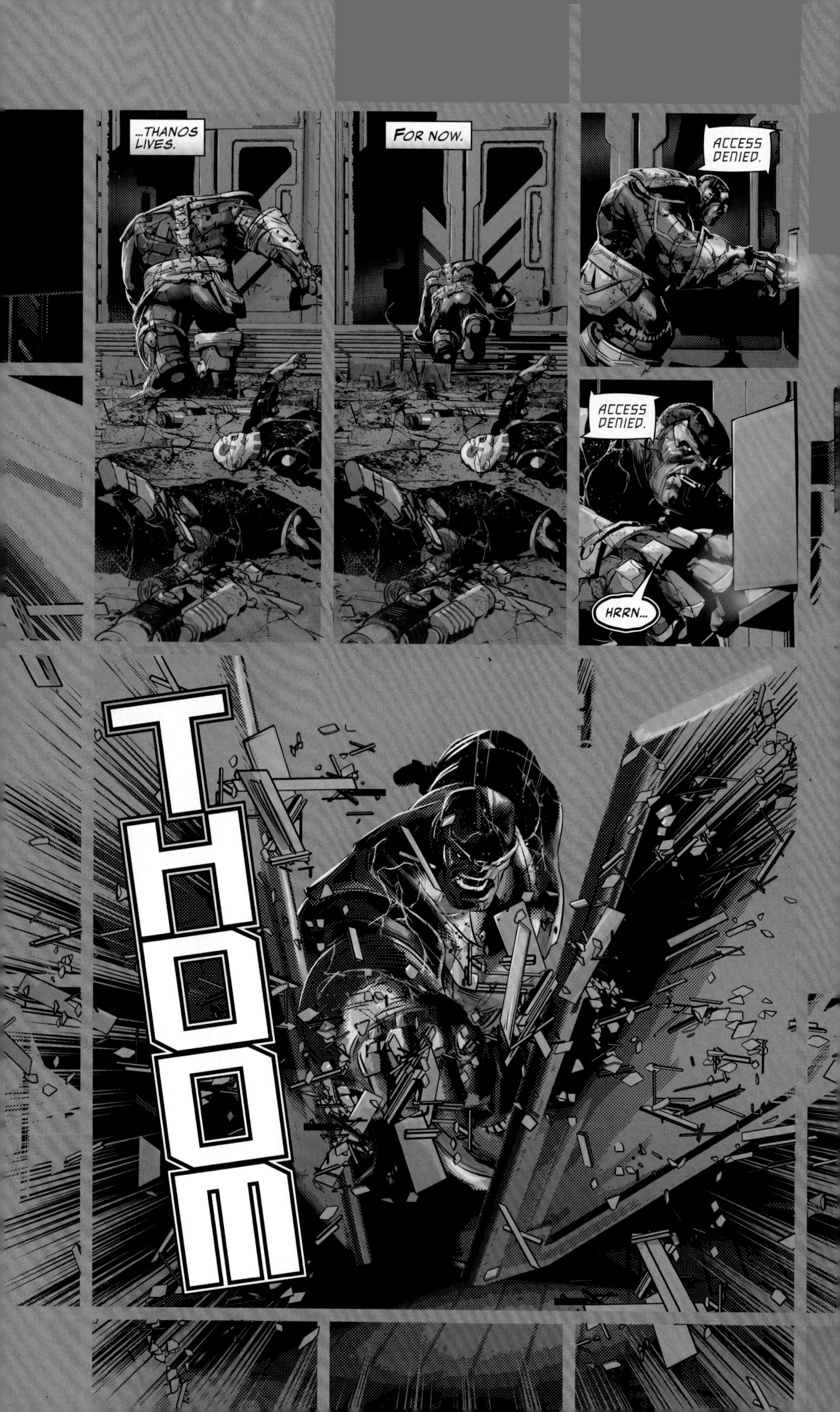
...THANOS LIVES.
FOR NOW.
ACCESS DENIED.
ACCESS DENIED.
HRRN...
THOOM

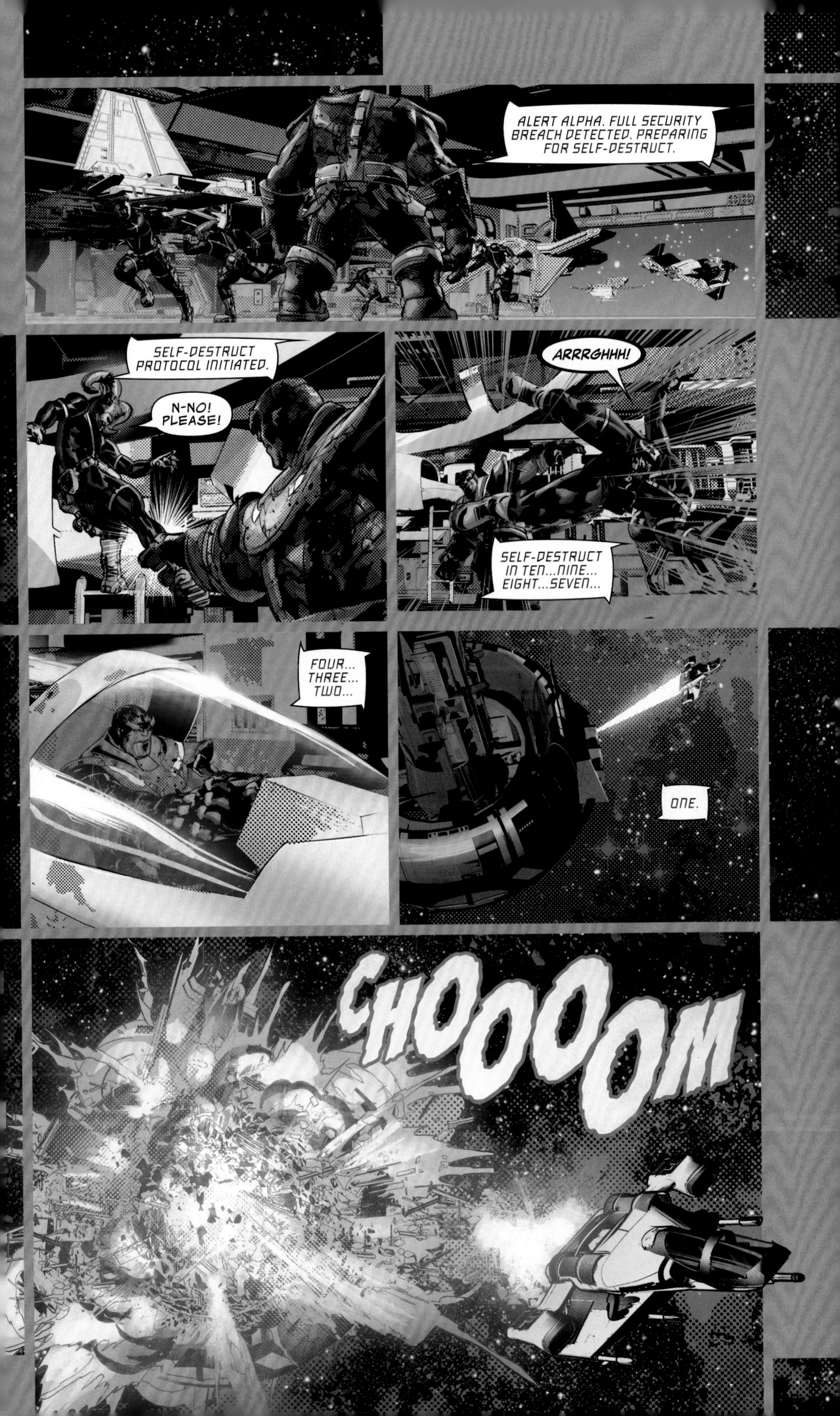

ALERT ALPHA. FULL SECURITY BREACH DETECTED. PREPARING FOR SELF-DESTRUCT.
SELF-DESTRUCT PROTOCOL INITIATED.
N-NO! PLEASE!
ARRRGHHH!
SELF-DESTRUCT IN TEN...NINE... EIGHT...SEVEN...
FOUR... THREE... TWO...
ONE.
CHOOOOOM

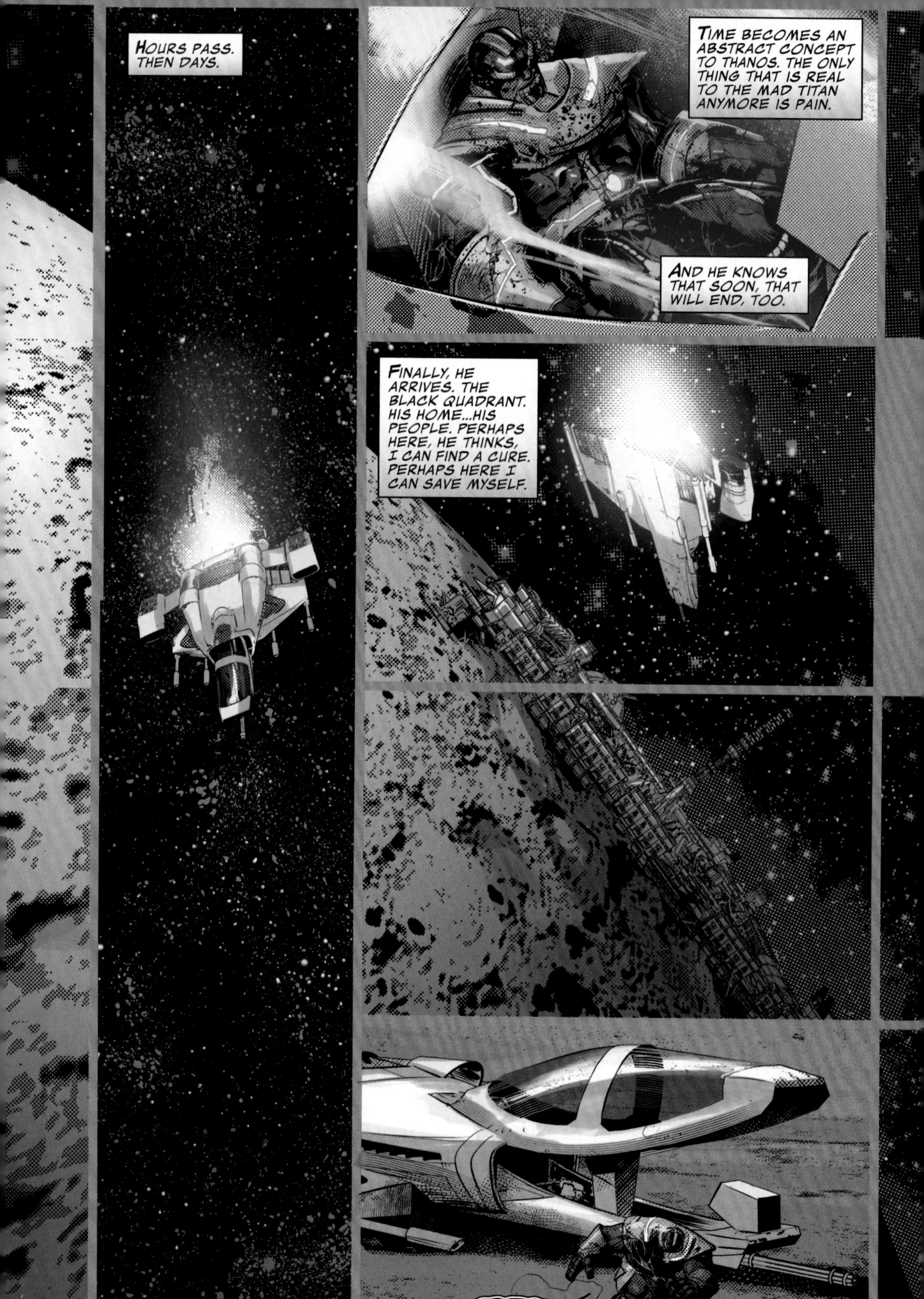
HOURS PASS. THEN DAYS.
TIME BECOMES AN ABSTRACT CONCEPT TO THANOS. THE ONLY THING THAT IS REAL TO THE MAD TITAN ANYMORE IS PAIN.
AND HE KNOWS THAT SOON, THAT WILL END, TOO.
FINALLY, HE ARRIVES. THE BLACK QUADRANT. HIS HOME...HIS PEOPLE. PERHAPS HERE, HE THINKS, I CAN FIND A CURE. PERHAPS HERE I CAN SAVE MYSELF.
I--I HAVE RETURNED...

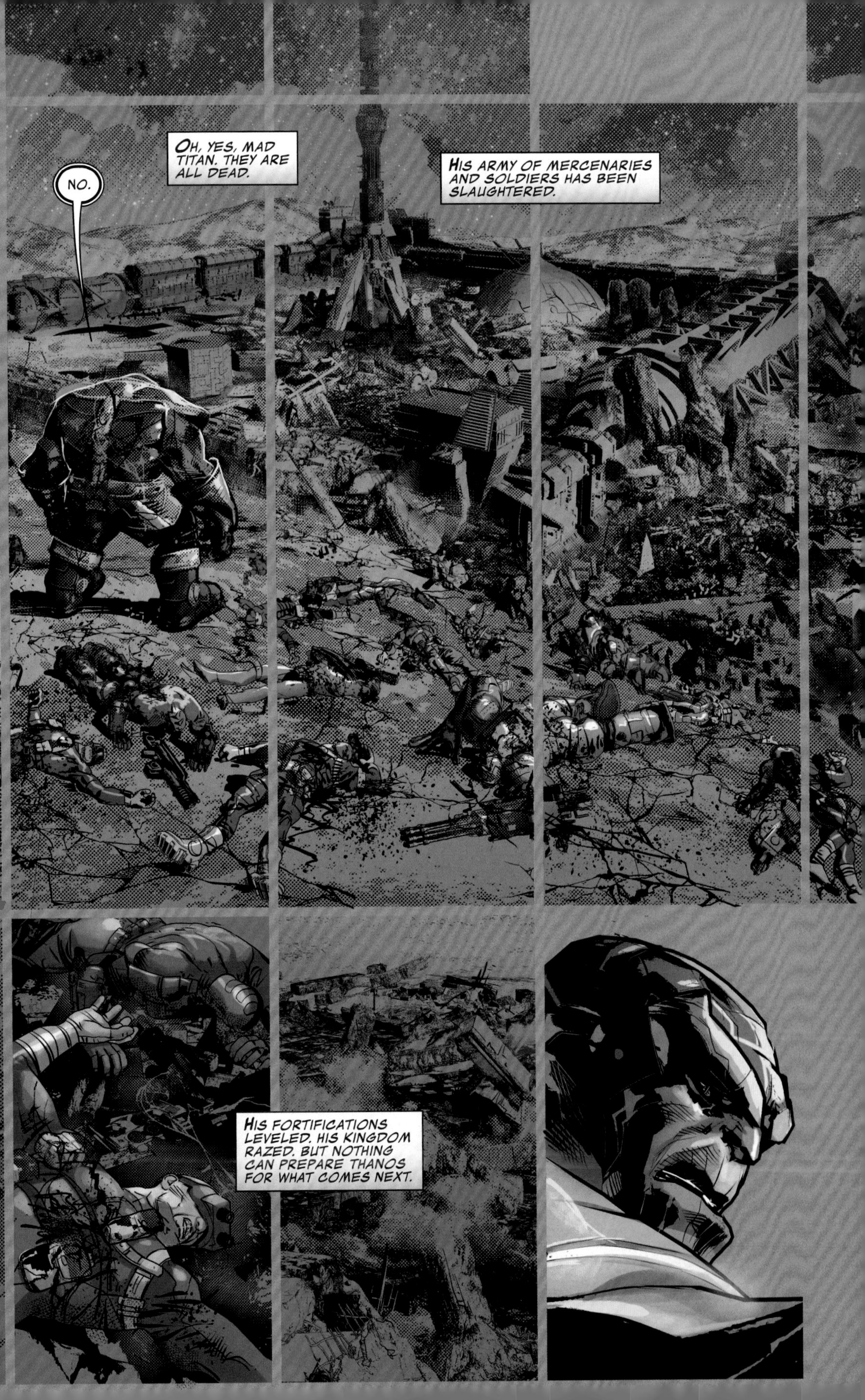
NO.
OH, YES, MAD TITAN. THEY ARE ALL DEAD.
HIS ARMY OF MERCENARIES AND SOLDIERS HAS BEEN SLAUGHTERED.
HIS FORTIFICATIONS LEVELED. HIS KINGDOM RAZED. BUT NOTHING CAN PREPARE THANOS FOR WHAT COMES NEXT.

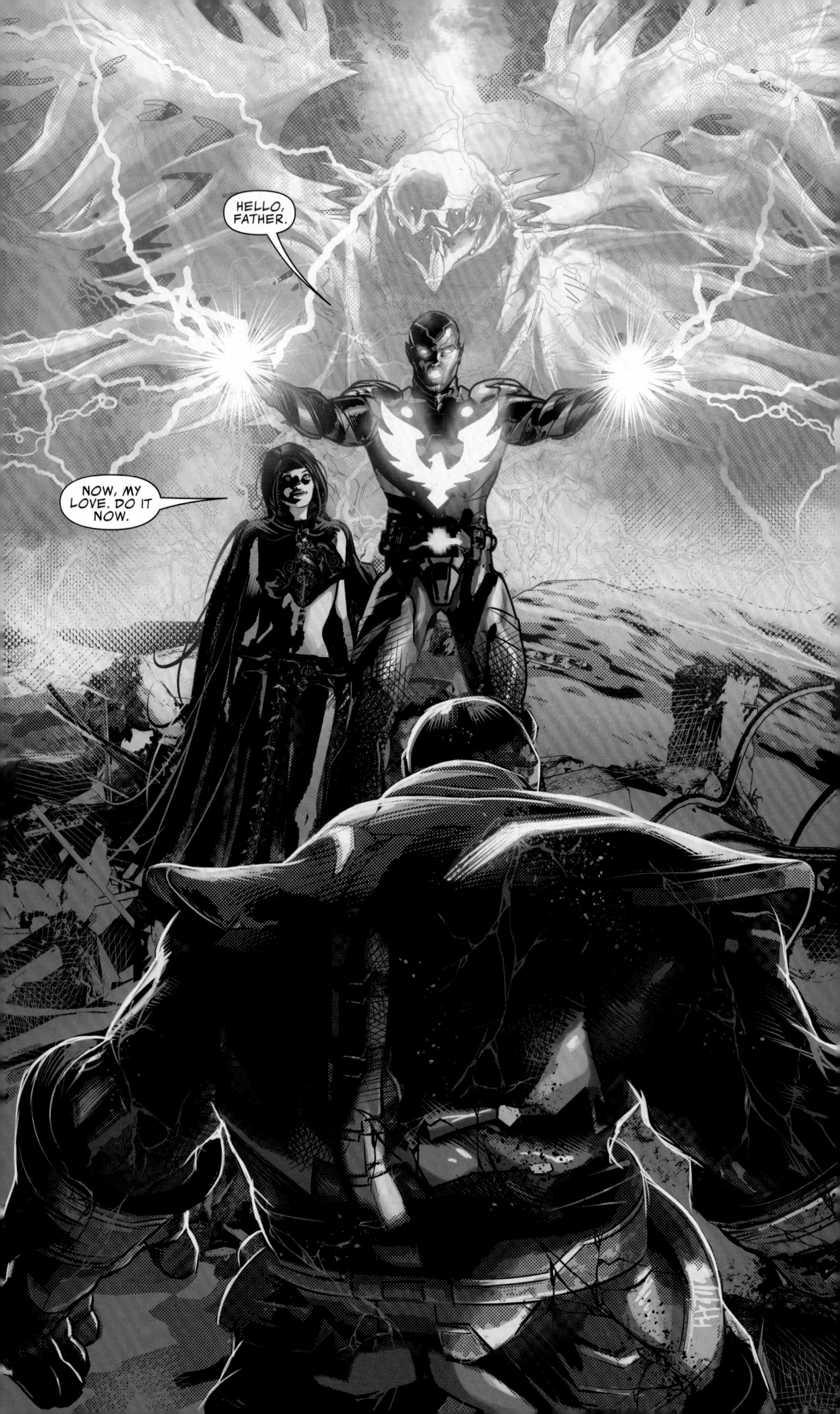
HELLO, FATHER.
NOW, MY LOVE. DO IT NOW.

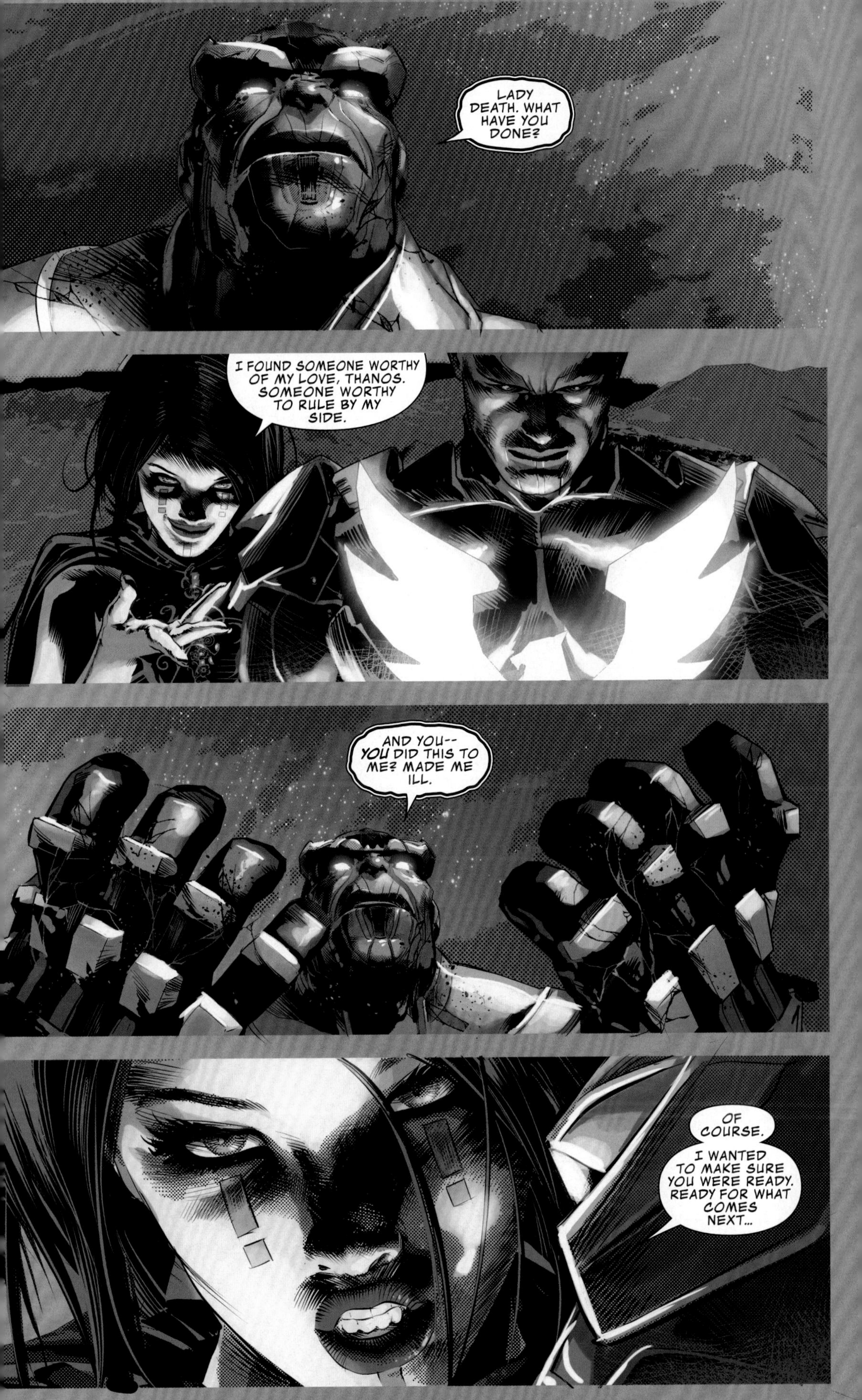
LADY DEATH. WHAT HAVE YOU DONE?
I FOUND SOMEONE WORTHY OF MY LOVE, THANOS. SOMEONE WORTHY TO RULE BY MY SIDE.
AND YOU-- YOU DID THIS TO ME? MADE ME ILL.
OF COURSE.
I WANTED TO MAKE SURE YOU WERE READY. READY FOR WHAT COMES NEXT...

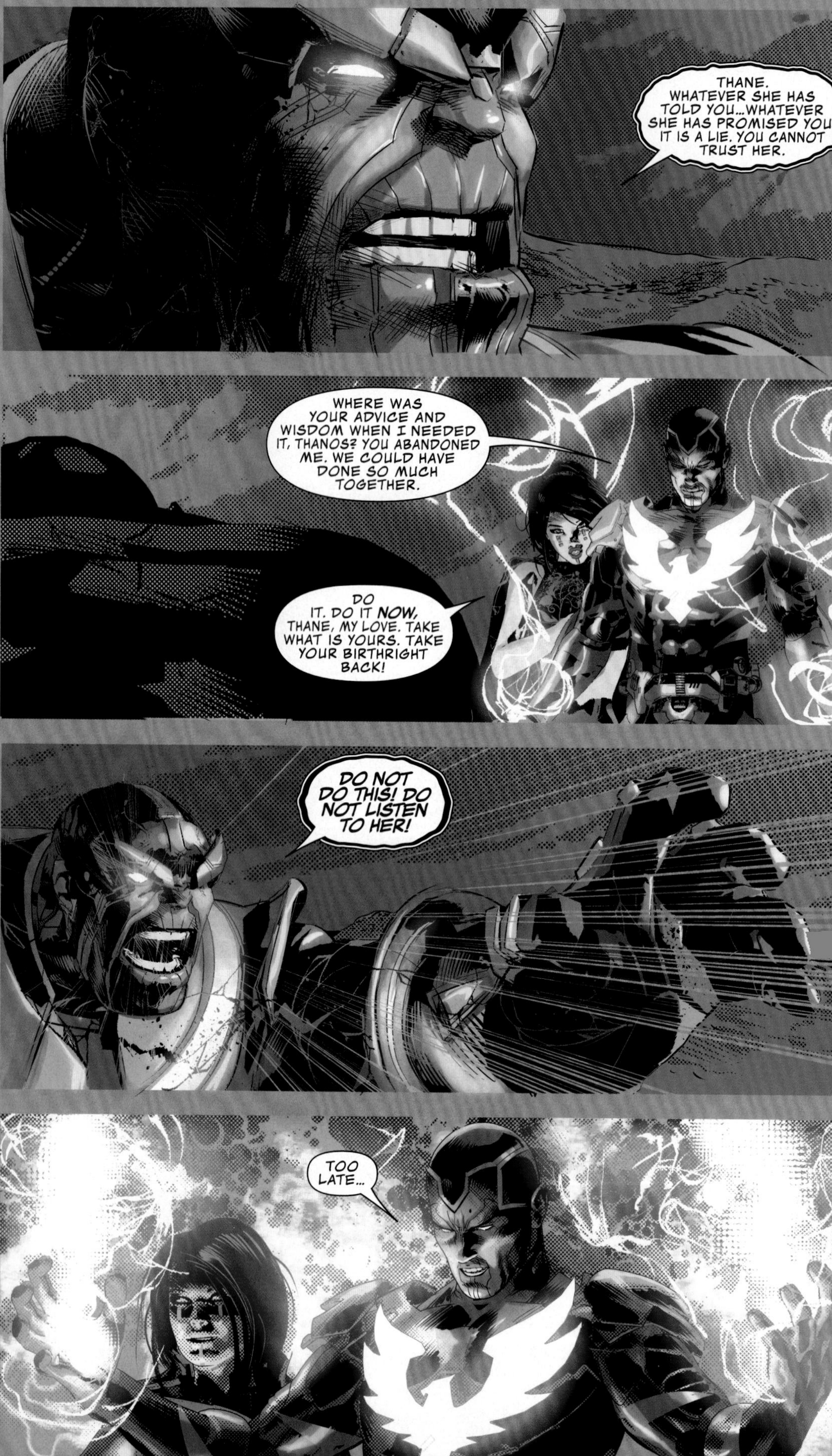
THANE. WHATEVER SHE HAS TOLD YOU...WHATEVER SHE HAS PROMISED YOU, IT IS A LIE. YOU CANNOT TRUST HER.
WHERE WAS YOUR ADVICE AND WISDOM WHEN I NEEDED IT, THANOS? YOU ABANDONED ME. WE COULD HAVE DONE SO MUCH TOGETHER.
DO IT. DO IT NOW, THANE, MY LOVE. TAKE WHAT IS YOURS. TAKE YOUR BIRTHRIGHT BACK!
DO NOT DO THIS! DO NOT LISTEN TO HER!
TOO LATE...

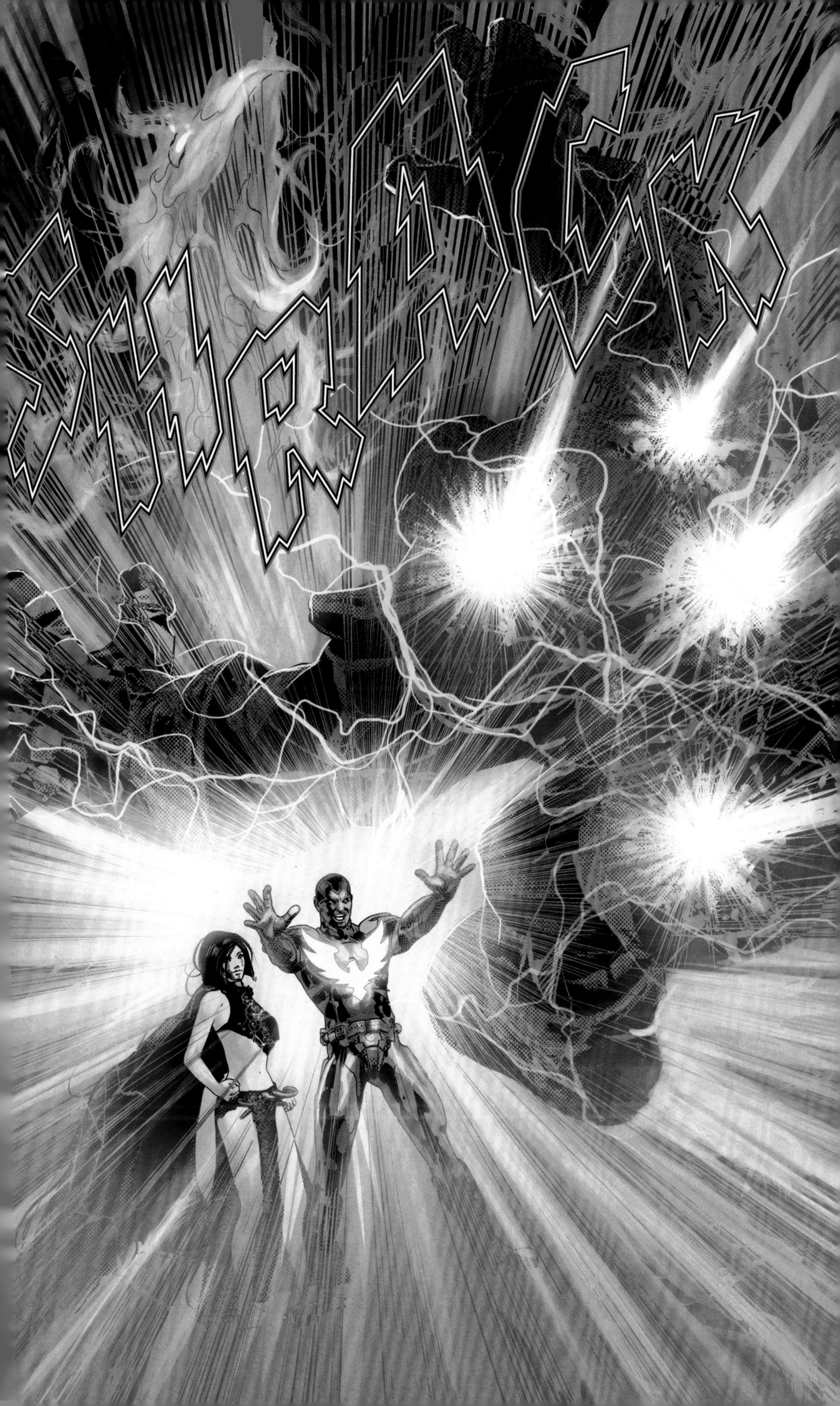

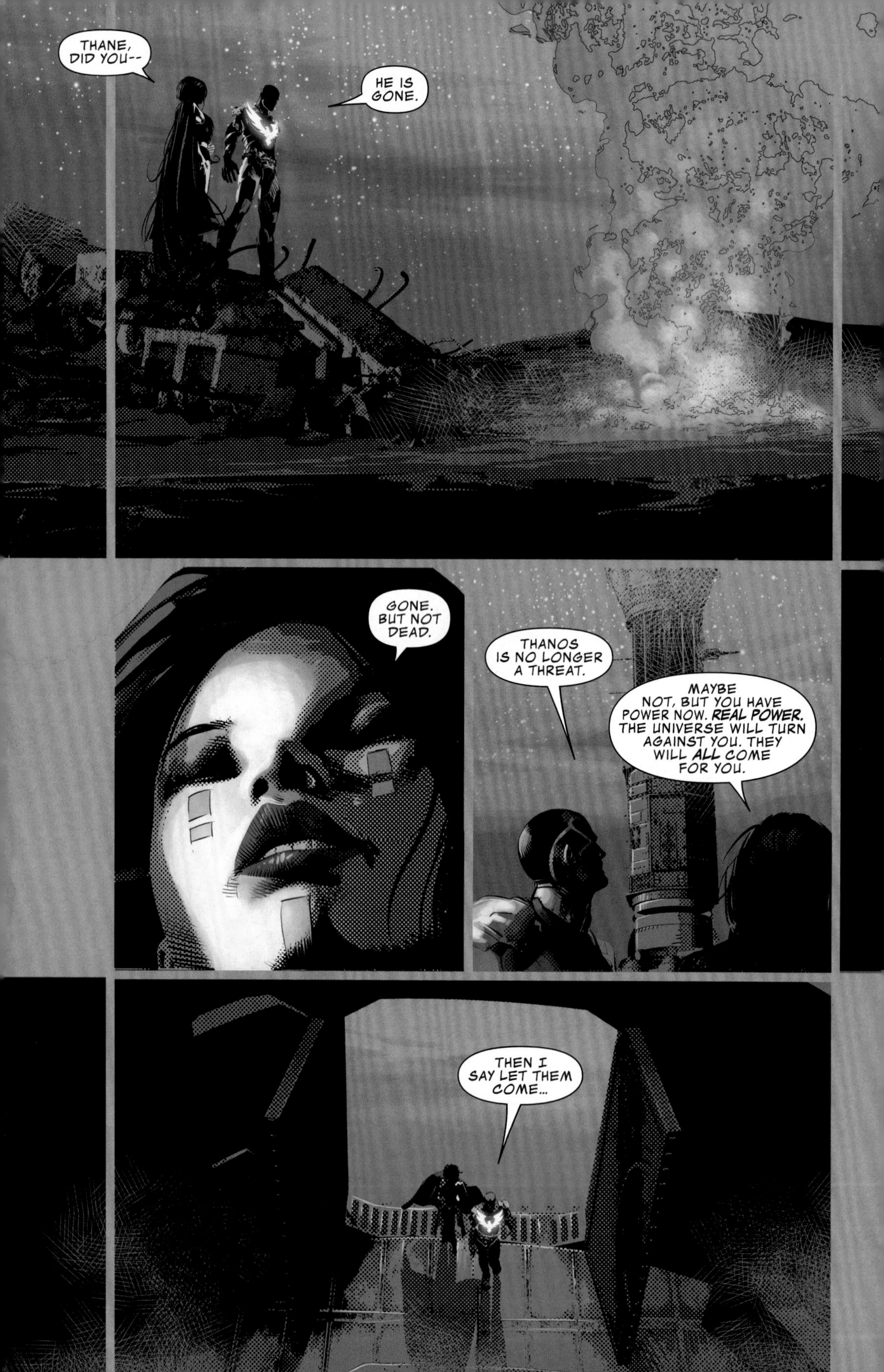
THANE, DID YOU--
HE IS GONE.
GONE. BUT NOT DEAD.
THANOS IS NO LONGER A THREAT.
MAYBE NOT, BUT YOU HAVE POWER NOW. REAL POWER. THE UNIVERSE WILL TURN AGAINST YOU. THEY WILL ALL COME FOR YOU.
THEN I SAY LET THEM COME...

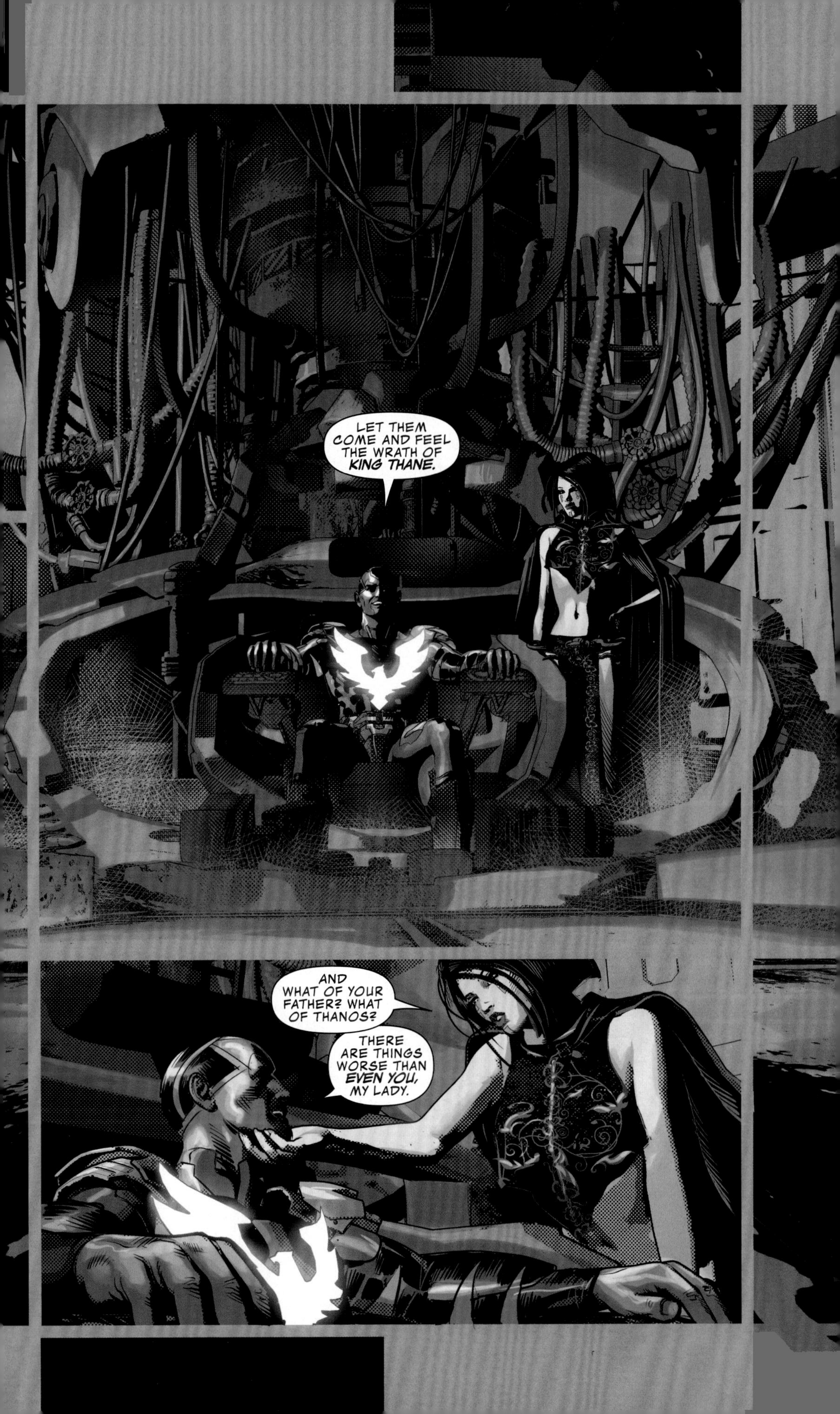
LET THEM COME AND FEEL THE WRATH OF KING THANE.
AND WHAT OF YOUR FATHER? WHAT OF THANOS?
THERE ARE THINGS WORSE THAN EVEN YOU, MY LADY.

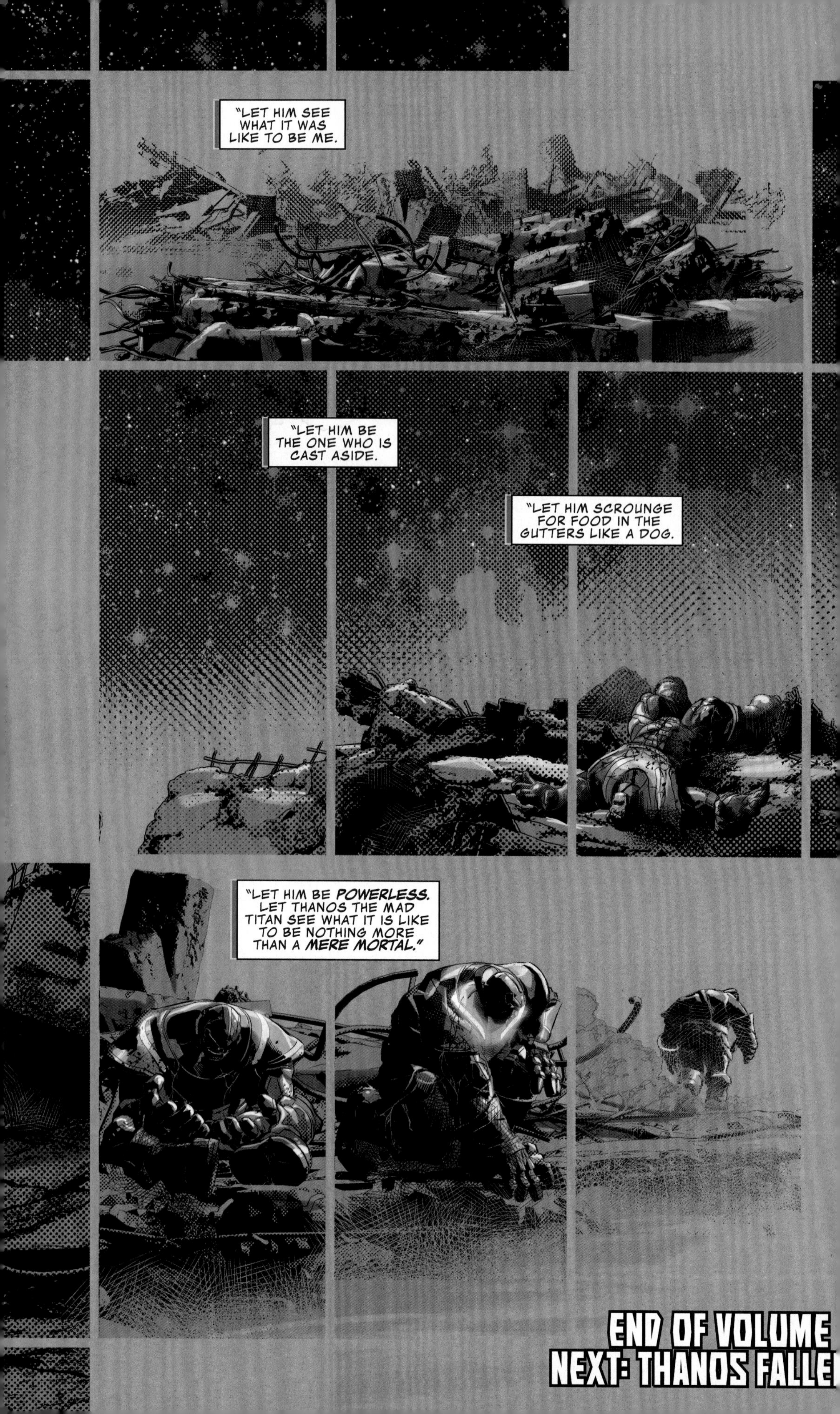
"LET HIM SEE WHAT IT WAS LIKE TO BE ME.
"LET HIM BE THE ONE WHO IS CAST ASIDE.
"LET HIM SCROUNGE FOR FOOD IN THE GUTTERS LIKE A DOG.
"LET HIM BE POWERLESS. LET THANOS THE MAD TITAN SEE WHAT IT IS LIKE TO BE NOTHING MORE THAN A MERE MORTAL."
END OF VOLUME
NEXT: THANOS FALLE

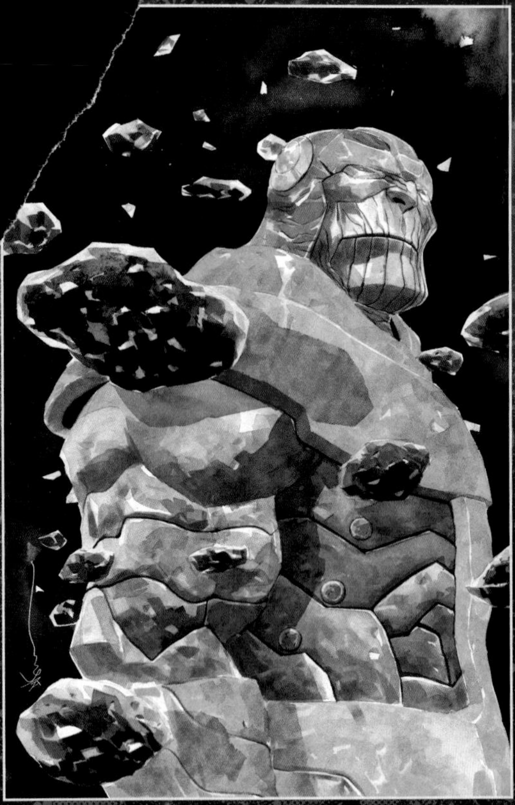

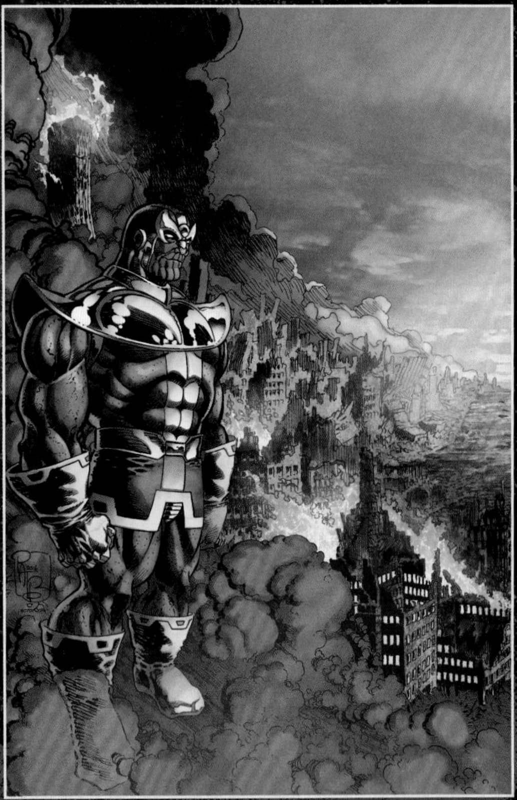

DUSTIN NGUYEN
NO. 2 VARIANT

PAT BRODERICK & CHRIS SOTOMAYOR
NO. 3 VARIANT

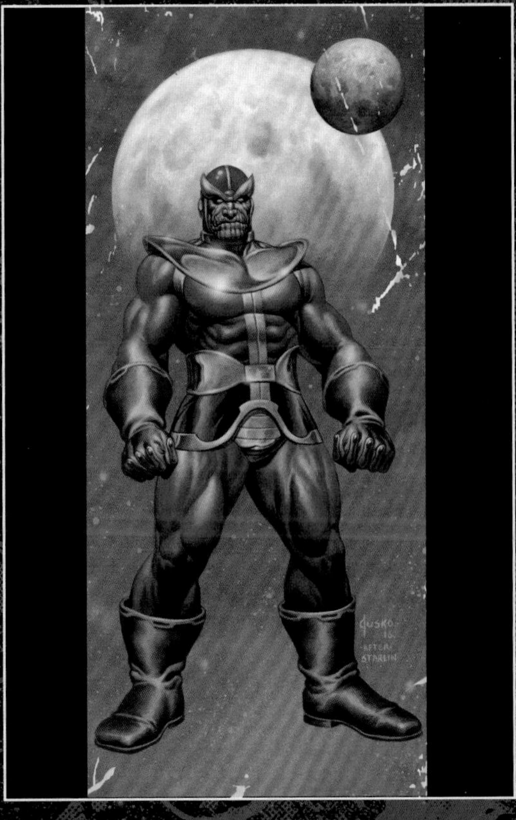

JOE JUSKO
NO. 4 CORNER BOX VARIANT

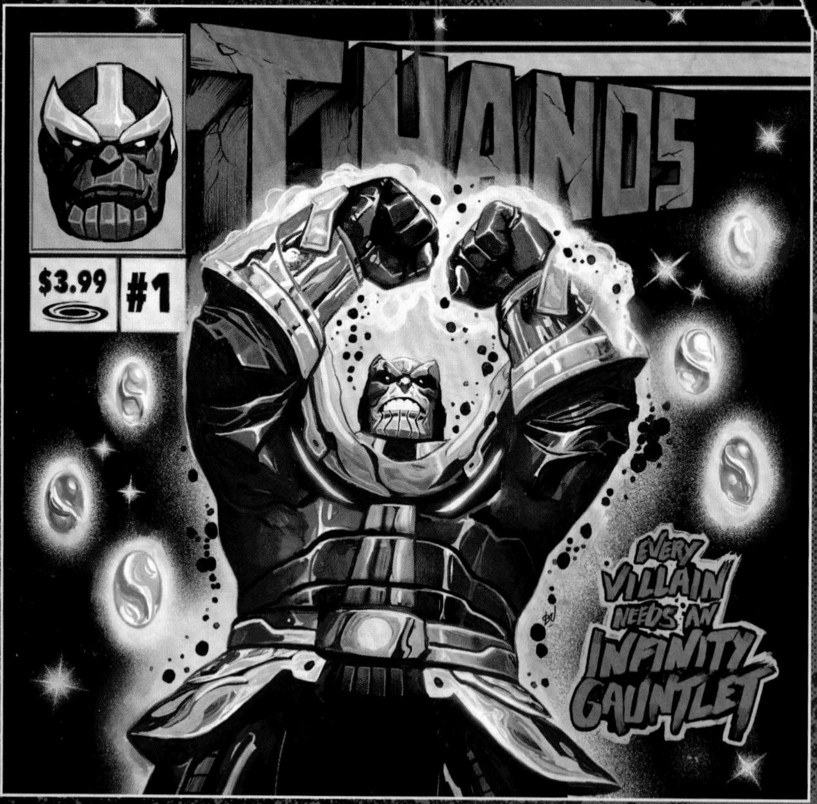
THANOS
$3.99
#1
EVERY VILLAIN NEEDS AN INFINITY GAUNTLET

MIKE DEL MUNDO

NO. 1 HIP-HOP VARIANT

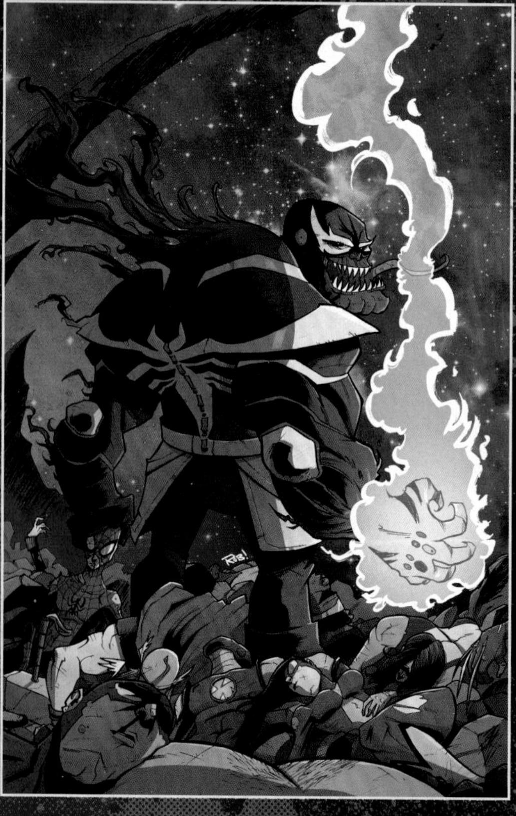

ROB GUILLORY

NO. 5 VENOMIZED VARIANT